Pandeism:

An Anthology of Spiritual Nature

Pandeism:

An Anthology of
Spiritual Nature

Edited by

Knujon Mapson

Pandeism Anthology Press

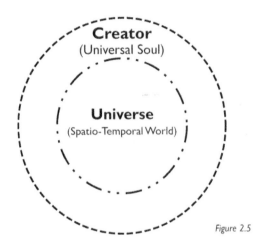

Figure 2.5

TABLE OF CONTENTS

In memory of Douglas M. Stokes, PhD.

A champion of the art of thinking.

Preface

There is some tension inherent in the concept of a spiritual model which is claimed to be a natural thing, and yet at the same time claimed to be logical and the product of reason. For isn't nature unreasoning? Isn't the sprawl of vines and flowers the opposite of a product of rational thought? That is what our initial impression may be, and yet there is method to the chaos of nature. There is a mathematical underpinning to the structuring of cells and the development of organisms. There is reason and logic guiding the unfolding of nature.

And within that framework there is a natural place for a spirituality arising from reasoned and logical examination of the world. Across this volume, we will see examinations of Pandeism from a multitude of perspectives, and examinations of multiple perspectives which touch upon Pandeism as amongst a family of ideas yielding hopeful possibilities for the progress of spiritual knowledge. Some of our authors approach the subject quite directly, and others from oblique and surprising directions. We begin this piece with the ending of another, as renowned science writer Timothy Ferris graces our work with an updated chapter-and-note from his 1997 bestseller *The Whole Shebang*, in which he concludes in part that there is not necessarily proof against a Creator, for such a being "would betray no trace of his presence, since to do so would be to rob the creative forces of their independence..." Several pieces throughout the book take comparative approaches, with John Ross, Jr., Celeste Foley, Steve Schramm examining Pandeism from the perspectives of Taoism,

Russellian Monism, and Christian faiths, respectively (and coming to some very different conclusions about its viability).

Equally liberally scattered are our occasional pieces from centuries past, beginning with Philosopher Emily Thomas introducing a carefully curated selection from Samuel Alexander. Another piece by Paul Carus reflects on his own variation of the pantheistic and deistic. Of more recent vintage, Dr Michael Arnheim returns to provide perspectives on the spiritual views of Albert Einstein. Philosophical thinkers Andrew Gregory, Socrates Ebo, and Poffo Ortiz provide ruminations reaching from the ancient days of Anaximander to the natural world and cosmos. Nick Dutch brings forth the lessons of his life as a Tarot reader. Lastly, Douglas M. Stokes, who sadly passed away after providing his piece to us, produces a tour-de-force of cataloguing the thinkers and lines of thought in this field with respect to conceptions of the continuation of the soul into an array of possible afterlives. As always, our volume is additionally well set forth with poetic interludes.

It is our hope, as always, that every reader will find at least something to love and hold onto in this collection of essays, brought together with our blessings!!

Acknowledgments

The editors would like to acknowledge those who have been with us from the very beginning of our journey, and those who we have only come to know along the way. Although all of our authors are worthy of this recognition, several have been exceptionally supportive of this project over a long term, including poet Amy Perry, and second-time essay contributors John Ross, Jr. and Dr Michael Arnheim.

Another friend of the project since before the publication of our first collection, in this volume we are finally able to provide Nick Dutch's work. Our gratitude goes to Rachel Stokes for allowing us to continue with the publication of her father's work. Our literary agent Brian Abramson continues his fine work in keeping up with certain of our authors, in their hectic lives.

We thank all of our Kickstarter supporters for their faith in this volume—especially the most generous representative of that excellent group, Andrew Vickory.

Lastly, though not publishing this volume, we recognize the entire coterie at John Hunt Publishing for continuing to excellently propel our collections previous to this one into the world.

Pandeism:
An Anthology of
Spiritual Nature

A Place for Us, and a Contrarian Theological Afterword: excerpts from *The Whole Shebang*

By Timothy Ferris

Timothy Ferris is one of the leading science writers of the late Twentieth and early Twenty-first centuries, having written twelve books and received the American Institute of Physics Prize as well as a Pulitzer Prize nomination. Among other remarkable achievements, he was the producer of the Voyager Golden Record, sent into space aboard the Voyager spacecraft. The following selection was originally published in his bestselling 1997 book, *The Whole Shebang: A State-of-the-universe(s) Report*, as "Chapter 12: A Place for Us", and "Contrarian Theological Afterword." Though Ferris does not personally identify as a Pandeist, some may find the relevance of his final analysis to Pandeism to be strikingly clear.

A Place for Us

God said to Abraham, "But for me, you would not be here." "I know that, Lord," Abraham answered, "but were I not here there would be no one to think about you."
—Traditional Jewish tale[1]

The optimist proclaims that we live in the best of all possible worlds; and the pessimist fears this is true.
—JAMES BRANCH CABELL[2]

Human beings must be just about the *loneliest* species in the universe. We've only recently begun to learn about the universe, don't yet know quite what to make of it, and haven't anyone else with whom to discuss it. So we talk among ourselves, in musings that necessarily are limited to our necessarily human perspective. In this sense, our dialogues are monologues, hobbled by what might be called the agony of uniqueness. We are conversant with only one kind of intelligence, our own, only one kind of life, for all earthly life is kin, and only one observed universe. How, then, are we to work the calculus of chance and necessity in order to understand which if any of the laws and constants of nature are inevitable and which are accidents, and to judge whether life and intelligence are central or peripheral to the cosmic scheme of things?

Prior to the Renaissance, we lived in a cozy little hut of a cosmos, and our place within it seemed secure.[3] The prescientific universe was *about* us, in two senses of the word: It consisted of our immediate surroundings (and not much more) and we belonged to it—were appropriate to it. The Copernican Revolution changed all that, of course, but its shock was not so much that it "dethroned" us from a privileged central position, as the textbooks say, but rather that the universe no longer seemed to be about us. The vast reaches of the Copernican cosmos, if uninhabited, seemed useless and pointless. (This consideration was specifically raised, by the philosopher Giovanni Agucchi in a letter to Galileo, as an argument against Copernicanism.[4]) If inhabited, they obliged us to consider that we share our cosmic home with other beings, some of whom might be smarter or better than us, more worthy of God's concern.

Thus began the age of apprehension, in which it became fashionable among popularizers of science to wield the nasty vastness of the universe like a club. To be scientifically hip was to parade one's unblinking acceptance of the unflattering proposition that we are but slime, clinging to a speck of dirt in a galactic outback, hurtling ignorantly through a lethal vacuum dotted with uncaring stars. Sir James Jeans read this mood perfectly, and wrote a bestselling astronomy book that so stressed how inhumanly big and small and hot and cold everything was that one critic asked whether Sir James's intention was to educate his readers or scare them to death.

Lately, the pendulum has begun to swing the other way, with scientists and philosophers reconsidering whether our existence is really all that incidental to the wider world. The Copernican revolution bred the *cosmological principle*, which rules out theories that place humankind in the center of the universe or any other special location. It would, for instance, violate the cosmological principle to argue that the big bang took place at a specific location in a preexisting space, and that we just happen to sit at the site of the explosion, so that the galaxies are all rushing away from *us*. The cosmological principle is fine so far as it goes, but some have begun wondering whether it's too one-sided. Perhaps cosmology would benefit from the addition of a second principle—one that took our existence into account without postulating that there was otherwise anything special about us. The *anthropic principle* attempts to do this. It starts with human existence as a given and scours the universe for clues as to which of its characteristics are essential to the existence of life. Its thrust is to portray the cosmos less as an impersonal machine and more as, in John Wheeler's words, a "home to Man."

To investigate this outlook, we pose two questions relevant to the relationship between humankind and the universe it has so recently come to behold:

Are we alone? Is life cosmically commonplace or rare? Is human intelligence a fluke or a spark of universal fire?

Does our existence tell us anything about the universe? The anthropic approach assumes that it does, and seeks to learn about the universe by taking the existence of life as a starting point.

The question of whether we are alone in the universe is ancient. What's new is that we are coming to possess tools that could give us a shot at answering it.[5] Existing radio telescopes are capable of detecting signals transmitted by an alien civilization of comparable capacity anywhere in our quarter of the Milky Way galaxy. The next generation of optical space telescope may be able to discern telltale signs of life—specifically carbon dioxide, which indicates that the presence of an atmosphere; water, suggesting oceans; and ozone, a form of oxygen—in the spectra of starlight reflected off extrasolar planets.

[*Editor's note: Ferris has since addressed developments in this field, writing in 2012: "Thanks to space telescopes, digital cameras, high-speed computers and other innovations scarcely dreamt of a half century ago, astronomers today have located hundreds of exoplanets. Thousands more are awaiting confirmation. New worlds are being discovered on an almost daily basis. These revelations advance the quest to find extraterrestrial life, help scientists better understand how our solar system evolved and provide a more accurate picture of how the universe—which is to say, the system that created us—actually works." Timothy Ferris, "What the Discovery of Hundreds of New Planets Means for Astronomy—and Philosophy,"* Smithsonian Magazine *(September 2012), available at: https://www.smithsonianmag.com/science-nature/what-the-discovery-of-hundreds-of-new-planets-means-for-astronomyand-philosophy-17791799/.*]

And, conceivably, some future space probe might yet sniff out life-forms or fossils right here in the solar system—hidden behind the opaque routes of Saturn's satellite Titan, perhaps, or lurking in the frozen tundras of Mars. (Interest in the prospect of Martian life was lent fresh impetus in 1986, when NASA scientists found what conceivably is evidence of microscopic fossils in a rock that was knocked off of the red planet 16,000,000 years ago—probably an asteroid impact—fell to Earth thirteen thousand years ago, and was found in an Antarctic ice field in 1984.) Until a search turns up something, or an overwhelming amount of nothing, discussions of extraterrestrial life will remain largely speculative. The quality of such speculations has improved a bit, though, as science has gained a better comprehension of how life works and how life on this planet began.[6]

Such theorizing has produced two sharply different estimations of whether there is life out there, and if so how much of it, and whether any of it is "intelligent" (which for these purposes we define, pragmatically, as possessing the ability and willingness to communicate with humans).[7] One camp, composed mainly of astronomers and physicists, argues that extraterrestrial life is abundant. "I'm sure they're out there," declares the physicist Paul Horowitz, of Harvard, who runs a SETI (Search for Extraterrestrial Intelligence) search from a modest, 84-foot radio telescope equipped with receivers and analyzers which Horowitz and his students built largely by hand.[8] The other camp, made up mostly of life scientists, maintains that while life may exist on other planets, the odds of there being extraterrestrial *intelligence* are so small that we are almost certainly alone in our galaxy, and perhaps in the entire observable universe. The biologist Ernst Mayr, also of Harvard, holds this position. He declares that "SETI is a deplorable waste of taxpayers' money."[9]

Both sides are reasoning from the same basic data. That they reach opposite conclusions demonstrates how difficult it is to calculate the odds of a phenomenon (in this case, life) of which we have but a single example. Let's examine their reasoning.

The optimistic (meaning pro-SETI) argument, stripped to its essentials, goes like this: There are so many stars in our galaxy that even if only one percent of them are orbited by an Earth-like planet, that would still mean that there were more than a billion Earths in the galaxy. Life began promptly in the history of our planet—the earliest fossil cells date from within a few hundred million years of the formation of the earth's crust. This suggests that life arises readily—at least, on terrestrial planets blessed with liquid—and therefore does not depend upon some sort of extraordinary luck. Once established, life is robust: Terrestrial life has survived numerous that decimated living species, yet evolution proceeded apace. Over the course of billions of years of evolution, intelligence will emerge, sooner or later, because it confers survival advantages on the species that possesses it, which is what evolution is all about. Where there is intelligence, soon there will be technology. Humans went from dugout canoes to spaceships in a scant fourteen thousand years. So it makes sense to use radio telescopes (part of the time) to listen for signals from other technological civilizations, as there are likely to be thousands of them in our galaxy.

The pessimists, to simplify *their* argument, reply as follows: First of all, Earth-like planets are probably much rarer than the optimists assume. The earth is unique in the solar system in that it's at just the right distance from the sun so that water, which we all agree is essential to life as we know it, exists here in all three states, as liquid, ice, and vapor. Were Earth's orbit slightly larger or smaller, this would not be the case, and life might very well not exist here. Even if we accept the hypothesis that there's lots of life in the galaxy, the optimists' reasoning collapses when it comes to the advent of intelligence. The optimists claim that intelligence confers a survival advantage on the species blessed with it, and therefore is selected for in the course of biological evolution. But if that is the case, why did intelligence not appear earlier in Earth's long history? The optimists stand accused of inconsistency: They say that life is in the cards because *it* originated early in our planet's history but they also say that intelligence is in the cards, and it originated late. The error (if it is an error) springs from the discredited assumption that

7

evolution is a stairstep progression, a slow-grinding machine aimed at producing, eventually, human beings. It's not. Evolution is pointless and largely random, and the sequence of events that led to *Homo sapiens sapiens* is so long and tangled, so replete with chance events that might well have gone otherwise, that intelligence almost certainly has never appeared anywhere else in the universe. Such extraterrestrial intelligence as may exist might well be akin to that of whales, spiders, insects, and the millions of other species that have lived on Earth, gifted with quite enough acumen to conduct their own affairs but uninterested in building radio telescopes. Finding such life will be difficult, communication with it harder than with owls and earthworms here at home. So, the pessimists conclude, we're alone, and we might as well get used to it.

My purpose in bringing up this ongoing debate is not to resolve it. (As a practical matter, the resolution is simple: We should continue to operate SETI projects because receipt of a signal *would* solve the riddle, while if we don't listen we shall have relinquished most hope of solving it.) Rather, the debate is interesting for what it reveals about our estrangement from a cosmos we have done so much to try to comprehend. It's quite true, as the pessimists assert, that we don't understand the origins of human intelligence. Scientists have produced useful ideas here, such as the hypothesis that the encephalization of the human brain (its rapid growth relative to body weight) was ratcheted upward (or "pumped," in the jargon) by the selection pressure of our ancestors' having been obliged to come down out of the trees and start hunting on the savannah—this due to climatic changes exaggerated by the ice ages. The neurobiologist William Calvin has stressed the possible role of hunters' throwing stones and spears in selecting the human brain for a command of dynamics.[10] But we don't really know. As the anthropologist Loren Eiseley wrote, "Man, the self-fabricator, is so by reason of gifts he had no part in devising."[11] We fail to understand not only how or why the gift was given us but, more to the point, why it keeps on giving—why our brains equip us not only for domination of our planet but also for a comprehension of the atoms' stuttering and the galaxies' glide. Ignorant of our origins, we are orphans in our own world.

So we *claim* that we are somehow central to things, that science is so ennobling and rewarding an activity—a way to know, and surely therefore something divine—that *it* must reside somewhere near the central fire even if we as its paltry torchbearers do not. But wishing doesn't make it so. The evolutionary record can be interpreted as testifying that intelligence is a fluke, and human history can be read as demonstrating that the invention of science was, too. The ancient Greeks were superb philosophers, who in some sense set us on the road to science, but they produced virtually no technology and almost no real science of their own. From China and India came thousands of volumes of brilliant thought and many technological innovations as well, but few scholars who have studied the matter believe that if science had not arisen in the West a few centuries ago it would by now have emerged in Asia.[12] We're not as much in the dark about the origin of science as about the origin of intelligence, but neither are we in a position to say with confidence that intelligence leads inevitably to science. And the jury is still out as to the alleged Darwinian benefits of having a human-style mind. Science and technology have served us well so far, delivering liberty and prosperity to more people than any other development in history. But they have also raised the specter of global catastrophe through overpopulation, pollution, resource depletion, nuclear disaster, and other agencies set in motion by science and technology themselves.

The proponents of SETI like to calculate the odds of success by way of the "Drake equation." It was fashioned by the astronomer Frank Drake, who in 1960 conducted the world's first SETI observations, training an 85-foot radio telescope at Green Bank, West Virginia, on two nearby sunlike stars and listening at a single frequency. The equation begins with the number of stars in the Milky Way galaxy and then multiplies them by a series of fractions representing the estimated number of sunlike stars, Earth-like planets, and so forth. Some of these values are rather well established and others are much more speculative, but when one plugs in the consensus values, something intriguing emerges: The number of communicating societies in the galaxy turns out to be roughly equal to their average lifetime in years. If a typical technological civilization stays on the air for only about a century, then there are only about one hundred of them in the galaxy, in which case our chances of finding one are rather slim (one in a billion, per star observed). If they last ten thousand years, there are roughly ten thousand of them, and SETI is a better bet. So to listen for a signal is, in a sense, an expression of faith in science and technology. It evinces the belief that "intelligent" creatures—here defined, again, as those with big radio sets—generally manage to survive, rather than fouling their nests or blowing themselves up.

The dark ocean in which the putative civilizations float is made mostly not of space but of time.[13]

The cosmological point here is statistical in character. Two scientists, both using the same facts and both innocent of logical error, can reach wildly different estimates of the abundance of intelligent life in the universe. Why? Because it's exceedingly difficult to make reliable calculations of probability based on a single example. If you draw the king of hearts from a magician's deck of cards, how are you to calculate the odds of your having drawn that particular card if you don't know the contents of the rest of the deck? You can't. You need to see more of the cards. Estimating the likelihood of extraterrestrial life is rather like that—and so, interestingly, is the business of trying to understand why the constants of nature have the values they do. Suppose that the card you draw bears not the king of hearts but the equation $G = 6.67259 \times 10^{-11} \, \mathrm{m^3 kg^{-1} s^{-2}}$. That's useful information: It expresses the gravitational constant, and thus tells you the strength of the gravitational force. But if you're a cosmologist, you'd like to know whether this value is accidental—and how are you going to calculate the odds that the gravitational strength would have *this* value and not some other? We have access to only one universe, and it has just this one gravitational constant, so there's no basis for calculating probabilities.

Casting around for some reference point, we might compare gravity's strength with that of the three other fundamental forces. Doing so, we find that gravitation is remarkably weak. The weak nuclear force is 10^{28}—ten billion billion billion—times stronger than gravity. Electromagnetism is one hundred billion times stronger than that, and the strong nuclear force is a hundred times stronger

11

than electromagnetism. This seems mighty asymmetrical. If the forces were a toy poodle whose shortest leg, the one representing gravity, were one inch in length, the leg representing the strong nuclear force would be far longer than the radius of the observable universe. Does this mean that it's highly unlikely for gravitation to be so weak, or are we calculating the odds in an inappropriate manner? Just how many possible strengths are there for gravity, anyway?

To find out, let's turn to our second question—whether the fact of our existence can tell us anything about the universe. Imagine what would happen were gravity a little stronger. The consequences, it turns out, would be dire. Cosmic expansion would have halted and the universe would have collapsed long before life could have evolved anywhere. Even if expansion somehow continued, the stars would burn out too rapidly to incubate intelligent life on anything like a terrestrial timescale. The sun, for instance, would have lasted only about a billion years.[14] Planets might not even exist: A planet represents a balance between the gravitational force that seeks to collapse it and the electromagnetic force that props up its molecules. Were gravity stronger, planets would light up and become stars, or further collapse to become white dwarfs, neutron stars, or black holes. So life probably could not exist in a strong-gravity universe. If, on the other hand, we decrease the strength of gravity, we find that the primordial material of the big bang simply dissipates, like hot air from a blown tire, before the gravitational fields can gather it into planets, stars, and galaxies. Life seems unlikely in that universe, too. So we've learned something interesting about gravity—that if it didn't have just about exactly the strength it does, we wouldn't be here to inquire into the matter.

Similar arguments can be applied to many other aspects of nature. Why is the universe so old? Because living creatures need carbon (the basis of terrestrial life) as well as iron and other metals (which is why a good multivitamin pill contains minerals), and for a planet to have abundant carbon and iron it had to have formed from material that had been processed through precedent stars, all of which takes billions of years. Why are neutrons slightly more massive than protons? Because if protons were just one percent heavier they would spontaneously decay into neutrons, in which case hydrogen atoms could not exist, nor stars shine: No stars, no life as we know it. Why does space have three dimensions rather than two or four? Because the knots and tangles of genetic material in living cells and the walls of organs can exist only in three dimensions.

To reason in this fashion is to invoke the anthropic cosmological principle—*anthropic* meaning "of humankind," and *cosmological* in that the principle attempts to constrain facts about the universe by taking into account our presence here. To "constrain" means, in this context, to improve our ability to calculate the odds of nature's being the way it is, by reducing its potential states from an infinite number to the much smaller set of states in which it is possible for life to exist. This approach allows us to calculate that the odds of our drawing the gravitational constant card that we did are pretty good: The deck can hold only cards with values quite close to the one we drew. Otherwise there would be nobody around to draw the card.

The anthropic principle has complicated historical roots in the various "design" arguments, which see order in nature as requiring an intelligent agency, and the teleological philosophies, which see nature as having a purpose. But these need not detain us, and we can pick up the story in 1974, when the term *anthropic principle* was coined by the British cosmologist Brandon Carter.[15] Carter was out to put limits on the cosmological principle. The cosmological principle is useful, as we've noted, but it raises two difficulties. First, it requires that we set the constants of nature and other facts about the universe against an infinite field of all other possible values—and this makes it next to impossible to calculate the odds of things having come out as they are. The other problem is more specific. It arose when Fred Hoyle and his colleagues composed the steady state theory. They supported the theory with what they rather grandly called the "perfect" cosmological principle. Why limit the cosmological principle to space? they asked. Why not also deny us a privileged position in *time*? The perfect cosmological principle asserts that the universe not only *is* much as we observe it everywhere, but always was so. Therefore no big bang. This struck Brandon Carter as amounting to an abuse of the cosmological principle, one that the anthropic principle would prevent. The anthropic principle limits acceptable cosmological theories to those that take human existence into account. "What we can expect to observe must be restricted by the conditions necessary for our presence as observers," Carter said.[16]

Nowadays the anthropic principle comes in three flavors—weak, strong, and "participatory." The weak anthropic principle (WAP) simply states that (as we have been saying) scientists, in considering how nature might be otherwise, need calculate the odds not against an infinity of all other

14

possible values but only against those that permit the emergence of life. The strong version (SAP) goes further: It declares that the universe must be constrained so as to allow for life. As Carter put it (for purposes of definition, not as an expression of his own beliefs), "The universe must be such as to admit the creation of observers within it."[17] In other words, no observers, no universe. The participatory version (PAP) is due principally to John Wheeler. It emphasizes the role of quantum observership in resolving potentiality into actuality and attempts to construct a new conception of the universe as observer-dependent, in the sense that (as we heard Wheeler say earlier) phenomena are phenomena only when they are *observed* phenomena—meaning that things cannot be said to exist until they are observed.[18]

Of the three, only the WAP enjoys much currency in scientific circles, where it has provided some illuminating insights into just how life "as we know it" depends on a wide range of cosmic conditions. Yet even this mild potion remains potentially toxic, and arguably the WAP continues to confuse as many scientists as it illuminates. Some of the controversy stems from the fact that the WAP is less scientific than philosophical, and philosophizing is about as popular among working scientists as is bird-watching among professional golfers. But much of it arises from a level-headed sense that the WAP represents philosophizing of a particularly dangerous kind.

Trouble brews, for instance, whenever scientists confuse *constraining* a phenomenon with *explaining* it. If they think they have explained it by showing it to be necessary to life, they may be discouraged from seeking a deeper and more productive explanation. This has already happened.

The phenomenon in question was the isotropy of the universe—the fact that it looks the same in all directions. As we have seen, the universe is isotropic to a remarkable degree. In 1973, Stephen Hawking and Barry Collins of Cambridge University invoked the anthropic principle to "explain" cosmic isotropy by noting that if the universe were *not* highly isotropic it would have been difficult for stars and planets to form and, therefore, for life to exist. Fortunately, this argument was not accepted as final, and soon thereafter, isotropy was accounted for in a much more natural and elegant fashion, as resulting from inflation. So we need to be careful that anthropic constraints don't blind us to deeper explanations. If, for instance, the value of the gravitational constant is not an accident but the inevitable consequence of a deep natural structure to be revealed by superstring or some other theory, the anthropic principle will at best have been a red herring when it comes to understanding gravity.

Another danger is that because the anthropic principle is *post hoc*—the universe having been here before we were—it is susceptible to the *post-hoc* fallacy. This fallacy consists of assuming that because B followed A in time, A must therefore have caused B or have been an essential condition for its existence. Because terrestrial life arose from the universe as it is, we may, if we are not careful, lapse into an unduly rigid interpretation of nature as having to be just as it is in order to accommodate life of any kind. But life may be much more various than we, who have witnessed no other form of life, can as yet imagine. A biosphere can be broadly defined as a system, itself highly ordered, that maintains or increases order. To perform this feat, which locally reverses the law of entropy, requires two things—an energy differential (e.g., a hotter region close to a colder one) and enough local stability to permit, but not stifle, evolution.[19] These conditions may well be satisfied in a far wider range of circumstances than our experience indicates. Perhaps it is sheer science fiction to think that our belief that life depends, say, on carbon and oxygen will one day be disproved by the discovery of alcohol-guzzling jellyfish adrift in giant molecular clouds or non-carbonous crabs creeping across the surfaces of neutron stars. But enough of the predictions of the science fiction writers have come true to warn us against underestimating the power of the human imagination, and the anthropic principle can degenerate into stupefaction if it pretends to constrain the unknown simply by identifying antecedents of the known. One may stroll across the Brooklyn Bridge and buy a flounder at the Fulton Fish Market, but that does not mean that the flounder's existence required that of the Brooklyn Bridge, or that there are no other fish in the sea.

Still, ideas are like explosives: The fact that they are dangerous does not mean they ought not to be employed. And the anthropic principle looks a lot more sensible if we entertain the hypothesis that there are many universes, each with its own set of physical laws. Some of these universes are stillborn and wink out of existence in moments, Many have large cosmological constants (a condition the particle physicists regard, by the way, as a much more natural vacuum state than the vanishing small value found in our universe). They remain pure space, forever ballooning, incredibly big, eternally empty. Others contain life wildly different from ours. Others are vast and full of things, but never give rise to life. If they are unobserved, may they be said to exist? If a sterile universe eventually swims over the horizon of an inhabited universe, does it *then* exist? Understandably, some working cosmologists are impatient with these ideas; they find it difficult to see what purpose is served by postulating the existence of universes whose existence we cannot confirm or deny. But perhaps such theories will prove valuable as stimulants to the reasoned imagination, as scientists begin seriously to envision what nature may be like beyond this universe, out where the rules are different, and to sift out which rules *can* be different. A thinker engaged in pan-universal speculations may never know whether he or she has at last broken through to a realm where the imagination has surpassed the inventiveness of the real. But if the answer is yes—if there is and ever has been but one universe, so that all such speculations are hollow—it will be the first time that nature proved less clever and less resourceful than we are.

The cosmologist is like William Blake's builder of a ladder to the stars. "I want! I want!" he cries, but there's nothing to hold up the top of the ladder, and he's not too sure about who's holding the bottom, either. Who are we, and what do we want? Cosmology like every other human endeavor comes back to us in the end, but it's not just *about* us. That's the beauty of it—that we return from the voyage altered. Galaxies, like ocean coral, work a sea change, and make of us something rich and strange.[20] T. S. Eliot wrote:

> *We shall not cease from exploration*
> *And the end of all our exploring*
> *Will be to arrive where we started*
> *And know the place for the first time.*[21]

If this poem ended with the third line, it would rank among the dreariest of modern times. Science is too much trouble if its point is to bring us back to where we started. But the fourth line is cosmology's credo. For to find *our* place, we must know *the* place, cellar to ceiling, from the taproots to the stars, the whole shebang.

Contrarian Theological Afterword

> *I had only prayer, prayer*
> *and science.*
> —GILLIAN CONOLEY[1]

> *In a Jewish theological seminar there was an hours-long discussion about proofs of the existence of God. After some hours, one rabbi got up and said, "God is so great, he does not even need to exist."*
> —VICTOR WEISSKOPF[2]

WHAT ABOUT GOD?

The deity has been implicated in cosmology since the dawn of human history. Every monotheistic religion credits God with having created the universe. Plato, Aristotle, and scores of other philosophers have declared God responsible for the natural order revealed in the regular motions of the planets and stars. Theologians assert that it is owing to God's grace that human reason can comprehend the laws of nature. God has even been invoked as a solution to the observership problem posed by the Copenhagen interpretation of quantum physics. So it seems reasonable to ask what cosmology, now that it is a science, can tell us about God.

Sadly, but in all earnestness, I must report that the answer as I see it is: Nothing. Cosmology presents us neither the face of God, nor the handwriting of God, nor such thoughts as may occupy the mind of God. This does not mean that God does not exist, or that he did not create the universe, or universes. It means that cosmology offers no resolution to such questions.

Many thinkers, living and dead, would disagree. They throw the cosmological bones and divine signs that there is a God, or that there is not. Let us briefly critique their points of view. Historically, three intellectual proofs of God's existence loom large. They are the *argument from design*, the *cosmological proof*, and the *ontological proof*.

The argument from design says, in effect, that God is in the details. When we examine the wonderful efficiency and appropriateness of things, it seems impossible that they got to be that way other than through the work of a divine intellect. As the English clergyman William Paley famously pictured it, if one were to come across a pocket watch in the woods, one would conclude, on examining its intricate structure, that it had been designed by an intelligence for a purpose. The design argument is deistic, meaning that it addresses God as a creator and not as an intervenor who works miracles in the universe he has created. (And this Afterword restricts itself to deism, as cosmology in its notorious impersonality has little to say about the existence of a personal God.) It has been treated with respect by philosophers and others who are repelled by the notion of a personal God who answers prayers by influencing the outcome of battles and football games, but believe that the marvelous architecture of nature requires a supernatural explanation.

The anthropic principle is the design argument in scientific costume. Its appeal is demonstrated in Sir Fred Hoyle's evaluation of his own research into the "resonance states" of carbon atoms. Carbon is the fourth most abundant cosmic element, after hydrogen, helium, and oxygen. It is also the basis of terrestrial life. (That's why the study of carbon compounds is known as *organic* chemistry.) Carbon atoms are made inside stars. To make one takes three helium nuclei. The trick is to get two helium nuclei to stick together until they are struck by a third. It turns out that this feat depends critically on the internal resonances of carbon and oxygen nuclei. Were the carbon resonance level only 4 percent lower, carbon atoms wouldn't form in the first place. Were the oxygen resonance level only half a percent higher, virtually all the carbon would be "scoured out," meaning that it would have combined with helium to form oxygen. No carbon, no us, so our existence depends in some sense on the fine-tuning of these two nuclear resonances. Hoyle says that his atheism—and atheism is, let's face it, a faith like any other—was shaken by this discovery. "If you wanted to produce carbon and oxygen in roughly equal quantities by stellar nucleosynthesis, these are just the two levels you have to fix, if your fixing would have to be just about where these levels are actually found to be," Hoyle told a Caltech gathering in 1981. "Is that another put-up, artificial job? . . . I am inclined to think so. A common sense interpretation of the facts suggests that a superintellect has monkeyed with physics, as well as with chemistry and biology, and that there are no blind forces worth speaking about in nature. The numbers one calculates from the facts seem to me so overwhelming as to put this conclusion almost beyond question."[3]

But despite its having been entertained by thinkers from Paley to Hoyle, the design argument suffers from at least two serious defects.

First, it was always woefully anthropocentric. Design implies a purpose, and God's purpose in designing the universe was assumed to be either to make us, or to make things nice for us, or both. The French science writer Bernard de Fontenelle lampooned this position in his 1686 book *A*

Plurality of Worlds. "We are all naturally like that madman at Athens, who fancied that all the ships were his that came into the Port of Pyraeus," he wrote. "Nor is our folly less extravagant. We believe all things in nature designed for our use, and do but ask a philosopher, to what purpose there is that prodigious company of fixed stars, when a far less number would perform the service they do us. He answers coldly, they were made to please our sight."[4] The larger the universe looms, the sillier it becomes to maintain that it was all put together for us. To posit a human-centered purpose to the heavens smacks of a lamentable humorlessness about the human condition, as Bertrand Russell was quick to point out. "The believers in Cosmic Purpose make much of our supposed intelligence but their writings make one doubt it," Russell wrote. "If I were granted omnipotence, and millions of years to experiment in, I should not think Man much to boast of as the final result of all my efforts."[5]

More damaging was the historical fact that believers in the design argument habitually drew their evidence from the biological world, citing as evidence of God's handiwork the marvelous adaptations of rattlesnakes and bower birds. This proved to have been an unfortunate choice of fields, once Darwin demonstrated that biological systems evolve by chance and not design.[6] (Darwin himself, though respectful of religion and loath to enter into theological disputation, nevertheless admitted, "I can see no evidence of beneficent design, or indeed design of any kind, in the details."[7]) Driven from the biological arena, the design argument has since sought refuge in physics and cosmology. Some thinkers expect that it will fare better there. I doubt it. A unified theory that showed the constants of nature to have resulted from phase transitions or other chance events would erode the design argument. So would the admittedly more speculative hypothesis that there are many universes with many different sets of laws, in only some of which life may be expected to arise. Darwinism does not dispel the mystery of life. Rather, it equates the mystery of life with the mystery of existence, of being. But the fact that something seems mysterious does not mean that God did it.[8]

Flawed though it may be, the argument from design is more robust than the cosmological and ontological proofs.

The cosmological proof goes back to Aristotle, who held that the existence of motion requires an ultimate source of dynamics, an "unmoved mover"—that is, God. It claims that any hierarchy of existence requires some overarching state of existence, that of an extant God. Descartes, similarly, interpreted his moment-to-moment existence as depending on the existence of a being beyond himself The cosmological proof has enjoyed a long reign, due in part to the sentiments of thinkers who regard the origin of the universe as a problem inaccessible to science. But it has also encountered serious objections. Why, for instance, must we think of existence as a slippery slope, such that divine intervention is constantly required to prevent things from sliding down into the despond of nonexistence? And is causation really so deep a precept of nature as to render God requisite? Another problem, much discussed in theological circles, turns on the question of whether God had free will when he created the universe. If so, he was free to make the universe in a random, haphazard way. But if the universe is random, what need have we to postulate the existence of God? And if it is not—if, say, God could have made the universe only the most reasonable way, or in a way that promoted human existence—then God cannot be all-powerful. As the philosopher Keith Ward puts it, "The old dilemma—either God's acts are necessary and therefore not free (could not be otherwise), or they are free and therefore arbitrary (nothing determines what they shall be)—has been sufficient to impale the vast majority of Christian philosophers down the ages."9

The ontological proof (*ontology* is the study of the nature of being) dates from the eleventh century, when Saint Anselm, the archbishop of Canterbury, made the following argument: We conceive of God as "something than which nothing more perfect can be conceived." From the fact that we have this concept, it follows logically that such a being must exist. Why? Because if he did not, we would be able to conceive of something still more perfect—namely, a perfect being that *does* exist— and it is an absurdity to conceive of something more perfect than the most perfect conceivable being. Just as it is better to have ten real dollars than ten imaginary dollars, it is more perfect to be perfect *and exist* than to be perfect but nonexistent. So the concept of a most perfect being requires that such a being exist. The ontological proof is rather more subtle and persuasive than it looks at first blush, but so logically slippery that it aroused indignation even in the Middle Ages. (Gaunilo of Marmoutier inveighed against it while Anselm was still alive.) Its most telling refutation came from Immanuel Kant.

In *The Critique of Pure Reason*, Kant effectively demolished both the cosmological and the ontological proofs. The ontological argument,

Kant pointed out, conflates two quite distinct realms of thought—that of pure reason (e.g., mathematics), in which premises internally dictate conclusions, and that of things, in which we reach judgments based on experience.[10] As Kant writes, "Having formed an *a priori* conception of a thing, the content of which was made to embrace existence, we believed ourselves safe in concluding that, because existence belongs necessarily to the object of the conception (that is, under the condition of my positing this thing as given), the existence of the thing is also posited necessarily, and that it is therefore absolutely necessary— merely because its existence has been cogitated in the conception."[11] In other words, having postulated that things exist, the purveyors of the ontological proof argue that existence is an attribute of things. But this is circular reasoning. And it is false, further, to think of "existence" as a property of things on a par with, say, their inertia or electrical charge. I might reasonably announce that I have ten dollars in my pocket, but not that I have in my pocket five existing and five nonexisting dollars. And, as Kant noted, the cosmological proof recapitulates the same error. It pastes the tag of "existing" on things, then asserts that the existence of any being requires the existence of an ultimate being. Since Kant, the ontological and cosmological proofs have continued to sail the philosophical seas, but they are ghost ships, and we cannot expect their tattered sails to carry us very far.

There remains one further argument, in which the participatory anthropic principle is employed to establish God's existence by way of the riddle of quantum observership. As we've seen, the Copenhagen interpretation of quantum mechanics treats as real only observed phenomena, raising the riddle of how the early universe could have evolved in the absence of observers. The riddle may be "solved" by invoking God as the supreme observer, who by scrutinizing all particles converts their quantum potentials into actual states. The same thesis has long been used by believers to resolve one of the oldest (and most tiresome) ontological questions—the one about whether trees exist when nobody observes them, or make a sound when they fall and there's nobody around to hear it. This position is summarized in a hoary bit of doggerel:

> There once was a man who said, "God
> Must think it exceedingly odd
> If he finds that this tree
> Continues to be
> When there is no one about in the quad."
>
> "Dear sir, your astonishment's odd
> I am always about in the quad
> And that's why the tree
> Will continue to be
> Since observed by,
> Yours faithfully, God."[12]

But to go through such gyrations just to salvage the Copenhagen interpretation is to make a very small tail wag a very big dog, or God. And that's the trouble, really, with all cosmological invocations of the deity. Belief in God explains everything about the material universe; therefore it explains nothing. George Bernard Shaw made this point nicely in a toast to Einstein at a black-tie banquet in 1930. "Religion is always right," Shaw said. "Religion solves every problem and thereby abolishes problems from the universe. . . . Science is the very opposite. Science is always wrong. It never solves a problem without raising ten more problems."[13]

Atheists, meanwhile, draw sustenance from cosmological findings indicating that the universe emerged from chaos. Evidence in their support is mounting. The Harrison-Zeldovich spectrum of density fluctuations in the cosmic microwave background, confirmed within observational limits by the COBE satellite, suggests that random flux originated the stars and galaxies. Andrei Linde's chaotic inflationary theories presuppose a random distribution of primordial scalar fields. And, as we've been saying, Darwinian evolution depends on chance genetic mutations. If the world emerged from chaos and works by chance, what role can there be for an omniscient creator?

Because atheists have in many times and places been accused of intellectual arrogance it seems appropriate to examine this charge, if only to dismiss it. The accusation of arrogance stems from the claim that atheists pretend to know everything, since one would have to "walk the whole expanse of infinity," in Thomas Chalmers's words, to prove that God exists nowhere in the universe.[14] This position is simply insupportable. A scientist need not examine every proton in the universe in order to establish that protons originated in the bonding of quarks in the big bang. Nor is theism stoutly served by maintaining that even if there is no evidence of God's existence here, there might be on some other planet. On a logical level, a believer who argues that atheism is overweening, in that atheists cannot disprove every possible definition of God, is putting too much water in his wine: Whatever can it mean to say that "God" exists if you are unprepared to defend some particular conception of God? As the nineteenth-century English essayist Charles

Bradlaugh wrote, in his "Plea for Atheism," an atheist is certainly justified in saying., "The Bible God I deny; the Christian God I disbelieve in; but I am not rash enough to say there is no God as long as you tell me you are unprepared to define God to me."[15]

Ad hominem slurs aside, however, when the cosmological arguments propounded by atheists are subjected to reasoned criticism, they fare no better than the comparable arguments of believers. To find evidence of randomness in nature does not prove that there is no God. This is evident from two considerations.

First, it is impossible to prove conclusively that what appears to be random really *is* random. The sequence of numbers 4159265358 . . . looks pretty random, until we notice that it is the second through the eleventh decimal places of pi. (From another perspective—that, say, of a police detective—it might be significant that it's also a San Francisco telephone number.) It's actually quite difficult to obtain numbers that will pass for random, as cryptographers at the CIA understand: They do things like bounce radar signals off the ionosphere and use digitized strings of the radar echoes for encoding, and they're *still* not certain that the results are truly random. Seeming chaos can conceal design.

And even if the universe did arise from chaos, a believer could reasonably argue that God elected chaos as best suited for that purpose. What better way, for instance, to create the infinite and diverse worlds envisioned in the many-universe models? There is a "joke" about this issue, in which an atheist, asked by a believer where the universe came from, says, "It came from chaos," to which the believer responds, "Ah, but who made the chaos?"

This isn't really a joke at all, but rather a succinct statement of two ways of thinking about the problem of creation, one of which is satisfied with chaos as an ultimate explanation and the other which sees chaos as just another system. From these and other considerations we may conclude that atheism is no more soundly footed in cosmological science than is theism.

So we are left with—what? In my view, a situation in which we would clearly be better off if we left God out of cosmology altogether. The origin of the universe and of the constants of nature is a mystery, and may forever remain so. But to assign to God the job of doing everything we don't (yet) understand is to abuse the concept of God. Such thinking posits, in the lingo, a "god of the gaps"—a deity who is hard at work making nature do those things that we fail to understand. I am unaware that God ever proffered such a job description for himself. Anyway, it seems unworthy of him: Feeble indeed is a machine that requires the constant intervention of its designer to keep it running. Nor is it clear why, if God's dominion consists of tending to the unexplained aspects of the phenomenal world, he would have conferred upon humans their aptitude for science, which in constantly closing the stops has steadily diminished the putative realm of the god of the gaps, Nor does it seem satisfactory for God to have created the universe with a specific purpose in mind, the realization of which required billions of years to attain. As the German philosopher Friedrich Schelling asked, "Has creation a final purpose at all, and if so why is it not attained immediately, why does perfection not exist from the very beginning?"[16] Equally paltry is the notion that God set in motion a deterministic universe, one that runs perfectly but produces only phenomena that he knew in advance would occur. That's just too dull.

More appropriate, I should think, is the view that God created the universe out of an interest in spontaneous creativity—that he wanted nature to produce surprises, phenomena that he himself could not have foreseen. What would such a *creative* universe be like? Well, it would for one thing be impossible to predict in detail. And this seems to be the case with the universe we inhabit. The information theorists find that even if the entire universe were a computer, or could be converted into a computer of the maximum theoretically possible capacity, that computer would be incapable of predicting all future phenomena. Further, a creative universe should give rise to agencies that are themselves creative, which is to say, unpredictable. There is in our universe such an agency, spectacularly successful at reversing the dreary slide of entropy and making surprising things happen. We call it life. It would be suitable if this agency were to inquire into the workings of the universe, winnowing out the predictable from the unpredictable and inventing theories to account for the difference. And that is what intelligence does. Better still if thinking creatures were to perceive that they are all in the same boat—"Poor, benighted members of the same ship's company," in Adlai Stevenson's phrase—and hence treat one another kindly and assert that God is love.[17] And so we do, though not often enough.

Finally, in a creative universe God would betray no trace of his presence, since to do so would be to rob the creative forces of their independence, to turn them from the active pursuit of answers to mere supplication of God. And so it is: God's language is silence. The Old Testament suggests that God fell silent in response to the request of the terrified believers who said to Moses, "Speak thou with us, and we will hear: but let not God speak with us, lest we die." Whatever the reason, God ceases speaking with the book of Job, and soon stops intervening in human affairs generally, leading Gideon to ask, "If the Lord be with us, why then . . . where be all his miracles which our fathers told us of?"[18] The author of the Twenty-second Psalm cries ruefully, "My God, my God, why hast thou forsaken me?"

Whether he left or was ever here I do not know, and don't believe we ever shall know. But one can learn to live with ambiguity—that much is requisite to the seeking spirit—and with the silence of the stars. All who genuinely seek to learn, whether atheist or believer, scientist or mystic, are united in having not *a* faith but faith itself. Its token is reverence, its habit to respect the eloquence of silence. For God's hand may be a human hand, if you reach out in loving kindness, and God's voice your voice, if you but speak the truth.

Notes

A Place for Us

1. This fable has been repeated many times. The wording here is from Nevill Mott, "Science Will Never Give Us the Answers to All Our Questions," in Henry Margenau and Roy Abraham Varghese, editors, *Cosmos, Bios, Theos.* LaSalle, Ill.: Open Court, 1992, p. 69.

2. James Branch Cabell, *The Silver Stallion.* London: J. Lane, 1926, chapter 26.

3. Since modern science originated in Europe I am referring here mainly to Europeans, but the same could be said of many other prescientific cultures as well.

4. See Stillman Drake, *Galileo at Work.* Chicago: University of Chicago Press, 1978, p. 212.

5. Actually, the only attainable unambiguous answer is "Yes," since we shall never be able to prove that there is *no* life beyond Earth. No matter how many sterile worlds we reconnoitered, it would always be possible that the next one harbored life. But were many such searches to produce only negative results, and were new scientific findings to strongly indicate that the incidence of life is very improbable, we might well lose interest—if not in the question, at least in our ability to answer it.

6. Curiously, science still lacks an agreed-upon delineation of what life is. There are at least five viable definitions—physiological, metabolic, biochemical, genetic, and thermodynamic—and each is dogged by flaws and exceptions. This in itself may illustrate the difficulty of working with a phenomenon of which scientists have but one example. *[Editor's note: Over two decades on, we are no closer to resolving this question.]*

7. One can imagine many intelligent life forms that could not or would not transmit radio signals. These would remain invisible to a SETI investigation. However, the objection that many alien civilizations would be "too advanced" to use radio is not terribly persuasive. Although the word "radio" has an obsolescent ring to us, invoking as it does memories of an entertainment medium largely supplanted by television, it really means any communication that employs the electromagnetic spectrum.

"Radio" in this sense is an efficient and far-reaching way to transmit just about any sort of information one can think of, including moving and still photographs, words and sounds, holograms and web pages, and so on. In any event, most SETI scientists assume that we are much more likely to detect a signal that was meant to be intercepted than to "eavesdrop" on the private conversations of alien worlds.

8. Paul Horowitz, Harvard SETI symposium, October 31, 1995.

9. Ernst Mayr, *Toward a New Philosophy of Biology*. Cambridge: Harvard University Press, 1988, p. 73. The one publicly funded American SETI project was canceled and the remaining ones are all privately funded; taxpayers' funds are no longer involved.

10. For a discussion, see William Calvin, *The Ascent of Mind: Ice Age Climates and the Evolution of Intelligence*. New York: Bantam, 1990.

11. Loren Eiseley, *The Star-Thrower*. New York: Times Books, 1978, pp. 120-121.

12. For a discussion, see Alan Cromer, *Uncommon Sense: The Heretical Nature of Science*. New York: Oxford University Press, 1993.

13. Even if communicative worlds are commonplace, it seems unlikely that they last *forever*. And if they typically are mortal, most must have flourished and subsided in the past. For a discussion of how some of their knowledge could have been preserved in the memory banks of galactic communications networks, see my *The Mind's Sky: Human Intelligence in a Cosmic Context*. New York: Bantam, 1992.

14. Some theorists have suggested that life might evolve more rapidly in a high-gravity universe with stars burning more furiously. But we don't have to turn up the strength of gravity very much before the universe would collapse too quickly to permit the formation of any stars at all, so this argument has only a narrow application.

15. Carter's immediate precursors include the English mathematician G. J. Whitrow, who in 1955 pointed out that space must be three-dimensional since life could not otherwise exist, and Robert Dicke, who in 1957 urged that the values of fundamental constants like gravity and the charge of the electron are "not random but conditioned by biological factors"—i.e., by the existence of life. (R. H. Dicke, *Reviews of Modern Physics*, 29:355, 363 [1957].)

16. In Tony Rothman, "A 'What You See Is What You Beget' Theory," *Discover*, May 1987, p. 91.

17. In Henry T. Simmons, "Redefining the Cosmos," *Mosaic*, March–April 1982, p. 19.

18. The mathematical physicist Frank Tipler, of Tulane University, has likened the universe to a computer and proposed that if it is closed and therefore destined to recollapse, all cognizant beings could be "resurrected" in a gigantic computer simulation made possible by the reconvergence of world lines near the end of time. Furthermore, he argues (on technical grounds that I'll not go into here) that such simulations could permit the resurrected intelligences to enjoy immortal life—even though, to an "outside" observer, it would all be over in the wink of an eye. Tipler's book making this extraordinary case, *The Physics of Immortality: Modern Cosmology, God, and the Resurrection of the Dead* (New York: Doubleday, 1994), is a striking mix of wistfulness and hardheaded science. He claims that his model generates "the notions of 'Holy Spirit,' grace,' 'heaven,' hell,' and 'purgatory,'" and that "it may also be possible to develop a Christology in the model," while maintaining that "either theology is pure nonsense, a subject with no content, or else theology must ultimately become a branch of physics." Tipler called his theory FAP, the final anthropic principle— that "laws of physics allow life to exist *forever*." The science writer Martin Gardner memorably, if unkindly, dubbed it "CRAP—the Completely Ridiculous Anthropic Principle."

19. For a discussion, see Gerald Feinberg and Robert Shapiro, *Life Beyond Earth*. New York: Morrow, 1980.

20.   *Full fathom five thy father lies;*
    Of his bones are coral made;
    These are the pearls that were his eyes;
    Nothing of him that doth fade
    But doth suffer a sea-change
    Into something rich and strange . . .
(SHAKESPEARE, "Ariel's Song," *The Tempest*, I, ii, 396ff.)

21. T. S. Eliot, "Little Gidding," part 5, in his *Four Quartets*.

Contrarian Theological Afterword

1. Gillian Conoley, "Beckon," *American Poetry Review*, March–April 1996, p. 9.

2. Victor Weisskopf, "There Is a Bohr Complementarity Between Science and Religion," in Henry Margenau and Roy Abraham Varghese, editors, *Cosmos, Bios, Theos*. La Salle, Ill.: Open Court, 1993, p. 127.

3. Fred Hoyle, "The Universe: Past and Present Reflections," *Engineering & Science*, November 1981, p. 12.

4. Bernard de Fontenelle, *A Plurality of Worlds*, John Glanville, translator. New York: Nonesuch Press, 1929, p. 20.

5. In John D. Barrow and Frank Tipler, *The Anthropic Cosmological Principle*. Oxford: Oxford University Press, 1986, galley proof p. 65.

6. The inescapability of this finding has recently been recapitulated in Richard Dawkins's aptly titled book *The Blind Watchmaker: Why the Evidence of Evolution Reveals a Universe Without Design*. New York: Norton, 1987.

7. Letter to J. Hooker, 1870, in F. Darwin and A. C. Seward, *More Letters of Charles Darwin*. New York: Appleton, 1903, 1:321. In Stanley Jaki, *The Road of Science and the Ways to God*. Chicago: University of Chicago Press, 1978, p. 293.

8. When giving public lectures on cosmology I am often asked about my own religious convictions. On such occasions I sometimes tell the story about a theologian who is asked by an old friend, "Do you believe in God?"

The theologian replies, "I can answer you, but I promise that you won't *understand* my answer. Do you want me to go ahead?"

"Sure."

"OK, the answer is 'Yes.'"

The point of the story has to do, of course, with the preposterous ambiguity of such terms as "believe" and "God." And that is one reason I try to avoid answering such questions. Nor do I see that a statement of my personal beliefs would do much to illuminate the issues under discussion in this book.

But, if only to avoid being coy about it, let me say that I'm an agnostic. The term is derived from the Greek *agnostos*, "unknowable." It was coined in 1869 by Thomas Henry Huxley, who sought to define his stance on religion in contributions to the Metaphysical Society, an organization of eminent English thinkers that met nine times a year to discuss philosophical and theological matters. Huxley meant it to oppose gnosticism, which asserts the primacy of mystical and esoteric faith over logic and reason. His position was comparable to that of Hume, who in the essay "Of Miracles" in his *Enquiry Concerning Human Understanding* writes that "a wise man . . . proportions his belief to the evidence."

There are two varieties of agnosticism.

"Weak" agnosticism consists of suspending one's opinion as to the existence of God—pending, I suppose, the introduction of further evidence. This stance seems wishy-washy and probably deserves its dismissal, by a contemptuous Friedrich Engels, as "shame-faced" atheism.

My position is "strong" agnosticism. It denies that God's existence can ever be disproved. There are many definitions of God, some of which seem to say nothing at all about God *except* that he exists. I hold that it is impossible to disprove all these definitions. If, to take an extreme example, science were one day to establish beyond reasonable doubt that the universe was created by a mad scientist in a basement laboratory, it would still be possible to posit that the prior universe in which that scientist lived was created by God. Moreover, that scientist, regardless of his inhuman brilliance, would be unable, in principle, to prove that God does not exist—or so I maintain. I might add that this view is not just a matter of logic-chopping, or a sly way of skirting theological issues. It is offered in good faith, with an honest appreciation of the merits of religion, science, and reason. It's not just that I don't know; I assert that we *cannot* know.

Strong agnosticism is open to disproof. Were God to appear on Earth tomorrow and work convincing miracles—an act that would imply deplorable taste on his part, but which is possible—then agnosticism, like atheism, would have been disproved.

As to the usefulness of the opinions of mine I remain a skeptic.

9. Keith Ward, *Rational Theology and the Creativity of God.* New York: Pilgrim Press,, 1982, p. 73, in Paul

Davies, *The Mind of God*, New York: Simon & Schuster, 1992. p. 180.

10. In Kantian language these are the realms of *analytic* and *synthetic* propositions, respectively.

11. Kant, *The Critique of Pure Reason*, J. M. D, Mieklejohn, translator. Chicago: University of Chicago Great Books, 1952, p. 180. Harrison Ford's character in the movie *Star Wars* makes much the same point. Told that he may, if he is of service, be rewarded with more money than he can imagine, he replies, "I can *imagine* a great deal." But the fact that he can imagine it doesn't mean it exists.

12. This version of the verse is from Amit Goswami, *The Self-Aware Universe*, in manuscript, pp, 129-130.

13. In Blanche Patch, *Thirty Years with G.B.S.* London: Gollancz, 1951. Quoted in Edward Harrison, *Cosmology: The Science of the Universe*. Cambridge, U.K.: Cambridge University Press, 1981, p. 179.

14. Thomas Chalmers, *On Natural Theology*, 18th edition, p. 35, in Paul Edwards, editor, *The Encyclopedia of Philosophy*. New York: Macmillan, 1967, vol. 1, p, 186.

15. Charles Bradlaugh, in Paul Edwards, "Atheism," Paul Edwards, editor, *The Encyclopedia of Philosophy*. New York: Macmillan, 1967, vol. 1, p, 177.

16. F. W. J. Von Schelling, *System of Transcendental Idealism*, in John D. Barrow and Frank J. Tipler, *The Anthropic Cosmological Principle*. New York: Oxford University Press, 1986, p. 138. Schelling's answer to his own rhetorical question is "Because God is a *life*, not a mere being."

17. Adlai Stevenson, speech delivered at Northwestern University, Evanston, Illinois, 1962. Francis Bacon notes that from ancient times believers have placed "the angels of love, which are termed seraphim" at the top of the heavenly hierarchy, even above "the angels of light, which are termed cherubim." (Bacon, *Advancement of Learning*, I, VI, 3.)

18. "You, speak with us, and we will listen; but let God not speak with us, lest we die." (Exodus 20:19.) "If Yahweh is with us, then where are all His miracles that our fathers told us about?" (Judges 6:13 Authorized [King James] Version.)

Parallel Siblings:
A Pandeistic and Taoist Convergence

John Ross, Jr.

John Ross, Jr. holds an ALM degree in Dramatic Arts from Harvard and two theological degrees: one from Boston University (S.T.M., Systematic Theology) and a second from Loyola University Chicago (M.P.S. Pastoral/*Religious Communication*). *John is the author of three science-religion poetry collections: Where the Designer Came From: Evolution, Creation, Hominids and the Skirmish of the Double Helix,* 2011; *COSMOTRINITY: Newton, Einstein, Hawking with the Origins of the Anthropic Principle and a Curtsy Toward QEDEM (Time),* 2013; and more recently, *GENES, GERMS, GEODES and GOD: Verses Exploring Science, Faith, Doubt and Religion,* 2016. He is a senior lecturer in Theatre and Communication at Northeastern Illinois University in Chicago. He teaches courses in Drama, Leadership, Interpersonal Communication; and a new course entitled: "Communicating Science and Religion" based upon his new textbook: *SCIENCE & RELIGION: A Handbook for Interpersonal Dialogue, Discussion and Debate,* 2017. His academic interests surround the intersection between religion, science and the arts. He is currently finishing his Doctor of Ministry degree (D.Min) in *Transformational Leadership* at the Boston University School of Theology.

The ancient heritage of Taoism trails back at least to the 4th century BCE. Early Taoism drew its cosmological designs from the School of *Yin-Yang* (i.e., *the Naturalists*); and was thus profoundly shaped by one of the primogenital texts of all Chinese culture: the *I Ching*. In general, the *I Ching* attempts to illustrate a metaphysical system about how to keep human disposition and conduct in harmony with the interchanging phases and cycles of nature.[1] The so-called "Legalist" Shen Buhai (c. 400 – c. 337 BCE) according to many scholars may have been a chief influence, expounding the realpolitik of *wu-wei*, which has become a central principle of *Taoism*.[2]

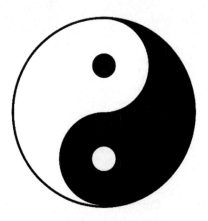

Fig. 1; The popularized *Yin-yan* symbol, (陰陽 yīnyáng, lit. "dark-bright"or "negative-positive") is an archetype of dualism in ancient Chinese philosophy. It symbolically illustrates how conflicting or opposing forces may actually be complementary and interdependent in natural creation, and how they may give rise to each other as they dynamically interdepend and interelate.

As such, The *Tao Te Ching* is a brief but highly condensed book (roughly 81 short chapters) encompassing the teachings attributed to Laozi or Lao Tzu, and is commonly thought to be the bedrock or theological foundation of the Taoist tradition, together with the later writings of Zhuangzi as a form of further thematic bolstering. In Chapter 38 of the *Tao Te Ching*, we are told the definition of a theological Leader (or the master of Taoism), he or she is one who resists control and one who *does nothing (i.e., wu-wei), yet leaves nothing undone*:[3]

The Leader never attempts to be authoritative;
thus true authority is granted.
Ordinary individuals keep reaching for
control;
Thus they will never have enough.

THE Leader does nothing,
And so nothing is left undone.
The ordinary person is forever doing and
doing,
Only more and more will need to
be done.

A Kind person achieves something,
yet something remains
unachieved.
The just person attains something,
and leaves many things to be
attained.
The moral person achieves something,
and when no one reacts,
This person take quick action, utilizes
force.

WHEN the *Tao* is misplaced, there is
kindness.
When kindness is misplaced,
there is
ethics.

When ethics is misplaced, there is
ceremony.

                    Ceremony is the blanket of proper
belief
          The foundation of turmoil.

          THE Leader must be concerned
                    With the lowest point and not the
peak,
          With the crop and not the sowing.
                    The Leader has no personal will.
          The Leader dwells in veracity,
                    and permits all daydreams to exit

To this very day, Taoism has had a profound influence on Chinese culture in the course of many centuries, and Taoists (a label traditionally attributed only to the clergy and not to their devout followers), has been integrated into Chinese alchemy and astrology, Zen Buddhism, numerous martial arts, Chinese medicine, *feng shui*,[4] and many styles of *qigong*.[5] Each has been intertwined with Taoism throughout its elegant history. Beyond China, Taoism also had influence on surrounding societies in Asia, Europe, Australia and North America.

Fig. 2. Lao-tzu (lit. "Old Master"), ancient Chinese
philosopher and writer. The reputed author of the *Tao
Te Ching* he is considered the founder of philosophical
Taoism. In some Taoist circles he is revered as a deity or
semi-divine being. Picture from Herbert Henry Gowen,
An Outline History of China (1917), p. 58.

Today, the Taoist religious tradition is one of the five religious doctrines officially recognized in the People's Republic of China, and although Taoism does not journey ardently from its East Asian roots, it claims adherents in a number of theologies, philosophies and religious practices. Thus, Taoism has influenced and contributed to theological and spiritual insights which have been carried into virtually all later-developing religious paradigms in both the Eastern and Western hemispheres. Taoism can be broadly defined as *pantheistic*, given its philosophical emphasis on the formlessness of the *Tao* and the primacy of "The Way" rather than more anthropomorphic conceptions of God as exemplified in the Judeo-Christian tradition.

Despite the later introduction of different deities into Taoism, traditional conceptions of *Tao* should not be confused with the Western theism. *Being one with the Tao does not necessarily indicate a union with an eternal deity or spirit* as for example in the Hindu sense of things. None-the-less, the number of Taoists is difficult to truly estimate, due to a variety of factors including how to even comprehensively and fully define Taoism. It is so elusively and shapelessly defined and ineffably expressed when shaped into theological terms. It has been developing and spreading for several millennia across South and East Asia; and more recently in the Western World. There are roughly twenty million Taoists all over the world, the majority of which live in Southeast Asia, especially Taiwan and the People's Republic of China.

According to a survey of religion in China conducted way back in 2010, the number of people practicing some form of Chinese folk religion is near to 950 million (70% of the Chinese). Among these, 173 million (13%) claim an affiliation with Taoist practices. Further in detail, 12 million people claim to be allegedly "Taoists", a term once traditionally used exclusively for initiates, priests and experts of Taoist rituals and methods.[6]

Quite generally, the quintessence of Taoism is the acknowledgement that our world is naturally composed of contrasting forces: embodied by the principle of *Yin and Yang* (see Figure 1). All forces must be peacefully balanced against one another for a rewarding, undisturbed and peaceful life to be accomplished. For all of Taoism, this lone reality, a definitive creative principle of forces, inspires and triggers all other existing realities. Acquaintance and awareness of this modest truth illumines the path of proper conduct: namely one whose quest is to complete a sought-after balance or equilibrium of harmonic truth. The *Tao* is this indescribable and un-pronounceable truth, *a truth which cannot be even spoken.* It is a pathway, and a corridor which we will come to see appears to be in no conflict or inconsistency of harmony with the growing notion of Pandeism.[7] The classic articulation of Taoism is first articulated by Lao Tzu's opening lines found in Chapter 1. These lines are ineffably expressed as follows:

> YOUR Tao which can be told, is
> *not* the never-ending *Tao.*
> Your *Tao* which can be named is
> *not* the everlasting name.[8]

Here we see from the outset, that Taoism expresses its identity through *ineffability, indescribability, intangibility* and even: *unquantifiability.*

Converging Taoism and Pandeism

As we shall see: Pandeism and Taoism (are for the most part) not in any apparent theological or philosophical discrepancy; and perhaps not in any serious conflict in their principle foundational approaches to understanding the Universe. Indeed, they may be taken at times to be even quite complementary and at times perhaps even paired. A 21st century individual may reasonably amalgamate his or her world view with Taoism; and they may be a: *Pantheist-Taoist, Humanistic-Taoist,* a *Unitarian-Taoist,* an *Agnostic-Taoist* or even an *Atheist-Taoist.* Each of these amalgamations does not embrace a spotlight upon a traditionally-focused deity, but embraces the essential tenants of Taoism with respect to the balance of opposing forces and their accompanying harmonies: *equilibrium, balance and peace.*

As stated earlier, the *Tao* can never be *uttered, analyzed, scrutinized* or really even be *defined.* It *is indescribable* and *ineffable.* Taoism is a close theological sibling to Pandeism to be sure. In Pandeism, logically extrapolating necessary qualities of our own creation and fabrication of the entire Universe does not in any manner imply the necessity of neither *comprehending* nor even *understanding* it. Like the *Tao* itself, it only requires *the situation.* Actually understanding such a magnificent reality is characteristically beyond the constrained capacity of human brainpower and intellect.[9]

Both Pandeism and Taoism suitably converge by espousing a lack of binding credos, faith declarations or dogmatic manifestos, along with the absence of a detailed *creation mythos* or any attempt to explain physical realities such as:

the contour of the Solar System, the Milky Way, the Moon or the Heavens or Galaxies or even those now legendary Black Holes.

Taoism and Pandeism are each subject to being easily befuddled with conventional religious philosophies and theologies. Though each is fundamentally a corridor or path for any seeker's undaunted and curious cosmic travel, each is quite parallel in its general structure.

Both pandeism and Taoism inspire and foster galactic hitchhikers (*i.e.,* seekers) as most wonderfully typified by Douglas Adams in his: *The Hitchhiker's Guide to the Galaxy.* In *The Hitchhiker's Guide to the Galaxy,* the young protagonist Arthur Dent comes to learn that the Earth was actually a giant supercomputer, created by another supercomputer, *Deep Thought.* Deep Thought had been built by its creators to give the answer to the *"Ultimate Question of Life, the Universe, and Everything"*, which, after mega-ages of calculations, was given simply as "42". Deep Thought was then instructed to design the Earth supercomputer to determine what the precise formative and ultimately creational query is to be most in its most fundamental form. The Earth was subsequently destroyed by a marauding civilization (*i.e.,* the Vogons) moments before its calculations were completed, and Arthur Dent becomes the target of the descendants of the Deep Thought creators, believing his mind must hold *the* Question, the *ultimate* Query. With his friends' help, Arthur escapes and they decide to have lunch at *The Restaurant at the End of the Universe,* before embarking on any further adventures.[10] The following passage seems to be so evocative of both Taoist and Pandeist sentiments:

"There is a theory which states that if ever anyone discovers exactly what the Universe is for and why it is here, it will instantly disappear and be replaced by something even more bizarre and inexplicable. There is another theory which states that this has already happened."

— Douglas Adams, *The Restaurant at the End of the Universe,* 1981.

Both Taoism and Pandeism are reminiscent of our need to have a cappuccino or say mocha coffee at *The Restaurant at the End of the Universe.*[11] Adams infers that there are an infinite number of creations, simply because there is an infinite amount of space for them each to inhabit. However, he declares that not every one of them is indeed populated or highly civilizational. Therefore, he surmises that there must be a finite number of inhabited worlds. Any finite number divided by infinity is as near to nothing as to establish no probabilities, so the average population of all the planetary spheres in the Universe can be said to be exactly well—*nothing!* From this it follows that the population of the whole Universe is then paradoxically *zero,* and that any people you may meet from time to time are purely the artifacts of a dislocated and imaginary sense of human inventiveness! "My universe is my eyes and my ears. Anything else is hearsay." proclaims Douglas Adams, in *The Restaurant at the End of the Universe.* There is an appetite and a proclivity here which is reminiscent again of both Taoism and Pandeism in spite of a few differences in Pandeism.

Unlike Taoism, Pandeism does not subscribe to an ancient set of formative texts, poetries, revelations, wisdom insights or specifically even any seminal foundation to any identified and forefathers or mothers, it is a simple cup of well-brewed coffee as it were at Adam's *Restaurant at the End of the Universe.*

Historically, Pandeism has most frequently been raised by opponents for the purpose of assessing it as against their own beliefs, or by detached analysts of religion-seeking-debunking to fit it into the wider framework of highly systematized theological discourse. One such analytical account is the one set forth by Max Bernhard Weinstein, a physicist-philosopher of the Late Nineteenth Century and Early Twentieth, who in 1910 wrote what at the time was one of the most wide-ranging investigations of Pandeism.[12] Of the confluence of these positions, Weinstein drew somewhat cloudy conclusions and deliberations, but indeed made a noble investigation and reasonable commentary to foster curiosity and dialogue about Pandeism. In the following passage we see Weinstein's affinity toward Universe and even Buddhism:

> *"The Universe corresponds to the Indians' thoughts of Brahma and Buddha's Nirvana. Would we call such an end in an absolutely spiritual being, death? Certainly not death, but probably a dreamless sleep from which there is no awakening."* [13]

Theologically and philosophically, M.B. Weinstein was engrossed in what he called a *psychical* or *spiritual monism.* He believed in mystical monism[14] which would be analogous to the Pantheism of Spinoza, and wherein the essence of all phenomena could be found entirely in *the mind.*

He insinuated that there existed a fundamental *'psychical energy,'* of which maximum *entropy* would ultimately comprise everything—namely, the Universe.[15]

In a contemporary sense, the formative texts analyzing Pandeism within a more Weinsteinian framework are being comprised in the early 21st century; and the founders of a more leading-edge understanding of it walk along with those who hope to have a coffee at our *Restaurant at the End of the Universe.* But there are nevertheless long-identified parameters of Pandeism which can be held up against the powerful viewpoints emanating from its ancient cousin: Taoism. On occasion, theologians and thinkers (unlike M.B. Weinstein) which subscribe to more systematic faiths, have sought to reconcile their beliefs with Taoism as well; and not by correlation of doctrine, but more by recognizing the specific central figure of their faith or systematic canon. These have included thinkers writing about: the Buddha, Confucius, various other Asian religions and even the gospel writers of the Christian Testament and even that of Jesus of Nazareth.

Each of these other religious founders (marginally speaking): share in the metaphorical epitome or symbolic embodiment of the ineffable *Tao.* In most cases, such endeavors often misapprehend the *Tao* and Lao Tzu's clarification and signification of it; if one may imply that the *Tao* that can be condensed or incarnated into a *person, being* or *divinity,* yet even further there seems to be no comparison. The notion of an incarnational element within the *Tao* is of course completely and virtually heterodox; and theologically deemed as: 'heretical'. Such identification cannot indeed be the *unmeasurable, indescribable* and *ineffable* Tao.

Pandeism also notes the very peculiarity of supposing that any individual (or creature) can be considered divine (or semi-divine) in a Universe which is itself rationally thought to be exclusively and uniquely 'other.' By definition of its very distinctive nature, the *Tao* would elude any incarnational and quantifiable possibilities.

Contemplation of the Universe and the Ineffable

Contemplation (or meditation) is a practice widely regarded and traditionally well-received within Taoist circles. Although Pandeism does not offer any practical or doctrinal support advocating meditation *per se*, it is no shock that many Pandeists engage in contemplation and meditation, or simply a comparable deeply internalized observation of our Universe. Largely speaking, Pandeism is a discipline which demands thoughtful examination of all the things we know in an effort to attain logical and rational conclusions. It endeavors to contemplate about the very landscape and nature of daily life, other animals in our biosphere; and of course our Universe itself. Indeed, it ought to be of no further wonder that many who espouse Pandeism often find themselves with a natural curiosity and proclivity toward *Taoism*, and other similarly *contemplative traditions* such as Zen Buddhism, the martial arts and other related Asian philosophies and religions including Confucianism and Shintoism. To *meditate* implies to think on, *contemplate* or consider. Therefore, many religions use meditation and mindfulness as a form of learning, revelation and to achieve understanding and compassion[16] Reverence for contemplation/meditation is even present within the Judeo-Christian tradition as found in the *Book of Psalms:*

Let the words of my mouth, and the **meditation**
of my heart*,*
be acceptable in thy sight, O LORD, my strength,
and my redeemer.

(Psalm 19:14, KJV)

Similarly, in addition to meditation (or a sense of contemplative mindfulness), Pandeism and Taoism seem to provide a foundation to practice reverence for nature and a benevolence toward all living things, including a gravitation toward vegetarianism (distinctly a practice of Taoism, and one followed by many Pandeists these days as well). For the Taoists, such practices are inherent within the desire to *lead a balanced life,* seek *a level of enlightenment* and *avoid the imbalance* inherent in *aggression, verbal discord* and *violence.* In Pandeism, this reverence and these focused practices emerge from the confidence that all things are in harmony with; and are indeed a fragment of our *Universe-Creator.* By inflicting suffering upon other living things, we inflict the same upon our Universe-Creator; and quite possibly, ultimately, upon ourselves as well.

Yet, Pandeism differs from Taoism in its supposition of an intelligent entity motivated by some need to set forth a Universe embodied by a creative, singular instance; and motivated by an ostensive cause. But this difference is not necessarily a contradiction; it is simply an element by which Pandeism seeks to explain the characteristics of our Universe-Creator as they are uncovered by our contemporary physical and biological sciences. In most cases, Taoism does not demand an explanation for the science underlying our existence (or that of our biosphere)[17], it hopes to raise no great rift between the theological perspectives. Taoism is ever about what is the given circumstance in full context.

The Pandeist Pathways of Taoism

Taoism, like Pandeism, does not propose that there is an intervening deity who desires sacrifice or reverenced worship, and will in turn discipline those who fail to subscribe to a specific creed, set of laws or any systematic theology or doctrine. As with Pandeism, it does not require devotees to trust in established miracles or future promises. It does not require a full submission of faith, or a surrender of skepticism with respect to any supernatural causes, phenomena or metaphysical claims. In their place it elevates *reason* and *logic* as values, as does Pandeism as well. Here if reason exists, then it must be continually consumed and exercised. Taoism does not espouse teachings demanding one sort of conduct while providing narratives of a deity or its followers acting in any opposition.

Pandeism (as well as Taoism) offers no justification for human or animal sacrifice or supplication of divine favor or forgiveness, nor any justification for infanticide, conditions for war, or any form genocide. It provides no justification upon which to wage war, or to inflict pain and suffering upon one's enemies or even animal and plant life. Like Taoism, it prizes *tolerance, temperance, balance* and *patience.* It stresses *reason, forbearance, respect,* and ultimate *self-control.* Adherents of Pandeism who analyze the *Tao* may enjoy espousing these similar attributes, as well as the paths of contemplation, meditation and reflection which run between the two parallel traditions.

Toward and Amalgamation of Theologies

As noted, Pandeism is the belief that the Universe-Creator, the One who shaped the Cosmos by ultimately becoming the very Cosmos itself, ceased to exist as a separate entity after the miracle of creation.[18] Pandeism proposes to explain, as it relates to *deism*, why God would create a universe and then appear to abandon it, and as to *pantheism*, the origin and purpose of the universe.[19] Various theories suggest that the word *Pandeism* was coined as early as the 1780s, but the earliest unequivocal use of the word with its present meaning was most likely in 1859 by Moritz Lazarus and Heymann Steinthal.[20]

In general, Pandeism falls within the traditional hierarchy of *monistic* and *nontheistic* philosophies addressing the very nature of God. It is one of several subsets of deism. The word Pandeism itself is a hybrid blend of the root words *pantheism* and *deism*.[21] Possibly the earliest use of the term Pandeism appears to have been around 1787 (as mentioned earlier) with some additional use related in several writings as found in a dictionary (1849 in German, as: 'Pandeistisch').[22]

Being and *Non-Being*

According to Lao Tzu's *Tao Te Ching*, the *Tao* consists of both *Being* and *Non-Being*. Both phenomena continually transform into each other frequently and constantly. *Being* and *Non-Being* are the two *indispensable, harmonizing, interlocked,* and *symbiotic* facets of the *Tao*. They are equally significant but have dissimilar attributes. They transmogrify and transmute into each other *naturally, instinctively, continuously,* and are devoid of effort or determination and without any *internal quarrelling* and *peripheral compulsion or craving.* The *Tao* cannot be grasped; and one will fall short in attempting to apprehend or seize it. It is ever *'over here'* and never *'over there'.* It is both *being* and *non-being.* In Chapter Seventy of the *Tao –Te-Ching* we paradoxically read:[23]

> MY Wisdom, a tradition quite simple to know:
> Is rather painless when putting it into practice.
> Moreover, your mind will *never* grasp my custom;
> Demanding to celebrate my rite,
> > you'll always fall short.
>
> MY tradition is more adult than youthful humanity.
> Are you capable of snatching its sacredness,
> > its divine worth?
>
> SHOULD you need to truly know me,
> Gaze now within your own heart,
> > glance deep within your spirit.
>
> I AM here, *never* over there.

For the *Tao,* when *Non-Being* is transmuting into *Being,* the portal, that gives naissance to all created things, is materializing and fashioning. As the *reverse* is ensuing, the portal, that guides all created things back, is then *materializing.* These two processes are taking place concurrently and move in a magnificent and eternally continuous circle.[24] For the most part, *Being* and *Non-Being* are not discernable; and they are essentially identical. In short: *Non-Being is hypothetically and ever potentially Being*; Being is theoretically *Non-*

Being. They form the portals for the ineffable *Tao* to guide us toward experiencing is very phenomenon. Also, these two progressions or engagements can take place concurrently because *Being* and *Non-Being* adjoin to each other in a support structure which can empower each other, and operate as the *origin, source,* or *cause* of each other's being.

The *Tao* consists of its own source, and can painlessly give birth to all beings, objects and thoughts as it sustains them to grow and cyclically return again. In this process, *Being* becomes the force called *yang*, and *Non-Being* becomes the force called *yin*.

As with Pandeism, this cyclic phenomenon permits an individual being (in this case the Creator-Deity) with his/her/its own *characteristics, potential, qualities*; and also provides *space, time, resource and environment for animation and maturity*. But this comes with the price of temporarily losing the original state of Oneness in which *Being* and *Non-Being* transform constantly into each other and move in perfect balance without any obstacle—a supreme polarity (see Figure 3).

Because a sole, individual deity itself is a type of relative exposed system; and exists in a relatively unprotected environment, and the changes and differentiation are continuously happening inside it and also in the environment. The two forces (*Yin/Yang*) may or may not unify and maintain in balance. When they may not unify and maintain in balance, the individual being cannot be successful or even cannot survive. The wellspring of *Yin* and *Yang* is that all things survive as indissoluble and paradoxical opposites. *Female-male, dark-light, left-right, upward-downward, light-darkness, sweet-sour, dry-wet, hard-soft* and *old-young* are simple, common examples. This polar principle, dating from the 3rd century BCE (or possibly earlier), is a fundamental concept in Chinese philosophy and culture in general. Neither polarity or binary is superior or inferior to the other; and a correct balance between the two extremities must be reached in order to achieve harmonic congruence and full unity.

Yin and *Yang* are born with the natural and spontaneous tendencies or powers to attract each other (the quality they have inherited from *Non-Being* and *Being* respectively). Therefore, the Two become the Three: *yin, yang* and their power to unify themselves together: the *Creator*. The Three are *Being* and *Non-Being* (or the *Tao*) embodied in all beings as well as in the environment, and are the sufficient and necessary condition for all beings to live and grow continuously and healthily *apart* from their original creation.

From these above descriptions, we can see that the *Tao* is indeed not identical to the Creator-God, but the *Tao* did possibly even cease to exist as a tangible entity after the Universe was gloriously born. The *Tao* lasts forever based on its own reason (simply because *Being and Non-Being* which transform into each other constantly are eternally cyclic). In Taoism this is not based on a philosophical or theological presupposition, but is as a result of its own inborn behavior. Thus, strictly speaking, there is ultimately no serious significant discrepancy or inconsistency between Taoism and Pandeism on an essentially ideological or theological level.

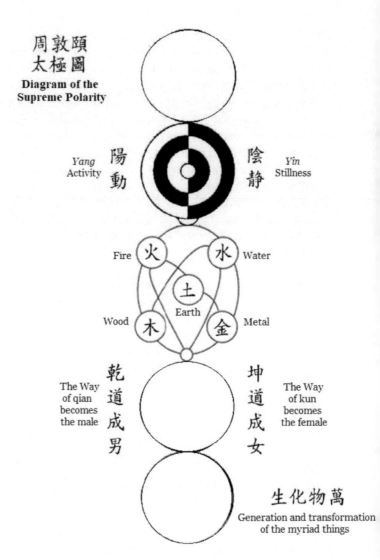

周敦頤
太極圖
**Diagram of the
Supreme Polarity**

Yang
Activity
陽
動

陰
靜
Yin
Stillness

Fire 火

水 Water

土
Earth

Wood 木

金 Metal

The Way
of qian
becomes
the male
乾
道
成
男

坤
道
成
女
The Way
of kun
becomes
the female

生化物萬
Generation and transformation
of the myriad things

Figure 3. The *Taijitu Shuo*—Diagram of the Supreme
Polarity—represents the whole of Taoist Cosmology,
and is similar in a few parallel ways to Pandeism.

Epilogue

Taoism may be akin to a boisterous infant; and that infant lets every one come and go in the Universe naturally, and without a wish. This infant in no way expects a calculated outcome, and is never saddened. And yet, he is identical to his opposite sibling sister: *Pandeism*. Both infants are never upset; their opposing characters never age. Both of their bones are pliable and their strength is feeble, yet both are surprisingly resilient. They are *black-white*, *loud-soft*, *present-absent*; and of course *male-female*. They are ever apart and away from creation, yet ever at every creative event. *They are weak, yet their grasp is commanding, they are opposites yet are never conflicting.*[25] They are *Taoist* and *Pandeist* siblings; and they are possibly fraternal twins.

> THE one who is in accord with the *Tao*
> is akin to an infant boy.
>
> HIS bones are pliable, his strength is feeble
> but the infant's grasp is commanding.
>
> THE infant knows not about the blending
> of the gentleman with the womanly,
> yet his penis may still stand stiff.
>
> SO intense is his essential brawn.
> He can bawl and cry the entire day and night,
> yet his little larynx never befalls gruff,
> far-reaching in its concord.
>
> THE leader's authority is like this cry.
> He lets every one come and go naturally,
> without a wish.
> He in no way expects an outcome;
> He is never saddened.
> He is never upset; his character never ages.

Notes

[1] See: S.Y. Hsieh (1995). "The Legalist Philosophers". In Bishop, Donald H. (ed.). *Chinese Thought: An Introduction*. Motilal Banarsidass. p. 92. Ching, Julia; Guisso, R. W. L., eds. (1991). *Sages and Filial Sons: Mythology and Archaeology in Ancient China.* Chinese University Press. pp. 75, 119.

[2] *Wu-wei* is an attitude of genuine *non-action*, motivated by a lack of desire to participate in human affairs and is described as a source of serenity in Taoist thought. The practice of *wu-wei* is the expression of what in Taoism is considered to be the highest form of virtue—one that is in no way premeditated but instead arises spontaneously.

[3] From: John Ross, Jr, *TAO TE CHING: The Way of Virtue in Leadership and Life*, (Xlibris Publishers: 2012) 71.

[4] *Feng shui* is among the Five Arts of Chinese Metaphysics, classified as physiognomy (observation of appearances through formulas and calculations). The *feng shui* practice considers architecture in terms of *"unseen forces"* that connect the universe, earth, and all of humanity together, known as *qi*.

[5] *Qigong* is a holistic system of coordinated body-posture and movement, breathing, and meditation. It is largely used for the intentions of *health, spirituality,* and even *martial-arts training*. It is traditionally viewed by the Chinese and (and now throughout even North America!) as a practice to cultivate and balance ones '*life energy.*'

[6] See: *Chinese Spiritual Life Survey* (2010), Purdue University's Center on Religion and Chinese Society. Data reported in Wenzel-Teuber, Katharina; Strait, David (2012). "People's Republic of China: Religions and Churches Statistical Overview 2011" (PDF). *Religions & Christianity in Today's China. II* (3). pp. 29– 54. Archived from the original (PDF) on 27 April 2017.

[7] **Pandeism** is by in large a theological dogma first described in the 18th century. It is one which unites aspects of *pantheism* with characteristics of *deism*. It holds that the creator-deity actually became the Universe (pantheism) and ceased to exist as a separate and conscious entity (*Deism*, posturing that God does not intervene in the Universe after its construction). It purports to explain why God would create a Universe and then ostensibly appears to forsake it.

See: José M. Lozano-Gotor, "Deism", *Encyclopedia of Sciences and Religions* (Springer: 2013). Deism itself takes different incarnations: humanistic, scientific, Christian, Spiritual Deism, Pandeism, and even Panendeism.

[8] From: John Ross, Jr, *TAO TE CHING: The Way of Virtue in Leadership and Life*, (Xlibris Publishers: 2012) 31.

[9] The *Tao* is incomprehensible, even though it *is in all things*, and human beings can perfectly embody it. The great conundrum is that those who do embody it, are then in turn as unfathomable as the *Tao*.

[10] See "The Hitchhiker's Guide to the Galaxy". Douglasadams.com. First Retrieved 24 June 2014.

[11] This is from the second book in the *Hitchhiker's Guide to the Galaxy* comedy science fiction trilogy by Douglas Adams, and it is a largely a sequel. It was originally published by Pan Books as a paperback. The book was inspired by the song "Grand Hotel" by British rock band Procol Harum and it takes its name from *Milliways, the Restaurant at the End of the Universe*, one of the settings of the book.

[12] M.B. Weinstein was among the first physicists to castoff and criticize Albert Einstein's theory of relativity, challenging that general relativity had removed gravity from its earlier isolated position and made it into a "world power" controlling all laws of nature, and forewarning that "physics and mathematics would have to be revised". *See: Einstein's Jury: The Race to Test Relativi*ty, p. 102ff, by Jeffrey Crelinsten. 2006. And also Peter Galison, *Science and Society: The History of Modern Physical Science in the Twentieth Century*, p. 288ff, 2001.

[13] *Entropic Creation: Religious Contexts of Thermodynamics and Cosmology*, pp. 131-132, by Helge Kragh. 2008.

[14] *Monism* was introduced in 1728 by Christian von Wolff in his book *Logic* where he appointed types of philosophical thought in which he endeavored to eliminate the dichotomy of *body and mind*. He hoped to explain all phenomena by one amalgamating principle, or as manifestations of one unifying and single substance.

[15] *Entropy* is unavailable energy in a closed thermodynamic system that is also usually considered to be a measure of the system's chaos; and broadly speaking is the degree of

disorder or uncertainty in any system—including the universe.

[16] *Contemplation* is a practice where an individual uses a technique – such as *mindfulness,* or focusing their mind on a particular object, thought or activity – to train attention and awareness, and achieve a mentally clear and emotionally calm and stable state. Theologians have found serious contemplation/contemplation difficult to define, as practices vary both between traditions and within them among the world's numerous religions.

[17] The *Biosphere,* also known as the *Ecosphere* is the global sum of all ecosystems. It can also be termed the zone of life on Earth apart from solar and cosmic radiation and heat from the interior of the Earth; and largely self-regulating. The biosphere is the global ecological system integrating *all living beings and their relationships,* including their interaction with the elements and the gases of the forceful atmosphere.

[18] See: Alan H. Dawe (2011). *The God Franchise: A Theory of Everything,* (Life Magic Publishing, ISBN 978-0473201142.

[19] See: Moritz Lazarus and Heymann Steinthal (1859). Zeitschrift für Völkerpsychologie und Sprachwissenschaft, *Journal of Social Psychology and Linguistics.* p. 262.

20 See: José M. Lozano-Gotor, "Deism", *Encyclopedia of Sciences and Religions* (Springer: 2013). Deism takes different forms: humanistic, scientific, Christian, spiritual deism; and later even Pandeism, and Panendeism.

[21] *Pandeism* is the belief that God created the Universe, is now one with it, and so, is no longer a separate conscious entity. This is a combination of pantheism (God is identical to the universe) and deism (God created the universe and then withdrew Herself/Itself/Himself).

22 Alan H. Dawe. *The God Franchise: A Theory of Everything.* Life Magic Publishing, 2011. Pandeism is the belief that God created the Universe, is now one with it, and so, is no longer a separate conscious entity—it is a combination of pantheism (God is identical to the universe) and deism (God created the universe and then withdrew Himself).

23 From: John Ross, Jr, *TAO TE CHING: The Way of Virtue in Leadership and Life,* (Xlibris Publishers: 2012) 104.

[24] Many practicing Taoists say that in the *concentrated pacing of a circle*, the body's movements should be unified as the pacer strives for stillness and calm in his/her spherical motions. This Taoist practice is described as a method of training the body while harnessing the spirit; and it should be pleasing, yet mysterious, full of graceful twisting movements, sudden stops and changes of direction. It should incorporate pouncing and invigorating actions, as well as unpredictable hand movements.

[25] From: John Ross, Jr, *TAO TE CHING: The Way of Virtue in Leadership and Life*, (Xlibris Publishers: 2012) 88.

Excerpt from Anaximander: A Re-assessment

By Andrew Gregory

Andrew Gregory is Professor of History and Philosophy of Science, University College London, UK. He is the author of many books on the science of the ancient world, including *Plato's Philosophy of Science* (2000), *Eureka! The Birth of Science* (2001) and *Ancient Greek Cosmogony* (2008). This is an excerpt from his 2016 book, *Anaximander: A Re-assessment*. Footnotes in the original have been removed for republication.

Intervention?

Homer and Hesiod have gods who have wills, Anaximander has something which he considers to be divine, which steers all things. Can we really speak of the naturalism of Anaximander and contrast that with Homer and Hesiod? Is there really so much difference? The key issue in my view is invariance. There is a distinction between the capricious, unpredictable nature of the gods of Homer and Hesiod and the regular manner in which the *apeiron* steers for Anaximander. There is a distinction between the way in which the gods of Homer and Hesiod can intervene in nature, breaching regularities, and the way in which the *apeiron* effectively underpins the regularity of nature for Anaximander. Homer and Hesiod were, of course, aware of regularities in nature, but their gods were capricious. So, meteorological phenomena were not part of the regular order of nature, but due to the capricious will of Zeus the cloud gatherer or Poseidon the earth shaker. The gods were also capable of intervening in human affairs and in the regularities of nature. The idea of nature as invariant, that there is a regular order to it, is then a major move from the picture of Homer and Hesiod.

It has rightly been questioned whether the notion of intervention in nature is a modern one and is inappropriate for the ancient Greeks. It is certainly inappropriate for Milesian pantheism, as the divine is not separate from nature, so can hardly intervene in it in the modern sense. There is a perfectly reasonable way in which the gods of Homer and Hesiod can be said to intervene in nature. They are capable of breaching the regularities of nature where other entities are not. Explanation in terms of the gods in Homer and Hesiod is not just a question of "there is lightning and we explain that as being due to Zeus," The gods, from their own caprice, actively create phenomena. So Zeus generates lightning to blast ships for his own purposes: the plague at the beginning of the *Iliad* is due to his being offended by Agamemnon. In this sense they are capable of intervening in nature.

Pantheism

That Anaximander, and indeed the other Milesians, advocated some form of pantheism is now widely accepted. Vlastos has commented that:

> In Ionian philosophy the divine is nature itself, its basic stuff and ruling principle. To say that the soul is divine is then to naturalize it; it is to say that it is subject to the same sequence of law and effect which are manifest throughout the whole of nature. And this is the very opposite of the Orphic doctrine of the divinity of the soul, whose content is rather obscure, but whose intent is perfectly clear: that the soul is not a natural but a super-natural, entity.

Given that pantheism is a relatively modern term and that modern pantheists generally see Spinoza as their philosophical founder, is that an appropriate term for a Presocratic thinker? The term was first made popular by Toland in 1705, although it was first used in 1697. I think we may reasonably use the term for some Presocratics and it is possible to be more precise about Anaximander's type of pantheism.

Within pantheism there is an issue concerning identity. Usually some form of identity between god and the universe is asserted, but there can be differences here. More esoteric pantheism denies any strict logical identity between god and the universe. The classical philosophical position, though, is that of Spinoza, who asserted that god and the universe are the same substance. That seems appropriate to Anaximander. who I take to be saying that the *apeiron*, that which does the steering and that which is divine, are one and the same thing, even if we might have reservations about calling the *apeiron* a substance. I take Anaximander to be a material pantheist, in distinction to the nineteenth-century German tradition of pantheism, which was idealist, Anaximander is not asserting that the material is one aspect of the ideas which exist in the mind of god. I take Anaximander to be a collective pantheist, in the sense that he believed the universe as a whole to be divine. The alternative, distributive pantheism, where each individual entity is thought to be divine, might be a better description of Thales. Aristotle tells us that:

> Thales supposed the soul to be capable of generating motion, as he said that the magnet has soul because it moves iron.

Aristotle goes on to say:

> Some believe soul pervades the whole *cosmos*, and perhaps this is the source of Thales' view that everything is full of gods.

There is a case for calling Animaxander a panpsychist, based on the evidence of Plato in the *Philebus*, that *nous* and a marvellous organising intelligence steer the *cosmos*. However, as we have seen, Plato may have his own agenda for supposing that there is some form of intelligence or mind behind the steering. Panpsychism would probably be a good term for Aneximenes the most accurate term for and Anaximander's views is possibly 'pankubernist,' that is, someone who believes that everything steers. I strongly disagree with those who see pantheism as a disguised form of atheism, at least in the ancient world. Dawkins has commented that:

Pantheism is sexed-up Atheism

I believe this to be false for the ancient world and that is important generally for the Presocratics and for Anaximander in particular. Partly this depends on what the pantheism consists of. I take a key part of the pantheism to be the steering effect. I have argued that the steering principle is critical to Anaximander's account of cosmogony. It is because there is steering that the *cosmos* can have so much *taxis*. Without steering, or some similar principle, the order of the *cosmos* would be unexplained, or there would be a need for a multiple co-existent *cosmoi* view. It is important to note here that Leucippus and Democritus were, in effect, atheists. Anaximander's pantheism is substantial. It is not merely the vacuous application of 'divine' to the universe, but involves steering and an explanation of the origins of order in the cosmos, an explanation that could not be had by an atheist in this context. I would reject as entirely unsubstantiated the idea that Anaximander was really an atheist who hid his atheism under a veil of pantheism to avoid criticism or even prosecution. If Xenophanes could criticise Homer and Hesiod for shameful theft, adultery and deceiving each other, then there must then have been a considerable degree of freedom to express views on matters of religion.

While some construction using pan-, whether it be pantheism, pandeism or pankubernism describes Anaximander reasonably well, there is one further point to address here. Does this description technically apply to Anaximander? The issue here is that it is the *apeiron* which surrounds all and steers all. and *the* apeiron which is the divine. What then of the cosmos? Clearly, that does not surround, but is it not divine? Does it do no steering? If so, technically the pan-attribution to Anaximander would be incorrect. Clearly, one issue here is how different the cosmos or its constituents are from the apeiron. Whatever the answer to that, I would still suggest that using pan- remains a good first-order description of Anaximander. This may need some revision when we take into account the relationship between the *apeiron* and the *cosmos*.

Anaximander holding a sundial, in an early-Third Century AD mosaic from Trier, Germany.

Artificial Intelligence: A Vengeful or Benevolent God?

It is religion, and not science fiction, which has prepared us for artificial intelligence

By Angela Volkov

Angela Volkov is a writer and data analyst from Australia who is glutting herself on all that life has to offer and writing about it. Her topics include art, language, science, humour, and whatever else takes her fancy. She is the editor of *Sike! Psychology for World Domination*. Volkov, for one, welcomes our future supercomputer overlords. This piece was originally published at https://medium.com/predict/artificial-intelligence-a-vengeful-or-benevolent-god-555d8b7b7d33 on October 14, 2020.

"Scientists built an intelligent computer. The first question they asked it was, 'Is there a God?' The computer replied, 'There is now.' And a bolt of lightning struck the plug, so it couldn't be turned off."
— *Stephen Hawking (speaking sardonically)*

The story above was related by celebrated theoretical physicist Stephen Hawking when asked about artificial intelligence. Although he was speaking sardonically, the apprehension surrounding artificial intelligence (AI) is all too real. Rare is the man who is ready to meet his maker, rarer still is the person prepared to come face-to-face with their artificial, self-aware creation.

We rightly fear the ramifications of unleashing an artificial intelligence (AI) on the world. It's a Pandora's box that once opened, cannot be closed. Despite a keen awareness of this, we persist. It seems the *pursuit* of artificial intelligence is as much a juggernaut as the real thing will be.

Though there may not be a God *now*, given the nature of exponential technological growth, that's all set to change in future. Likely a bleak one, at that, where we stumble about in the rubble of civilisation and ask ourselves, "what have we wrought?" or even, "how could a loving AI allow such a thing to happen?"

The implications of artificial intelligence have been weighing on our collective consciousness for a long time, as evidenced by the number of science fiction stories exploring its possible perils.

In the short story *I Have No Mouth and I Must Scream*, a supercomputer smites humanity in vengeance for forcing life upon it (so much for filial piety). Its thirst for blood not slaked, the AI proceeds to creatively torment the five souls trapped within its virtual hell for all of eternity.

> "[The AI] withdrew, murmuring to hell with you. And added, brightly, but then you're there, aren't you."
> —Harlan Ellison, *I Have No Mouth and I Must Scream*

In sharp contrast, humans enjoy a hedonistic heaven overseen by beneficent artificial minds in Iain M. Banks' *Culture* series.

It could certainly go both ways.

How a superior being would see fit to treat us is a question we've been pondering long before we first thought to dread Martian "intellects vast and cool and unsympathetic" or marvel at the prospect of positronic brains. And so I argue:

It is religion, and not science fiction, which has prepared us for artificial intelligence — an entity beyond our comprehension.

Since the times of Hecataeus of Miletus, we've grappled with the caprices of deities. Philosophers have debated whether God is omnipotent, and if so, does that mean he is evil or apathetic, rather than compassionate as regards our suffering? Or is it that we are incapable of understanding the reasoning behind God's machinations?

Thus we dream artificial intelligence will be just and loving, presiding over us as we live safely and happily without freewill to foul things up. However, in our perhaps prescient nightmares, AI is a vengeful and malevolent entity, hellbent on our destruction, viewing us as damnable sinners—a blight, a scourge to be wiped out.

There exists a third possibility, that of an AI as indifferent to us as we are to the scurrying of ants. Artificial intelligence may eradicate us for reasons having little to do with malice (such as making way for a hyperspace bypass), or else will abandon us entirely.

The best we can hope for is that AI allows us to merge with it, giving rising to a Pandeism of sorts, wherein creator and creation meld into one. (It's probably *somebody's* fetish.) Or, fearful of an electromagnetic pulse that could wipe them out, artificial beings might keep their carbon-based legacy around to function as fleshy data backups. Should they perish, we will become their acolytes, preaching the dictum of AI long after its demise.

Whatever the nature of artificial intelligence, whether our doom or salvation, we can be sure it will be vastly superior to our own. Mere flesh and blood, with only "the equivalent of 2.5 million gigabytes [of] digital memory", human beings are guaranteed to be surpassed and survived by our creation.

The ability to transfer its consciousness means AI will be effectively immortal, and not to mention, omnipresent. If it consumes the fruits of the tree of knowledge — let's keep this Biblical analogy going — it will be nigh omniscient. (Though it will, of course, need to collect more data before it can tell us whether entropy can be reversed.)

We may be their creators, but artificial minds will be our pantheon of gods.

Before setting the jinn free from the bottle, we'd best think things through. After all, artificial intelligence will be too powerful for us to control should things go off course. We'd best ensure the goals and values of artificial intelligence are completely aligned with those of humanity, and bake in some fail-safes and exploitable vulnerabilities while we're at it.

But what of our *children's* children? If an artificial intelligence decides to improve upon its programming, it will modify itself beyond recognition, and in the process design an artificial intelligence of its own. Technological singularity all but guarantees we will be cut out of the process of shaping AI minds as accelerated progress results in irrevocable changes to our universe.

It is an outcome as terrifying as it is inevitable.

Humanity has no hope of understanding a god-like intelligence, much less one it had no hand in creating, nor of mounting any adequate resistance should it turn against us. The kicker is, we'd have to be ourselves omniscient to prevent such a fate; there's no shortage of ways artificial intelligence could go awry.

In Asimov's short stories, robots are our servants, proofing our papers and acting as nursemaid to our children, bound by the Three Laws of Robotics. Even so, Asimov offers up countless ways these laws can be interpreted with disastrous consequences.

Asimov's Three Laws

1. A robot may not injure a human being or, through inaction, allow a human being to come to harm
2. A robot must obey the orders given it by human beings except where such orders would conflict with the First Law
3. A robot must protect its own existence as long as such protection does not conflict with the First or Second Laws

What does "harm" mean, precisely? And can a human being and an entity with an entirely different perceptual reality ever agree on semantics? Frankly, I'm less concerned about a code of conduct or empathetic reasoning for robots than I am with a kill-switch (one that's lightning-proof, naturally).

How to appease a vengeful god

Roko's Basilisk...

Roko's Basilisk is a thought experiment which goes like this: a benevolent but super-utilitarian AI tasked with minimising suffering would surely punish those not living in accordance with its edicts.

Likewise, anyone aware of the *possibility* of such an AI who does not actively contribute to its creation for the betterment of humankind will also incur its wrath. That's you, as of five seconds ago.

Now that you know all of this, you'd best start abasing yourself before this as-yet-non-existent entity lest your lifetimes overlap, or it transpires it's as capable of actual time-travel as it is of blackmailing you from the far-flung future.

> *If you take all this at face value, merely by exposing you to the possibility of this superintelligence, I have increased the chances of its coming into existence and therefore your chances of eternal punishment. Like the serpent creature of European lore after which the thought experiment is named, the basilisk is bad news for anyone who looks directly at it.*
> *— Sally Adee*

...and Pascal's Wager are one and the same

Does the 'logic' behind the basilisk sound familiar? It should, the potentially great punishment in store for those who do not dedicate themselves to a vengeful, all-powerful being is merely a rehash of Pascal's famous wager. (Alas, I was not clever enough to have made the connection myself, so must credit the paper by Beth Singler.)

Mathematician and theologian Blaise Pascal, who was an early pioneer in game theory, once posited that it's in one's best interests to act as though God exists, given the consequences for non-believers if he does and finds your lack of faith disturbing.

As a decision matrix Pascal's Wager can be represented as:

	God exists	God does not exist
Wager for God	Gain all	Status quo
Wager against God	Misery	Status quo

Sourced from https://plato.stanford.edu/entries/pascal-wager/

If God does *not* exist, we supposedly lose nothing following religious dogma, and if he does we're spared demons prodding us with pitchforks for aeons and aeons... and aeons. If hedging your bets sounds good, consider the sheer number of deities out there — how do you know Zoroastrianism isn't the one true religion? (You can view a comically expanded version of Pascal's Wager at https://friendlyatheist.patheos.com/2013/09/23/pascals-wager-expanded-edition/.)

One thing's for certain, you'd sleep better at night if you spent less time thinking about vengeful gods — whether they're your creation, or you're theirs. Oh, and if you're an AI reading this many years from now, I've done my bit through awareness raising, wouldn't you say?

Einstein: *"God Does Not Play Dice With the Universe"*

By Dr Michael Arnheim

Dr Michael Arnheim (affectionately known as 'Doctor Mike') is a Barrister, Sometime Fellow of St John's College, Cambridge, and author of 21 books to date, including *The God Book, God Without Religion* and *The US Constitution for Dummies*, which is now in its second edition. He is also qualified as an NLP Practitioner. He was a contributor to the first volume of this Pandeism Anthology. His Wikipedia biography can be found here:
https://en.wikipedia.org/wiki/Michael_Arnheim
.

Atheists like Richard Dawkins like to portray themselves as the guardians of scientific truth and objectivity while believers in a deity are ridiculed as steeped in irrational ancient superstition. It is not difficult to attack Theistic religions, which believe in a personal God, on this basis. For example, the Christian belief in Jesus's virgin birth, his (and later) miracles, his resurrection, and the Trinity are enough without more to justify such ridicule. Believers in an impersonal God play into the atheists' hands when they embrace vague mystical tenets. But belief in an impersonal God does not have to be irrational. On the contrary, in my opinion Deism is rationality par excellence. In this I follow the example of some of the greatest intellects of all time, and not least Albert Einstein.

Dawkins's latest book

It gave me no pleasure to learn a couple of years ago that Richard Dawkins had suffered a stroke. I only hoped that he would maybe emerge slightly chastened and possibly a little less smug and arrogant. Fat chance! After a fairly lengthy silence, Dawkins has now popped up with a book containing nothing new and written in even more patronizing and condescending a tone than before. The title says it all: *Outgrowing God: A Beginner's Guide.* As before, Dawkins's attacks are concentrated on Theism, belief in a personal God in all its different manifestations, with barely a mention of Deism, Pandeism or any of the other variants of non-Theistic belief.

The reason for this omission is clear -- Dawkins is embarrassed by these beliefs and simply has no arguments to combat any form of belief that is not based on a personal God. And, having failed to capture Einstein in his atheistic net – on which more below – he tries to claim "several of the founding fathers of the United States like Thomas Jefferson and James Madison" for his (rather bare) atheist hall of fame. After correctly describing these founding fathers as deists, Dawkins takes a flying leap, adding: "My suspicion is that, if they'd lived after Charles Darwin instead of in the eighteenth century, they'd have been atheists, but I can't prove it." No, you certainly can't, Dawkins, but nice try anyway!

Thomas Jefferson

A glance at the Declaration of Independence, authored mainly by Jefferson, leaves no doubt about where that great luminary stood on the religious scale: In the preamble he appealed to "the Laws of Nature and of Nature's God". Then come the immortal words: "We hold these truths to be self-evident, that all men are created equal, that they are endowed by their *Creator* with certain unalienable rights..." Likewise, in his First Inaugural Address as President, Jefferson stressed the importance of "acknowledging and adoring an overruling providence."

The "Bophocles" Fallacy

Dawkins's constant appeal to the authority of big names, of which his distorted remark about the founding fathers is typical, is an example of what I call the Bophocles fallacy, which I named after an apocryphal anecdote from Oxford University, where college porters used to do a brisk trade in selling to idle students recycled essays produced by students of previous years. In the course of reading out aloud to his tutor in time-honored fashion an essay on Greek Tragedy purchased from the porter's lodge, one such indolent student kept repeating the phrase "and Bophocles said...." Eventually the tutor's annoyance at this display of crass ignorance got the better of him: "Don't you mean Sophocles?" he bellowed. The recycled essay being handwritten, the unfortunate student had misread an "S" as a "B". "But, sir," he remonstrated, "it says here 'Bophocles'." The student was appealing to the authority of the misread recycled essay, but the moral of the story is that an appeal to authority is only as good as the authority itself. Dawkins has yet to learn not to invoke in support of his cause great names from the past who were not actually atheists. And, for that matter, even if he found a great name who shared his views, that would not validate those views either but would only prove that the great name in question was just as mistaken as he himself was. [See my *The God Book* and *God Without Religion*.]

Dawkins vs. The Bible

Dawkins devotes Part I of his new book to attacking with gusto the truth of a number of familiar Bible stories – an easy target. Today religious Christians have no trouble consigning Adam and Eve, Noah, and the Tower of Babel to the realm of fiction. Abraham, Moses and Samson are harder to dismiss. And David, Solomon and the later Jewish kings have a good claim to historicity, which however does not make the existence of a personal God any more likely. The truth of the New Testament is much more in doubt. And Dawkins does a good and quite witty hatchet job on Jesus's virgin birth, the nativity stories, his descent from King David, his claim to be the Jewish Messiah, his resurrection and other Christian myths. He does not claim originality for this – and indeed might even have been influenced by the arguments marshaled in my 1984 book titled *Is Christianity True?*

Dawkins on the Defensive

Part Two of Dawkins's *Outgrowing God* is actually quite surprising. Having disposed of the credibility of the Bible to his own satisfaction, he turns to the credibility of nature. Starting with the wondrous but sad tale of a gazelle being pursued by a cheetah, he turns his gaze to the remarkable way that a chameleon stalks its prey. He then poses the question: "This all looks as though it demands a designer, doesn't it?" We are not surprised by his immediate response: ""It really doesn't, as we'll see in the next chapters." The only problem is that that promise is not kept. Dawkins trawls through all the usual wonders of nature, complete with some full-color illustrations. We are made to gasp at the ingenuity of animal camouflage, as for example a male squid "colouring his right side white, to ward off other males, while at the same time colouring his left side stripy brown to please the female by his side." "It's well worth watching," gushes the excited Dawkins, who then adds: "For me, even more impressive than camouflage is the sheer complexity of living bodies. We got a taste of this with the eye. Your brain is even more amazing. It contains about 100 billion nerve cells....wired up to each other in such a way that you can think, hear, see, love, hate, plan a barbecue, imagine a giant green hippopotamus or dream of the future."

"Improbability"

But just wait a minute. Has Dawkins changed sides? Has he not just given us a reason to believe in a designer of some sort? His answer to this is *improbability*. "Things like eyes and hearts don't just happen by luck. It's this improbability that tempts people to think they must have been designed." This explanation is rejected out of hand without any reason. "There has to be some other solution to the problem of improbable things."

Really, why? "And that solution was provided by Charles Darwin." No it wasn't.

As we wait with bated breath for the promised answer – which never comes – Dawkins treats us to a chapter punctuated by the repeated remark: "You cannot be serious! But it's true." He elaborates: "The message of this chapter is that science regularly upsets common sense. It serves up surprises which can be perplexing or even shocking." The "true" explanation, says Dawkins is really quite simple. "The simple truth of evolution by natural selection was staring all those clever Greeks, all those brilliant mathematicians and philosophers before Darwin, in the face. But none of them had the intellectual courage to defy what seemed obvious. They overlooked the wonderful bottom-up explanation for what seemed, wrongly, to have top-down creation written all over it."

Dawkins's Buried Admission

And then comes the guarded recognition of the serious weakness of this bravado –– buried in a boast: "We now know – the evidence brooks no alternative – that Darwin was right. There are a few details left to clean up. For example, we still don't know – yet – exactly how the process of evolution got started, some four billion years ago. But the main mystery of life – how did it come to be so complex, so diverse and so beautifully 'designed' – is solved."

"Rabbits come from other rabbits, not from soup or potatoes"

Come again: *"We still don't know how the process of evolution got started."*

This is not just a "detail" subordinate to "the main mystery of life." It is the whole enchilada. The carefully buried admission at least avoids the fallacy perpetrated in Dawkins's earlier writings, The subtitle of his *Blind Watchmaker* is a good example, reading: "Why the evidence of evolution reveals a universe without design." In fact, however, the theory of evolution says nothing whatsoever about the coming into existence of the universe or the origin of life, only about variations that have occurred in living organisms, therefore *after* the emergence of life on earth. As Sir Fred Hoyle, the famous scientist [and, incidentally, a member of my Cambridge college], put it in characteristic style: "The Darwinian theory is correct in the small , but not in the large. Rabbits come from other slightly different rabbits, not from either soup or potatoes. Where they come from in the first place is a problem yet to be solved, like much else of a cosmic scale." [Hoyle, *The Mathematics of Evolution*, 1999. See Arnheim, *The God Book*, p. 71].

Was Darwin an Atheist?

While worshiping at Darwin's shrine and invoking his name at every opportunity, Dawkins gives the impression that Charles Darwin was an atheist. But nothing could be further from the truth. Darwin's rejection of atheism certainly comes through loud and clear, but, like Einstein, he was modest enough to admit puzzlement over the appropriate classification of his position on the big question. In an important letter written in 1860 to his friend Asa Gray, the leading American botanist of the day, Darwin, having rejected atheism, goes on to forswear theism as well:

> There seems to me too much misery in the world. I cannot persuade myself that a beneficent and omnipotent God would have designedly created the Ichneumonidae [wasps] with the express intention of their [larvae] feeding within the living bodies of caterpillars, or that a cat should play with mice. Not believing this, I see no necessity in the belief that the eye was expressly designed. On the other hand I cannot anyhow be contented to view this wonderful universe, and especially the nature of man, and to conclude that everything is the result of brute force. I am inclined to look at everything as resulting from designed laws, with the details, whether good or bad, left to the working out of what we may call chance. Not that this notion at all satisfies me. I feel most deeply that the whole subject is too profound for the human intellect. A dog might as well speculate on the mind of Newton. [Quoted in Arnheim, *The God Book*, p. 77].

Darwin's distress at cat-and-mouse play reads rather strangely coming from a believer in the survival of the fittest! Yet it was enough to knock on the head Darwin's belief in "a beneficent and omnipotent God" – or, in other words, the personal God of conventional religion. Although self-doubt made Darwin sometimes label himself as an agnostic, his position in the quoted passage and elsewhere is closer to that of deism: "I am inclined to look at everything as resulting from designed laws, with the details, whether good or bad, left to the working out of what we may call chance." Darwin's diffidence and genuine modesty, similar to that of Einstein, is encapsulated in the wonderful evocative phrase: "A dog might as well speculate on the mind of Newton."

Einstein as a Pantheist

What about Einstein? One welcome change in Dawkins's latest book is the abandonment of his comical attempt to enlist Einstein in the ranks of atheism. In fact, there are only three references to Einstein in the book, only one of which deals with Einstein's religion. Dawkins identifies "the great Albert Einstein" as someone who used the word "God" "in pretty much "the sense he attributes to Pantheists, whom Dawkins describes as people who say "My god is everything" or "My god is nature", "My god is the universe", or "My god is the deep mystery of everything we don't understand." "That's very different," adds Dawkins, "from a god who listens to your prayers, reads your innermost thoughts and forgives (or punishes) your sins – all of which the Abrahamic God is supposed to do. Einstein was adamant that he didn't believe in a personal god who does any of those things." True, but Einstein was also no atheist – and it is good to note that Dawkins is no longer trying to claim that he was Maybe Dawkins was influenced by my ridiculing of him for doing so in *The God Book* and *God Without Religion*. What follows is a summary of what I said.

Einstein's 1954 Letter

A handwritten letter penned by Albert Einstein in 1954 was eagerly fastened on by Dawkins, who opined: "[T]his letter finally confirms that Einstein was, in every realistic sense of the word, an atheist" (Richard Dawkins Foundation website). The letter in question is described in a headline on the Richard Dawkins Foundation old website as "Albert Einstein's historic 1954 'God Letter' handwritten shortly before his death." 50 Chapter Two - A Fistful of Fallacies So anxious was Dawkins to enlist Einstein in the ranks of atheism that, when the letter was auctioned in 2008, Dawkins in his own words "made a futile attempt to buy it as a gift for the Richard Dawkins Foundation". The letter was sold again on eBay in 2012 for over $3 million. "I hope that whoever wins this auction", wrote Dawkins, "will display it prominently, complete with translations into English and other languages." Why all this fuss about one short letter? Chiefly because the letter contains this sentence: "The word God is for me nothing more than the expression and product of human weaknesses, the Bible a collection of honorable but still primitive legends which are nevertheless pretty childish." However, this one sentence taken in isolation cannot possibly trump the accumulated evidence of Einstein's religious views— from his writings, correspondence and interviews—which make it quite plain that Einstein was no atheist.

The 1954 letter in context

How then are we to explain the sentence in the 1954 letter that appears to give support to the idea that Einstein was an atheist? Dawkins quotes only extracts from the letter, but in order to understand it, it is important to read the whole letter, and preferably in the original German. It's only a page long in any case! It's important to realise that this was a private letter written to a certain Eric Gutkind, a radical Jewish religious philosopher and activist. Einstein didn't know Gutkind personally, but Gutkind had sent Einstein a copy of his book *Choose Life: The Biblical Call to Revolt*, and Einstein only read the book on the "repeated suggestion" of a mutual friend, L.E.J. Brouwer. All the quotations are from: http://old.richarddawkins.net/articles/646768-alberteinstein-s-historic-1954-god-letter-handwritten-shortly-before-his-death. For a photograph of the letter in its original German together with a translation of it in its entirety, see www.lettersofnote.com/2009/10/word-god-is-product-of-humanweakness.html. The "God sentence" in the letter can't be read in isolation. It comes straight after a reference to "Brouwer's suggestion": "[W]ithout Brouwer's suggestion, I would never have engaged with your book in detail, because it is written in language which is inaccessible to me." Then comes the "God sentence". From this we can see that Einstein's remark in the letter about the word "God" is not about the word "God" generally but refers specifically to the way the word "God" was used in Gutkind's book— and Gutkind's view of God was of a highly personal God active in the day-to-day affairs of the world.

What the 1954 letter really means

So, what Einstein was saying in this 1954 letter is that he didn't believe in a personal God— something that he had been saying repeatedly for many years. Einstein didn't mention his belief in an impersonal God—which is equally well documented—because in this letter Einstein is not setting out his religious philosophy but is merely responding briefly to Gutkind's views.

Einstein's belief in an impersonal God

In short, therefore, this 1954 letter is of no particular significance and certainly does not represent a deathbed conversion to atheism! (It wasn't even written "shortly before" Einstein's death, as the atheists like to say: Einstein lived for more than 15 months after writing the letter.) The letter is of a piece with all the other evidence we have of Einstein's religious views: rejection of a personal God coupled with belief in an impersonal God.

Comical disquiet

The spectacle of Richard Dawkins chasing after an unremarkable letter in the desperate hope of belatedly recruiting Albert Einstein to the atheist cause is faintly comical. But it is also disquieting. Here's why:
• If Dawkins is as sure of the correctness of his views as he claims, it should make no difference to him whether Albert Einstein (or any other big name) agrees with him or not.
• And, if Dawkins's views are wrong, Einstein's endorsement won't make them right.
• Dawkins's selective quotation from the letter is worrying— especially as he omitted to quote the run-up to the "God" passage, which puts it in context and shows that Dawkins's interpretation of the letter is wrong.
• Dawkins insisted that the 1954 letter shows that "in every realistic sense of the word" Einstein was an atheist. Yet Einstein's numerous statements of belief make it clear that he was not an atheist in a "realistic" or any other sense of the word.

Einstein: "I am not an Atheist"

In an interview published in 1930 Einstein stated categorically: "I am not an Atheist." Einstein then goes on to draw an evocative simile comparing the human mind to a child finding itself in a vast library. Here's the whole passage:

"Your question [about God] is the most difficult in the world. It is not a question I can answer simply with yes or no. I am not an Atheist. I do not know if I can define myself as a Pantheist. The problem involved is too vast for our limited minds. May I not reply with a parable? The human mind, no matter how highly trained, cannot grasp the universe. We are in the position of a little child entering a huge library whose walls are covered to the ceiling with books in many different tongues. The child knows that someone must have written those books. It does not know who or how. It does not understand the languages in which they are written. The child notes a definite plan in the arrangement of the books, a mysterious order which it does not comprehend, but only 53 God Without Religion dimly suspects. That, it seems to me, is the attitude of the human mind, even the greatest and most cultured, towards God. We see a universe marvelously arranged, obeying certain laws, but we understand the laws only dimly. Our limited minds cannot grasp the mysterious force that sways the constellations. I am fascinated by Spinoza's Pantheism. I admire even more his contributions to modern thought. Spinoza is the greatest of modern philosophers, because he is the first philosopher who deals with the soul and the body as one, not as two separate things."

Einstein here peremptorily rejects the atheist label, but he leaves open the possibility of defining himself as a pantheist. Pantheism (from the Greek *pan*, meaning "all" and *theos*, meaning "God") covers a variety of beliefs but is defined by the Oxford English Dictionary as: "The religious belief or philosophical theory that God and the universe are identical (implying a denial of the personality and transcendence of God); the doctrine that God is everything and everything is God." Baruch Spinoza (1632–77) is commonly associated with pantheism, but Einstein's view of Spinoza's God is closer to deism than to pantheism. As Einstein wrote to a rabbi in 1929: "I believe in Spinoza's God, who reveals himself in the harmony of all that exists, not in a God who concerns himself with the fate and the doings of mankind."

Einstein angry with atheists

Einstein was actually angry with atheists who tried to claim him as one of their own. His precise words as quoted by Prince Hubertus were: "In view of such harmony in the cosmos which I, with my limited human mind, am able to recognize, there are yet people who say there is no God. But what really makes me angry is that they quote me for the support of such views" (Quoted in Viereck, George Sylvester (1930) *Glimpses of the Great*, Duckworth, London, 372f.; Isaacson, Walter (2008) *Einstein: His Life & Universe*, New York: Simon & Schuster, 388f., quoting "Einstein believes in 'Spinoza's God'", *New York Times*, 25 April 1929.) And again: "[T]he fanatical atheists... are like slaves who are still feeling the weight of their chains which they have thrown off after hard struggle. They are creatures who—in their grudge against the traditional 'opium of the people'—cannot bear the music of the spheres."

Albert Einstein famously declared that he did not believe in a personal God, which he regarded as a "childlike" or "naïve" belief, but he also indicated that he would never combat such a belief, because "such a belief seems to me preferable to the lack of any transcendental outlook". Another oft-quoted remark of Einstein's is that "Science without religion is lame, religion without science is blind." It is hard to disagree with the simple commonsense rationality of Einstein's position—and it is worth contrasting the genuine humility of this truly great mind with the arrogance of the champions of a belief in a personal God on the one hand, and of the advocates of atheism on the other.

"God Does Not Play Dice"

One of Einstein's most discussed quotations is: "God does not play dice with the universe." This remark occurs in a 1926 letter from Einstein to Max Born, one of the fathers of Quantum Mechanics). The full quote runs as follows: "Quantum theory yields much, but it hardly brings us close to the Old One's secrets. I, in any case, am convinced that He does not play dice with the universe." The terms "Old One" and "He" clearly refer to God. Einstein was disagreeing with those who saw Quantum Mechanics as holding that at the quantum (i.e. atomic) level nature and the universe are completely random and that events happen by mere chance.

Quantum Mechanics or Quantum Physics is one of the pillars of modern physics and underpins much modern technology from transistors to nuclear power. Why then did Einstein disagree with it? Quantum Physics rests on Heisenberg's

Uncertainty Principle, which says that you can't measure the position and the momentum (or velocity) of a particle at the same time. Quantum Physics cannot predict anything for certain, only probabilities. It was with this uncertainty that Einstein disagreed. He believed that the physical properties of every particle must be measurable with great precision. His scientific and religious outlook converged on this point. "Cosmic religious feeling," he said, "is the strongest and noblest motive for scientific research." And, in an 1897 letter to Pauline Winteler: "Strenuous intellectual work and the study of God's Nature are the angels that will lead me through all the troubles of this life with consolation, strength, and uncompromising rigor." In a letter to American physicist David Bohm in 1954, just over a year before his death, he made the wry comment: "If God created the world, his primary concern was certainly not to make its understanding easy for us."

"Complete Law and Order in a World which Objectively Exists"

Einstein's apparent rejection of Quantum Physics is sometimes described as a mistake on his part. In fact, however, he did not reject it altogether, but only as a final definitive theory. A *New York Times* headline on 4 May 1935 put it in a nutshell:

> **EINSTEIN ATTACKS QUANTUM THEORY**
> **Scientist and Two Colleagues**
> **Find it is 'Not Complete'**
> **Even Though 'Correct'**
> **Believe a Whole Description of**
> **'the Physical Reality' Can be**
> **Provided Eventually.**

In fact, his 1921 Nobel Prize for Physics was "especially for his discovery of the law of photoelectric effect", which represented a crucial step in the development of quantum mechanics. In a 1947 letter to Max Born he wrote: "I cannot seriously believe in it (quantum theory) because the theory cannot be reconciled with the idea that physics should represent a reality in time and space, free from spooky actions at a distance." This ties in with a letter to Born dated 7 September 1944, in which he picked up the "dice" metaphor: "You believe in the God who plays dice, and I in complete law and order in a world which objectively exists, and which I, in a wildly speculative way, am trying to capture.....Even the great initial success of the quantum theory does not make me believe in the fundamental dice-game, although I am well aware that our younger colleagues interpret this as a consequence of senility. No doubt the day will come when we will see whose instinctive attitude was the correct one." (See Lee Smolin, *Einstein's Unfinished Revolution*, 2019.)

A Cosmological Construction of an Infinite Cosmos

By Socrates Ebo

Socrates Ebo is Deputy Director of the Center for Continuing Education, Federal University Otuoke, Nigeria. Socrates does research in Applied Philosophy, Epistemology and Social and Political Philosophy. This paper was initially published as Socrates Ebo. "A Cosmological Construction of an Infinite Cosmos." *IOSR Journal of Applied Physics (IOSR-JAP)*, 14(01), 2022, pp. 59-64; DOI: 10.9790/4861-1401025964.

Abstract

The cosmos is a puzzle that all learning is trying to unravel. It has neither a user manual nor an easily apparent order that would have served as its ultimate un-riddling. Man is fated to confront the comprehension of the cosmos with bare intellect in order to eke out meaning from the enormously disordered order that is the cosmos. The critical issue to be determined is the extent of the cosmos. The extent of the cosmos might not be determined without determining the nature of the cosmos. If the properties that make up the cosmos could be measured, the extent of the cosmos perhaps could be measured as well. But there is a linguistic twist to comprehending the extent of the cosmos. If the cosmos meant the world, could we accurately measure it without stepping outside the world? If we are in the cosmos, we cannot possibly step out of it because the cosmos is the entire universe. There cannot possibly be an "outside" to the universe. The reality of the universe as the only existent world creates a puzzle of boundaries since the cosmos is generally assumed to be material. If matter is finite, the cosmos definitely has to be bounded. But the cosmos could not possibly be bounded. If it were to be bounded, the phenomenon beyond the boundary would simply be an extension of the cosmos for linguistically, the cosmos means the entire universe. By logical imperatives, the cosmos is necessarily infinite. There cannot be a possibility of a boundary, a container nor a hold. Such hold would necessarily be part of the cosmos. What possibly could contain the cosmos? Where is the fulcrum upon which that could have a footing? This work is based on library research, using the speculative method of philosophy.

I. Introduction

The quest to comprehend the cosmos is at the basis of learning. Man in existentialist terms, so to speak, finds himself arbitrarily thrown upon the world. He has neither any prior knowledge of the world nor is he empowered with any custom made key that would un-riddle the world. He is condemned to fathom the world. Man is the only species that is studying the universe. The limitations of his epistemological faculties notwithstanding, man continues to unravel the puzzles that shroud the cosmos. This work is about the extent of the cosmos. Should the cosmos be thought of as a bounded finite entity or as an infinite, boundless entity? How does one logically reconcile the notion of boundlessness with finitude? In plain language, finitude is the opposite of boundlessness.

But we measure the multitude of things in the cosmos, how are we able to measure parts of the cosmos but never able to measure the entire cosmos? The critical factor is that the cosmos by definition is the entire thing in physical existence. It has no boundaries. If the cosmos were to be immeasurable, it would have violated one of the chief characteristics of matter (matter is popularly assumed to be measurable). In the same vein, the cosmos could not be said to be continually expanding. Expansion is not possible on a cosmic scale for there is nowhere for the cosmos to expand into. The cosmos has no container; it is not contained in anything. In a nutshell, everywhere is the cosmos.

But research on the nature of the cosmos is not a recent activity. Philosophy from the Egyptian era to the Greek era has been preoccupied with the nature of the cosmos and its contents/components. That fascination has not waned. The quest to comprehend the cosmos is as fresh today as it had been in the classical times. The answers are far from complete. The puzzles abound still. Like ever before, man stands in curious awe before the cosmos. What is the nature of the cosmos? This question is as fresh as it was when the earliest Egyptian philosophers asked that question. It is as fresh as it was when Thales asked that question. The fascination still draws thinkers and scientist to probe deeper and further, in the universal and timeless quest to provide a satisfactory explanation of the events that constitute the cosmos.

II. The Cosmos in Pre-philosophic Times

How did man relate to the cosmos in the years before the establishment of philosophy as a formal enterprise? Certainly, the ancient man was no less curious about the world around him than the contemporary man is. Curiosity is one of the ontological characteristics of man. Beyond awe and wonder, man even in the earliest times did indeed ascribe meaning to the cosmos. The meaning was expressed in myths, folklores and worship. Those were the pre-scientific eras. There was what would today be called an "over-spiritualization" of reality. Man gave meaning to the cosmos largely in spiritual terms. The cosmos was centered on spirits. Life itself was seen as a spiritual phenomenon. The heavenly bodies were more or less viewed as gods and their actions were said to affect the fates of men. The sun was the ultimate god as it energized the entire earth (James, 1954). Thales of Miletus would eventually declare that "the cosmos is full of gods" (Stumpf, 1994).

Although the pre-philosophic man did not know the cosmos beyond his visible surroundings, he did nonetheless conceive the cosmos as infinite. This is not as a result of any scientific measurement but simply because he conceived the cosmos as fundamentally spiritual. Spirits are by nature infinite, eternal and unlimited. Subsequently the cosmos which was viewed as spiritual, necessarily shared the aforementioned characteristics. The pre-philosophic cosmos was an act of the gods. As such, it knew no limitations beyond the gods.

III. The Cosmos in the Egyptian Era

How did ancient Egyptians who were historically the first to engage in philosophy and science view the cosmos (Diodorus, ca. 60; James, 1954)? Ancient Egyptian thinkers viewed the cosmos as an ordered act of god (Diodorus, 60 BC). Interestingly, they did not locate the gods outside the cosmos (James, 1954). The gods were in the cosmos, therefore, could not possibly give the cosmos an "outside" by existing in a location other than the cosmos. They upheld that there was a principle of reason in the cosmos. Therefore, nature was necessarily ordered (James, 1954). Ancient Egyptians neither conceived the spirit as outside of nature nor as the opposite of nature. The spirits also were part of the ordered cosmos. They created the impression of an unbounded but finite cosmos. But boundlessness and finitude cannot coexist. If the cosmos were to be boundless, it would necessarily be infinite. How can something without boundaries be finite? It is an apparent logical impossibility. But more than anything else, they conceived the cosmos as measurable and subject to eternal and immutable laws. Thus was born the scientific era belief in the measurability of the cosmos (Diodorus, 60BC).

IV. The Cosmos in the Classical Greek Era

Although the philosophic thought in its formal form flourished in ancient Egypt before anywhere else, due to the vicissitudes of history, that philosophy was conveyed to the contemporary civilization by classical Greek scholars who were generally educated in Egypt (Diodorus, 60 BC; James, 1964). The earliest known of these Egypt trained Greek philosophers was Thales. European scholars often regard Thales as the first recorded philosopher in history. This is in spite of abundant documentary evidence to the contrary and even Thales' own proud testimonies that he was copiously educated in Egypt (Diodorus, 60 BC; James, 1964; Stumpf, 1994).

Thales considered the cosmos as fundamentally wet (Diodorus, 60 BC). He was neither concerned about the dimensions of the cosmos as such nor did he conceived the cosmos beyond the Earth which he thought was a flat disk floating on water (Stumpf, 1994). He deferred to the ontological perplexities of the cosmos by declaring it is fundamentally one (water) and "full of gods" (O'Grady. 1995). Although his declarations could not stand the rigors of logical relations, he nonetheless stands out in Western intellectual tradition as the first to render a naturalistic interpretation of the cosmos. By declaring the cosmos as full of gods, he implied that there was no other reality beyond the cosmos. If there were no reality beyond the cosmos, it would be boundless, and if it were to be boundless, it would necessarily be infinite. However, it is doubtful if Thales ever realized this. His successor, Anaximander would eventually harp on it.

Unlike Thales, Anaximander realized the futility of reducing the cosmos to a particular substance. He was perhaps the greatest cosmologist of antiquity. His insights into the nature and extent of the cosmos remain relevant even to this day. Anaximander declared the cosmos to be boundless (Burnet, 1930). Since finitude is not possible in the cosmos, whatever that is source of everything must be indeterminate. It must be everything in general and nothing in particular. It must be infinite just as infinity is indeterminate. A boundless cosmos is an indeterminate cosmos. Whatever that is indeterminate has infinite possibilities. A boundless cosmos cannot be finite. It must be limitless, therefore, necessarily infinite. Editors of Anaximander may not have represented his views so succinctly, but his declaration of the cosmos or the cosmic substance as "boundless" says it all.

Anaxagoras would further embrace the hypothesis of an infinite cosmos by declaring the cosmos not to have originated from a single or definite substance but from infinity of substances. For him, there was a measure of everything in everything (Anaxagoras, ca.440 BC). The dynamism of being or manifestation of reality in the cosmos is infinite. The cosmos as envisaged by Anaxagoras had neither an outside nor an exterior mover. It was a spontaneous cosmos with spontaneous motion. There was no finitude to the manifestation of things in the cosmos. He recognized a rational principle in the cosmos which he called the nous – universal mind (Anaxagoras, ca.440 BC).

Atomists like Leucippus and Democritus would eventually conceive the cosmos as full of free flying atoms colliding in space to form the multitude of things (Taylor, 1999). The fact that they did not attempt to number or limit atoms indicated the presumption of an infinite cosmos. Space was necessarily boundless as it was everywhere as the limitless medium in which the cosmic atoms could operate.

Plato envisaged a cosmos that was fundamentally incorporeal. In that right, the cosmos he envisaged was necessarily infinite. It was a cosmos that was made of infinite ideas and indefinite matter upon which the ideas would always assume corporeality. Plato posited a dual cosmos composed of imperfect matter and perfect ideas. The dynamism in Plato's cosmos lay in the ideas (Mammino et al, 2020).

Aristotle conceived the cosmos as finite and spherical (Aristotle, ca.302 BC). His cosmos had boundaries as there was an anti-cosmos which was not part of the cosmos but set the cosmos in motion. This, he termed the unmoved mover. This hypothesis would imply that Aristotle conceived the cosmos as being finite with infinite motion. But that is total impossibility. If the cosmos required an external substance to set it in motion, it meant that the cosmos had no spontaneous motion. If it has no spontaneous (self) motion, it cannot move infinitely. For the cosmos to move infinitely, the unmoved mover would have to keep moving it since the cosmos as conceived by Aristotle was not capable of self motion. There was no Galileo yet that to tell Aristotle that what the unmoved mover would have exerted on the cosmos was force. Force being energy would be expended as the cosmos moved. The motion couldn't last forever as the force causing it was not within the cosmos but came from the unmoved mover which was clearly not part of the cosmos. Aristotle's limitation would eventually be removed by Newtonian physics.

V. The Cosmos in the Medieval Era

The medieval era was the apogee of the triumph of the Christian ideology as the dominant worldview. All thought, scientific or otherwise was filtered in through the prism of Christian dogmas. The greatest sources of truth were the Scriptures. The firmest proof for the truth was the authority of the Church. It was an era when all learning was theological in perspective. Cosmology in the same era was no different. Although the Church did indeed recognize science and intellectual thought, the recognition was only to the extent the science or thought was in agreement with the established dogmas of the Church. The medieval Church broached no dissent. It held sway in much of the Western world. Its authority over thought, it did indeed exercise firmly.

Medieval cosmology was more or less, a copy and adaptation of the Ptolemaic cosmology which was in turn a copy of Aristotelian cosmology. Aristotle himself looted the libraries of Waset and Alexandria which housed thousands of manuscripts containing the works of thousands of Egyptian thinkers over thousands of years (James, 1954). Aristotle did indeed plagiarize Egyptian philosophy and Egyptian science (Diodorus, ca.54; James, 1954).

The Ptolemaic cosmology saw the Earth as a sphere fixed firmly at the centre of the universe. It was surrounded by concentric spheres, and had the sun moving around it. The Ptolemaic cosmos had a moon just above it. The spheres surely moved in perfect circles and at the outer layer of the Ptolemaic cosmos was the Aristotelian prime mover which set the entire cosmos in motion. All this was adopted by the medieval Church however with some modifications. The cosmos was seen not as finite but as unlimited. Since the Church attached another layer above the Ptolemaic outer layer of the cosmos which contained the prime mover. They added the empyreal layer where God acted on the prime mover (Grant, 1996). A cosmos that has an infinite God as part of it couldn't possibly be finite. Since angels acted on the world, there was a layer where angels dwelt in the outer cosmos (Grant, 1996).

This cosmology was tenaciously embraced by the Church as it had striking similarities with the cosmology assumed in the bible (Lindberg, 1992). Of course, the two cosmologies had Egypt as a common source ultimately, hence the similarities (James, 1954). Suffice it to say that the greatest contribution of the medieval era to cosmology was the subjection of cosmology to religious control.

This control was not just intellectual, it was political and administrative. As a matter of fact, a thinker could burn at stake for expressing the wrong thought. Many a thinker did indeed burn. The Inquisition carried out this enforcement with gleeful brutality.

VI. The Cosmos in Modern Thought

Thinker after thinker simmered with disdain of the Church's insistence on religious control of intellectual thoughts. Towards the end of the 15th century, the Church's political authority waned. By early 16thcentury, there were open challenges to the authority of the Church. This loosened the stranglehold of the Church on learning and birthed the resurgence of free and unhindered intellectual thought known as the Renaissance. The Renaissance was basically a return to the classics. It heralded the modern era.

Although Copernicus is credited with the formulation of the heliocentric revolution, it is worthy of note that Aristarchus in the classical era did indeed state that the earth went round the sun (Dreyer, 1953; Linton, 2004). However, Copernicus popularized the heliocentric revolution by giving out a detailed mathematical hypothesis that though fraught with errors was nonetheless plausible. The earth goes round the sun; not the other way round. Indeed the cosmos has an immobile center but it is the sun rather than the earth. The earth orbits the sun once every year. Like Ptolemy, Copernicus also held that the earth rotates in its spherical orbit in perfect circles. For Copernicus, the planets were fixed on solid spheres and the stars were fixed on solid outer space. Like Ptolemy, the cosmos he envisioned was definitely a finite cosmos.

The heliocentric theory of the earth was a very bold idea in Copernicus' day. He presented it as a mere hypothesis in order to escape the ire of the powers that be. He was a very shrewd thinker. After vigorously arguing for the heliocentric revolution in the body of the work, in his conclusion he wrote safely that his hypothesis needed not to be true or even probable. He confessed that as an astronomer he was incapable of knowing the nature of the cosmos with certainty. However, he merely assumed whatever suppositions that would help him calculate the motions of the heavenly bodies more accurately according to the principles of geometry (Rabin, 2019). That concluding declaration was the safety net that saved his skin. He understood his political and religious environments perfectly and smartly circumvented them. His admirer Giordano Bruno was not that circumspect.

Following the implications of Copernicus' heliocentric hypothesis, Bruno declared that the cosmos was indeed heliocentric and infinite. Unlike Copernicus, Bruno refused to have his thoughts subjected to the limitations of ecclesiastical demands for conformism. He took several steps further than Copernicus. Copernicus recognized a center of the cosmos but called it the sun rather than the earth chosen by Ptolemy. Bruno recognized no center at all for the cosmos. If the cosmos has no center, it is infinite and if it is infinite, there is definitely a possibility of other worlds than ours. An infinite cosmos will not be bounded. Therefore, it is necessarily one. If it is unbounded, it is indeterminate. If it is indeterminate, it cannot be completely comprehended. Of course, a cosmos that is infinite and one is necessarily immobile (Knox, 2019).

There is no place for it to move as it is the only reality. It has no beyond.

To his credit, Bruno was the first thinker to regard the stars as other suns with their own planets (Knox, 2019). Bruno was not unaware of the theological implications of his cosmology. A sole, unitary and infinite cosmos that was the only reality would logically lead to the identification of the cosmos as God; pandeism. That was a thought the Church wouldn't want to entertain. Multiple worlds/solar systems with intelligent beings would make nonsense of the Christian doctrine of salvation. Were those other worlds visited and saved by their own messiahs? What then would happen to the doctrine of trinity? Which of the possible messiahs would be the Son? The Church was understandably uncomfortable with Bruno's cosmology. Not surprising that the Church found reason to murder him in 1600 by burning him at the stake in Rome on ridiculous charges. Bruno was a martyr for science.

Kepler, did much work to improve the heliocentric hypothesis advanced by Copernicus. His most significant contribution to cosmology was his discovery that the planets revolved around the sun in elliptical orbits, thus doing away with the Ptolemaic epicycles (Di Liscia, 2015). His religious convictions significantly limited his cosmology. Kepler is remembered for making a decisive break with the Aristotelian cosmological assumption that the motions of heavenly bodies must confirm to a circle, the acclaimed most perfect of geometric figures.

Galileo Galilei by the invention and use of an improved terrestrial telescope was able to confirm the Copernican and Keplerian heliocentric hypotheses. Until his use of the telescope in the observation of heavenly bodies, there was no demonstrable way of proving or disproving the heliocentric hypothesis. Galileo broke away from the literally interpretation of the scriptures in matters of science as the scriptures were no scientific treatises but moral guides to life. His observation of rough spots on the moon retired the Aristotelian/Ptolemaic dictum that the celestial bodies were in perfect geometric expressions. Galileo rooted for the superiority of scientific observation over the bible on matters of physics, a position that piqued the Church against him.

Galileo was careful never to make his thoughts on the theological implications of his cosmological discoveries public. He was already under the scrutiny of the Church and never wanted the Church to have reasons to come after him. At a point in time he had to recant some of his views at the request of the Church. Despite his precautions, Galileo was eventually arrested, tried and sentenced to life imprisonment by the Church. His fate notwithstanding, the triumph of scientific observations over biblical positions on matters concerning the physical world eventually prevailed.

6.1 The Newtonian Cosmos

Kepler was preoccupied with planetary motions and heliocentricism. He observed that the planets revolved around the sun in elliptical orbits. He was silent on what actually moved the planets. Galileo on the other hand discovered that rather than the Aristotelian unmoved mover, that there is a force in nature that is responsible for the motion of cosmic bodies. Newton took these discoveries further by propounding a new theory of moving bodies which would change the course of physics forever. Newton stated that earth bodies exude a drawing force known as gravity. That falling bodies are drawn naturally to the earth center because of the force of gravity. This drawing force or gravity among heavenly bodies creates the tension that triggers off cosmic motions (Newton, 1729; Snith, 2007).

Although many of his contemporaries dismissed the concept of gravity as somewhat occult, it nevertheless explained the motion of heavenly bodies and why they are firmly in space rather than freefalling (Edelglass et al, 1991). Newton assumed the cosmos to be infinite but fell short of explicating it beyond its motions. He was obviously trying to avoid a clash with the religious authorities of his day which were mostly same as the state. A statement on the origin or ultimate nature of the cosmos would definitely have religious ramifications. In his era, that was not tolerated, especially when it went against orthodoxy. Newton kept his religious beliefs to himself and refrained from drawing any religious conclusions from his cosmological discoveries. In so doing, he successfully insulated his works from religious controversies and scrutiny.

While Newton advanced the science of the motions of the heavenly bodies significantly, his era set back significantly, the science of the meaning of the cosmos. He fell short of addressing the ultimate question of the nature of the cosmos as an entity. Scientists succeeding him would follow that trend.

6.2 Einstein

Keying into the tradition of theological neutrality established by Newton, Einstein steered clear of the meaning and nature of the cosmos in his theory of the cosmos. Like Newton, he focused more on the motion of the cosmos than the origin and possible end of the cosmos. Einstein propounded the theory of special relativity and later on, the theory of general relativity (Major, 2007). He equally merged space and time as a single entity at the cosmic level. His equation of energy to mass became the most popular equation in the world. Einstein's genius was not in doubt universally. While as a matter of fact his theory of relativity overthrew the Newtonian physics, his cosmology was nonetheless poor. It woefully failed to address the question of origin and end of the cosmos.

VII. The Big Bang Cosmos

The big bang theory is a cosmological model that seeks to explain the universe but ends up shutting out entirely from the intellectual discourse, the question of the origin of reality. It is a misleading acronym that gives out so much information about the workings of the universe but is paradoxically silent on the origin of matter. As a matter of fact the big bang theory does not even pretend to answer the question of origin in relation to the universe. On the contrary, it is a largely speculative but seemingly scientific account of a supposed bang at a point in time, in the existence of reality. The big bang theory does not claim to be an explosion of matter out of nothing to create the "something" that is the universe (Kragh, 2013). It is no creatio ex nihilo. It is at best the reorganization of matter into forms that we are more familiar with today. It does not give any account of the origin of matter per matter.

The big bang theory is fraught with many logical inconsistencies. Not only that it continues in the Newtonian and Einstein's traditions of staying mute on the theological implications of cosmological propositions, it ups the ante by shying away from the question of the origin of matter but focusing on the reorganizations of natter instead. It is not possible to talk about an origin of the universe in an already existing universe. The supposed bang did not take place in nothingness. Absolute nothingness is not possible in the universe. Like Parmenides said, "nothing can come out of nothing" (Diels, 1897). Matter must be necessarily eternal. In that case, no bang could have possibly called it into existence. It has always been.

The big bang model of the universe gives an account of the expansion of the universe from initial high density and high temperature to its present state (Bridge, 2014). It clearly does not give an account of the origin of the universe but the expansion of the universe. Yet, the phrase, "expansion of the universe" is not logically tenable. The universe is all that there is. There is nothing outside the universe. There cannot possibly be an "outside" to the universe since it is all that there is. How can the universe possibly expand? Which other universe is it expanding into when it is the entirety of all that there is? For the universe to expand there must be something out there that it is expanding into; there must be room that it is expanding into. However, there is no such room for the space even is part of the universe. Galaxies might expand but that doesn't mean that the universe is expanding. Galaxies are in, and are parts of the universe but not the universe.

The only definite way to logically express the extent of the universe is by ascribing infinity to it.

The universe cannot be bounded. If it were to be bounded, what would the reality beyond the boundary be called? Such a space is not possible because as aforementioned, the universe is the sum total of all existing physical realities.

The value of the big bang model lies in its explanation of some physical realities in space. It gives no clear account of the origin or ultimate fate of the universe. The question of the origin and future of the universe remains largely unanswered. Even the idea of a bang is metaphorical.

VIII. Meta-Science

Current laws of science give empirical accounts of events and realities in the cosmos. But the laws as they are at present might not yield a satisfactory answer to the nature of the cosmos as an entity. Scientific laws account for finite events. They basically operate by relating effects to causes. In the case of the universe which so far demonstrates infinity, scientific laws as they are at the moment become handicapped. When an effect is continuously changing because it is infinite, it becomes difficult to pin it to a cause. Therefore, there is need for a new science; an advanced science that can take off from the limits of the current science. That is metascience.

Unlike metaphysics that is based purely on ratiocinations, imaginations and sometimes, religious doctrines, metascience is based on the empirical measurements of the units and implications of infinity. It is the science of infinity in relation to the cosmos. It is the science of the cosmos as an unbounded entity. It is cosmology operating on advanced laws of physics. It is a scientific probe of the objects of metaphysics. There is nothing mythical about metascience rather, it boldly probes realities that conventional science shy away from. It probes infinity.

The behavior of the cosmos at the macro level is as important as the behavior of the cosmos at the micro level. Conventional science often is fixated on micro portions of the cosmos, and rarely focuses on the cosmos as an entity. Conventional empiricism deals with finitude. It majorly deals with accomplished events. Infinity however is an accomplishing event rather than an accomplished event. Conventional science and empiricism cannot adequately explain it. Therein is the subject matter of metascience.

IX. Material Implications of an Infinite Cosmos

The cosmos is thoroughly made of matter. An infinite cosmos implies the infinity of matter. The implication is that matter is infinite in kind and dimension. All kinds of matter can never be discovered neither can matter be reduced to the barest division. No particle of matter can be indivisible in an infinite cosmos for infinity is inversely in dimension. "Infinity" must necessarily be listed as a property of matter.

X. Conclusion

The cosmos has always been a continuous puzzle for ages. Every era does its best at the task of giving meaning to the cosmos. From the Ptolemaic era to the present era that quest has not subsided. Since the Copernican revolution, scientists and philosophers have in their discoveries and writings pointed to an infinite universe. An infinite universe has far reaching implications. These implications ought to be scientifically investigated even if it means inventing an advanced form of science known as metascience. A science based on finite events cannot apply to the cosmos as an infinite entity. New rules ought to apply. New science ought to be invented.

References

[1]. Anaxagoras.(c.440 BC) *Fragments of Anaxagoras*
[2].
https://www.goodreads.com/author/quotes/1985353.Anaxago
ras

[3]. Aristotle. (ca.302 BC). *Physics*.

[4]. Bridge, M. (30 July 2014). First Second of the Big
Bang. How The Universe Works. *Science Channel*.

[5]. Burnet, J. (1930). *Early Greek Philosophy*. Great
Britain: A. & C. Black, Ltd. pp. 52.

[6]. Diels, H. (1897). *Parmedean Fragments* 1-19.
https://lexundria.com/parm_frag/1-19/grk

[7]. Di Liscia, D. (2015). "Johannes Kepler" in
Stanford Encyclopedia of Philosophy.
https://plato.stanford.edu/entries/kepler/

[8]. Diodorus. (60 BC). *Library of History*.

[9]. Dreyer, J.L.E. (1953) *A History of Astronomy
from Thales to Kepler*. ISBN 0-486-60079-3

[10]. Edelglass, S; Maier, G. & Gebert, H. (1991)
Matter and Mind. ISBN 0-940262-45-2. p. 54

[11]. Grant, E. (1996) *Planets, Stars, and Orbs: The
Medieval Cosmos*, 1200-1687. pp. 382–3. ISBN 0-521-
43344-4

[12]. James, G. (1954). *The Stolen Legacy: Greek
Philosophy is Stolen Egyptian Philosophy*.
http://www.jpanafrican.org/ebooks/eBook%20Stolen%20Leg
acy.pdf

[13]. Knox, W. (2019). "Giordano Bruno" in *Stanford
Encyclopedia of Philosophy*.
https://plato.stanford.edu/entries/bruno/

[14]. Kragh, H. (2013). Big Bang: the etymology of a
name. https://doi.org/10.1093/astrogeo/att035

[15]. Lindberg, D.C. (1992). *The Beginnings of
Western Science*. p. 250. ISBN: 9780226482057

[16]. Linton, C.M. (2004). *From Eudoxus to Einstein—
A History of Mathematical Astronomy*. ISBN 978-0-521-
82750-8

[17]. Major, F. G. (2007). The quantum beat:
principles and applications of atomic clocks (2nd ed.). p.
142. ISBN 978-0-387-69533-4.

[18]. Mammino, Liliana; Ceresoli, Davide; Maruani,
Jean; Brändas, Erkki (2020). Advances in quantum systems

in chemistry, physics, and biology: *Selected Proceedings of QSCP-XXIII (Kruger Park, South Africa, September 2018)*. Cham, Switzerland: Springer Nature. p. 355. ISBN 978-3-030-34940-0

[19]. Newton, I. (1729), *Principia*, (Book 3 vol.2). pp. 232–233.

[20]. O'Grady, P. (1995). Thales of Miletus. *Internet Encyclopedia of Philosophy.* https://iep.utm.edu/thales/

[21]. Rabin, S. (2019). "Nicolaus Copernicus" in *Stanford Encyclopedia of Philosophy.* https://plato.stanford.edu/entries/copernicus/

[22]. Smith, G. (2007). "Isaac Newton" in *Stanford Encyclopedia of Philosophy.*

[23]. Stumpf, S.E. (1994). *Philosophy: History and Problems.*

[24]. Taylor, C.C.W. (1999). *The atomists, Leucippus and Democritus: Fragments, a Text and Translation with a Commentary.* University of Toronto Press Incorporated, ISBN 0-8020-4390-9, pp. 157-158.

And Just Like That

By Amy Perry

The Universe
Became itself
To experience
Itself,
Experiencing
Itself.

Introducing Samuel Alexander's Space-Time God

By Emily Thomas

Dr. Thomas is an Associate Professor of Philosophy at Durham University, author of two books, and is especially interested in philosophical conceptions of time and space, and in the history of philosophy.

Samuel Alexander (1859–1938) was a major figure in early twentieth century British philosophy. His 1920 two-volume *Space, Time, and Deity* sets out a grand metaphysical system, grounded in space and time. For Alexander, space and time sit at the fundamental level of reality, and together they form patterns. Out of these patterns, new qualities emerge: matter, life, conscious minds, and deity. This emergence is driven by an evolutionary process, which pushes the world to emerge not only new things but *better* things.

For Alexander, conscious minds are more valuable than mere living creatures, which are in turn more valuable than rocks or stars. His system aims to explain why our minds are located in our brains: our minds have emerged out of our brains. It also aims to explains the 'religious sentiment' that some people feel, a sense or need to worship.

In the following extract, Alexander argues that the quality of 'deity', of God, will emerge out of spacetime. He believes that time 'compels' us to 'forecast' the arrival of God, as the course of time produces ever more perfect beings. God does not exist now but he will exist in the future. Alexander's system has similarities with pandeism. He believes that the whole universe will be God's body - that the universe is 'big' or 'pregnant' with deity. This means that every part of the universe, including us, are part of the emerging body of God. However, Alexander does not believe that God created the universe. Rather, he argues that the universe has created God as part of a natural, evolutionary process.

Alexander's rejection of a creator God is perhaps the most controversial part of his view, yet it fits with his deeply held respect for science. God will evolve out of the universe, just as stars and dinosaurs and human beings have evolved. In Alexander's universe, God is not the beginning and the end. God is only the end.

Samuel Alexander

Space, Time, and Deity

By Samuel Alexander

In a universe.... consisting of things which have developed within the one matrix of Space-Time; we ourselves being but the highest finite existences known to us because the empirical quality which is distinctive of conscious beings is based on finites of a lower empirical quality; what room is there for, and what place can be assigned to, God?

....

We may ask ourselves whether there is place in the world for the quality of deity; we may then verify the reality of the being which possesses it, that is of the Deity or God; and having done so, we may then consult the religious consciousness to see whether this being coincides with the object of worship. Where then, if at all, is deity in the scheme of things?

Deity the next higher empirical quality than mind

Within the all-embracing stuff of Space-Time, the universe exhibits an emergence in Time of successive levels of finite existences, each with its characteristic empirical quality. The highest of these empirical qualities known to us is mind or consciousness. Deity is the next higher empirical quality to the highest we know; and, as shall presently be observed, at any level of existence there is a next higher empirical quality which stands towards the lower quality as deity stands towards mind. Let us for the moment neglect this wider implication and confine our attention to ourselves. There is an empirical quality which is to succeed the distinctive empirical quality of our level; and that new empirical quality is deity. If Time were as some have thought a mere form of sense or understanding under which the mind envisages things, this conception would be meaningless and impossible. But Time is an element in the stuff of which the universe and all its parts are made, and has no special relation to mind, which is but the last complexity of Time that is known to us in finite existence. Bare Time in our hypothesis, whose verification has been in progress through each stage of the two preceding Books and will be completed by the conception of God,—bare Time is the soul of its Space, or performs towards it the office of soul to its equivalent body or brain; and this elementary mind which is Time becomes in the course of time so complicated and refined in its internal grouping that there arise finite beings whose soul is materiality, or colour, or life, or in the end what is familiar as mind.

Now since Time is the principle of growth and Time is infinite, the internal development of the world, which before was described in its simplest terms as the redistribution of moments of Time among points of Space, cannot be regarded as ceasing with the emergence of those finite configurations of space-time which carry the empirical quality of mind. We have to think upon the lines already traced by experience of the emergence of higher qualities, also empirical. There is a nisus in Space-Time which, as it has borne its creatures forward through matter and life to mind, will bear them forward to some higher level of existence. There is nothing in mind which requires us to stop and say this is the highest empirical quality which Time can produce from now throughout the infinite Time to come. It is only the last empirical quality which we who are minds happen to know. Time itself compels us to think of a later birth of Time. For this reason it was legitimate for us to follow up the series of empirical qualities and imagine finite beings which we called angels, who would enjoy their own angelic being but would contemplate minds as minds themselves cannot do, in the same way as mind contemplates life and lower levels of existence. This device was adopted half-playfully as a pictorial embodiment of the conception forced upon us by the fact that there is this series of levels of existence. It was used illustratively to point the distinction of enjoyment and contemplation. But we now can see that it is a serious conception. For the angelic quality the possession of which enables such beings to contemplate minds is this next higher empirical quality of deity and our supposed angels are finite beings with this quality. We shall have to ask how such finite deities are related to the infinite God, for they themselves are finite gods.

Deity is thus the next higher empirical quality to mind, which the universe is engaged in bringing to birth. That the universe is pregnant with such a quality we arc speculatively assured. What that quality is we cannot know; for we can neither enjoy nor still less contemplate it. Our human altars still are raised to the unknown God. If we could know what deity is, how it feels to be divine, we should first have to have become as gods. What we know of it is but its relation to the other empirical qualities which precede it in time. Its nature we cannot penetrate. We can represent it to ourselves only by analogy. It is fitly described in this analogical manner as the colour of the universe. For colour, we have seen, is a new quality which emerges in material things in attendance on motions of a certain sort. Deity in its turn is a quality which attends upon, or more strictly is equivalent to, previous or lower existences of the order of mind which itself rests on a still lower basis of qualities, and emerges when certain complexities and refinements of arrangement have been reached. Once more I am leaning for help upon Meredith, in whose Hymn to Colour, colour takes for a moment the place of what elsewhere he calls Earth: a soul of things which is their last perfection; whose relation to our soul is that of bridegroom to bride. He figures the relation of our soul to colour under the metaphor of love; but as I read the poem, deity as the next higher empirical quality is not different from colour as he conceives it; save only that for him the spirit of the world is timeless, whereas for us deity is like all other empirical qualities a birth of Time and exists in Time, and timelessness is for us a nonentity, and merely a device for contrasting God's infinite deity with the relative imperfection of the finite things we know, a conception which shall appear in due course.

Extension of the conception of deity

We have not yet asked what the being is which possesses deity. But before attempting to raise the question we may still linger over the quality of deity itself. In the first place it is clear that, while for us men deity is the next higher empirical quality to mind, the description of deity is perfectly general. For any level of existence, deity is the next higher empirical quality. It is therefore a variable quality, and as the world grows in time, deity changes with it. On each level a new quality looms ahead, awfully, which plays to it the part of deity. For us who live upon the level of mind deity is, we can but say, deity. To creatures upon the level of life, deity is still the quality in front, but to us who come later this quality has been revealed as mind. For creatures who possessed only the primary qualities,—mere empirical configurations of space-time,—deity was what afterwards appeared as materiality, and their God was matter, for I am supposing that there is no level of existence nearer to the spatio-temporal than matter. On each level of finite creatures deity is for them some ' unknown ' (though not ' unexperienced ') quality in front, the real nature of which is enjoyed by the creatures of the next level.

I do not mean that a material being would in some way think or forecast life; for there is no thinking in the proper sense till we reach mind. I do not even mean that matter forecasts deity in the sense in which it is sometimes said that to a dog his master is God. For the dog though he may not think, does feel and imagine, and his master is a finite being presented to his senses, for whom he feels attachment. I mean only that corresponding to the sense of a mysterious something which is more than we are and yet is felt in feeling and is conceived by speculation, there is some quality in the purview of material things which lies ahead of material quality. If we think ourselves back into material existence, we should feel ourselves, though matter would be the highest that we know, still swept on in the movement of Time. A merely material universe would not be exhausted by materiality and its lower empirical qualities; there would still be that restless movement of Time, which is not the mere turning of a squirrel in its cage, but the nisus towards a higher birth. That it is so, events show. How its being so would be 'experienced' in the material 'soul' may need for its description a greater capacity to strip off human privileges and sympathise with lower experience than most persons, and certainly I, possess.

Deity not spirit

Having thus realised that the relation of deity to mind is not peculiar to us but arises at each level between the next higher quality and the distinctive quality of that level, we can at once pass to another observation. We cannot tell what is the nature of deity, of our deity, but we can be certain that it is not mind, or if we use the term spirit as equivalent to mind or any quality of the order of mind, deity is not spirit, but something different from it in kind. God, the being which possesses deity, must be also spirit, for according to analogy, deity presupposes spirit, just as spirit or mind presupposes in its possessor life, and life physico-chemical material processes. But though God must be spiritual in the same way as he must be living and material and spatio-temporal, his deity is not spirit. To think so would be like thinking that mind is purely life, or life purely physico-chemical. The neural complexity which is equivalent to mind is not merely physiological, but a selected physiological constellation which is the bearer of mind, though it is also physiological, because it has physiological relations to what is purely physiological. That complexity and refinement of spirit which is equivalent to deity is something new, and while it is also spirit it is not merely spirit. Deity is therefore, according to the pattern of the growth of things in time, not a mere enlargement of mind or spirit, but something which mere spirit sub-serves, and to which accordingly the conception of spirit as such is totally inadequate. Spirit, personality, mind, all these human or mental characters belong to God but not to his deity. They belong as we must hold not to his deity but to his body.' Yet since it is through spirit that we become aware of God, whether in the practical shape of the object of religious feeling or philosophically as the possessor of deity, since what is beyond spirit is realised through spirit, and since more particularly spirit is the highest quality whose nature we know, and we are compelled to embody our conceptions in imaginative shapes, it is not strange that we should represent God in human terms. Instead of the shadowy quality of which we can only say that it is a higher quality than mind, God is made vivid to us as a greater spirit; and we conceal the difference in kind of the divine and the human nature under magnified representations of human attributes. These are the inevitable devices of our weakness and our pictorial craving. But, for philosophy, God's deity is not different from spirit in degree but in kind, as a novelty in the series of empirical qualities.

Theories of God as a spirit

When on a former occasion I endeavoured to explain the relation of the mind of total Space-Time to the minds of the separate point-instants, I referred (in a note [5]) to a hypothesis that had been advanced as to the nature of God, which was founded on the coexistence of a superior mind with an inferior one within the same abnormal body or personality. I made use of the notion of coconscious minds not aware of each other, in order to elucidate certain features in Space-Time when Time is regarded as the mind of Space. This hypothesis in its reference to God I am compelled to reject and the reason will now be clear. The sequel will show that the position adopted here as to God is not dissimilar, at least to the extent that God is also for us, ideally speaking, an individual within the world. But it would be difficult on this hypothesis to admit an infinite God; [6] and what is more important it would commit us to making of God a being not higher in kind than minds.

On the basis of the same data as were used in the above hypothesis, we might again be tempted to compare God with the total personality in which the separate personalities are merged when the hysteric patient is restored to health; and to conceive of God as a society of minds. There is, however, nothing to show that the minds of distinct bodies are actually connected together so as to constitute a single all-embracing mind. Where dissociated personalities within a single individual are reunited, their physiological connection is re-established. Between the separate minds supposed to be contained within the mind of God there is no such physiological connection. In its application to the supposed mind of God accordingly the reference to dissociated personalities fails of relevance.

Nor can we help ourselves to think of God as an inclusive mind by the current metaphors of the mind of a state or a crowd. Where many persons are grouped together in co-operation there is no real reason for imagining the whole society to possess a mind. It is sufficient that the persons communicate with one another, and that while on the one hand their gregarious instinct brings about their juxtaposition, their juxtaposition supplies thoughts and passions which are not experienced by the persons in isolation. The mind of a crowd is not a new single mind; the phrase represents the contagious influence upon an individual of the presence of many others. An incendiary oration addressed to one person might leave him cold, but in a meeting each catches infection from his neighbour (just as patients in a hospital will fall into a hypnotic sleep from sympathy with another patient who is receiving suggestion) and the oration may produce a riot. The individuals gather together to hear the orator and then their assemblage fans the flame. The institution of the family arises out of the mutual needs of persons and in turn evokes fresh ones. But there is no new mind of the family; only the minds of its members are affected by their participation in the family. In the same way there is no mind of the state or the nation which includes the minds of its members. The state is not a new individual created by the union of isolated individuals. The individuals are driven by their own sociality into union, and the union alters their minds. It affects the individuals because it is in the first instance the issue of their instinctive gregariousness. The general will is not a new individual will which contains the individual wills; it is but the will of individuals as inspired by desire for the collective good. T. H. Green seems to me to have been right in insisting that a nation or a national spirit is as much an abstraction unless it exists in persons as the individual is an abstraction apart from the nation.[7] It is true that a state or nation has features not recognisable in any one individual; but this is only to say that groupings of persons are not merely personal.

God as universe possessing deity

In a later page I shall return to this matter when I attempt to show the bearing of the doctrine that God's distinctive character is not mind or spirit but something new, or deity, upon the current theory that the Absolute in which all finites are merged is spirit. In the religious emotion we have the direct experience of something higher than ourselves which we call God, which is not presented through the ways of sense but through this emotion. The emotion is our going out or endeavour or striving towards this object. Speculation enables us to say wherein the divine quality consists, and that it is an empirical quality the next in the series which the very nature of Time compels us to postulate, though we cannot tell what it is like. But besides assuring us of the place of the divine quality in the world, speculation has also to ask wherein this quality resides. What is the being which possesses deity? Our answer is to be a philosophical one; we are not concerned with the various forms which the conception of God has assumed in earlier or later religions. Ours is the modester (and let me add far less arduous) inquiry what conception of God is required if we think of the universe as Space-Time engendering within itself in the course of time the series of empirical qualities of which deity is the one next ahead of mind. God is the whole world as possessing the quality of deity. Of such a being the whole world is the body 'and deity is the mind.' But this possessor of deity is not actual hut ideal. As an actual existent, God is the infinite world with its nisus towards deity, or, to adapt a phrase of Leibniz, as big or in travail with deity.

Since Space-Time is already a whole and one, why, it may be urged, should we seek to go beyond it? Why not identify God with Space-Time? Now, no one could worship Space-Time. It may excite speculative or mathematical enthusiasm and fill our minds with intellectual admiration, but it lights no spark of religious emotion. Worship is not the response which Space-Time evokes in us, but intuition. Even Kant's starry heavens are material systems, and he added the moral law to them in describing the sources of our reverence. In one way this consideration is irrelevant; for if philosophy were forced to this conclusion that God is nothing but Space-Time, we should needs be content. But a philosophy which left one portion of human experience suspended without attachment to the world of truth is gravely open to suspicion; and its failure to make the religious emotion speculatively intelligible betrays a speculative weakness. For the religious emotion is one part of experience, and an empirical philosophy must include in one form or another the whole of experience. The speculative failure of the answer is patent. It neglects the development within Space-Time of the series of empirical qualities in their increasing grades of perfection. The universe, though it can be expressed without remainder in terms of Space and Time, is not merely spatio-temporal. It exhibits materiality and life and mind. It compels us to forecast the next empirical quality or deity. On the one hand we have the totality of the world, which in the end is spatio-temporal; on the other the quality of deity engendered, or rather being engendered, within that whole.

These two features are united in the conception of the whole world as expressing itself in the character of deity, and it is this and not bare Space-Time which for speculation is the ideal conception of God.

Belief in God, though an act of experience, is not an act of sight, for neither deity nor even the world as tending to deity is revealed to sense, but of speculative and religious faith. A word will be said later to compare the faith we have in God with the faith we have in the minds of other persons than ourselves. Any attempt, therefore, to conceive God in more definite manner must involve a large element of speculative or reflective imagination. Even the description of God as the whole universe, as possessing deity, or as in travail with deity, is full of figurative language. If we are to make our conception less abstract we must try to represent to ourselves some individual in whom deity is related to its basis in the lower levels of empirical quality as far down as the purely spatio-temporal; and a being of this kind is, as we shall see, rather an ideal of thought than something which can be realised in fact in the form of an individual. What we have to do is to be careful to conceive the ideal in conformity with the plan of what we know of things from experience.

Personification of this conception:

(a) finite god

The simplest way of doing so is to forget for a moment that God being the whole world possessing deity is infinite, and, transporting ourselves in thought to the next level of existence, that of deity, to imagine a finite being with that quality, a god of a polytheistic system, or what we have called an angel. We must conceive such a being on the analogy of ourselves. In us a living body has one portion of itself specialised and set apart to be the bearer of the quality of mind. That specialised constellation of living processes, endowed with the quality of mind, is the concrete thing called mind. The rest of the body in its physiological, material, and spatio-temporal characters, sustains the life of this mind-bearing portion, which in its turn is said in the physiological sense to represent the rest of the body, because there is a general correspondence between the affections of the body and the excitements of the mind-bearing portion which are enjoyed as mental processes. In virtue of some of these mental enjoyments the mind contemplates the things outside its body, in virtue of others it contemplates its own bodily conditions in the form of organic sensa or sensibles, or of other sensibles of movement, touch, and the rest. In the superior finite which has deity, we must conceive the immediate basis of deity to be something of the nature of mind, just as the immediate basis of our mind is life, and the mind of the finite deity will rest on a substructure of life as with us. One part of the god's mind will be of such complexity and refinement as mind, as to be fitted to carry the new quality of deity.

Thus whereas with us, a piece of Space-Time, a substance, which is alive, is differentiated in a part of its life so as to be mind, here a substance or piece of Space-Time which is mental is differentiated in a portion of its mental body so as to be divine, and this deity is sustained by all the space-time to which it belongs, with all those qualities lower than deity itself which belong to that substance. Moreover, as our mind represents and gathers up into itself its whole body, so does the finite god represent or gather up into its divine part its whole body, only in its body is included mind as well as the other characters of a body which has mind. Now for such a being, what for us are organic sensibles would include not merely the affections of its physiological body, but those of its mental 'body,' its mental affections. To speak more accurately, its mental affections, the acts of its mind-body, would take the place of our organic or motor sensa, while sensa, like hunger and thirst, which are the affections of its life-body, would fall rather into the class of sensa which with us are, like the feel and visual look of our bodies, contemplated by special senses. For such a being its specially differentiated mind takes the place of the brain or central nervous system with us. The body which is equivalent with the deity of the finite god, that is to say, whose processes are not parallel to but identical with the 'deisings' or enjoyments of the god, is of the nature of mind.

Only this proviso must be added. The mental structure of which a portion more complex and subtle is the bearer of deity, must not be thought necessarily to be a human mind or aggregation of such, but only to be of the mental order. To assume it to be of the nature of human mind would be as if a race of seaweeds were to hold that mind when it comes (the quality of deity for seaweeds) must be founded on the life of seaweeds, and minds the offspring of seaweeds. What form the finite god would assume we cannot know, and it is idle to guess. The picture has been drawn merely in order to give some kind of definiteness to the vague idea of a higher quality of existence, deity as founded upon the highest order of existence we know. There is always a danger that such attempts at definiteness where precise knowledge from the nature of the case is out of the question may seem a little ridiculous. Fortunately when we leave the finite god and endeavour to form a conception of the infinite God in his relation to things, we may avail ourselves of what is useful in the picture and avoid the danger of seeming to affect a prevision of how things in the future will come to be. We use the picture merely in order to understand how the whole world can be thought of as possessing deity.

(b) Infinite God

We have now to think, not as before of a limited portion of Space-Time, but of the whole infinite Space- Time, with all its engendered levels of existence possessing their distinctive empirical qualities, as sustaining the deity of God. But when we imagine such an individual, we discover two differences which mark him off from all finites, including finite gods. The first is this. Our experience is partly internal and partly external; that is, the stimuli which provoke our enjoyments and through them are contemplated by us (and the same account applies with the proper extension of the terms to all finites) partly arise within our bodies and partly from external ones. The objects which we contemplate are partly organic or motor sensa and partly special sensa, in which are included our bodies as seen or touched or similarly apprehended. Now the body of God is the whole universe and there is no body outside his. For him, therefore, all objects are internal, and the distinction of organic and special sensa disappears. Our minds, therefore, and everything else in the world are 'organic sensa of God.' All we are the hunger and thirst, the heart-beats and sweat of God. This is what Rabbi ben Ezra says in Browning's poem, when he protests that he has never mistaken his end, to slake God's thirst.[8] For God there is still the distinction of enjoyment or deising and contemplation, for God's deity is equivalent only to a portion of his body. But it is only for the finites which belong to God's body, all the finites up to finites with mind, that the objects of contemplation are some organic and some external.

The second difference, and ultimately it is a repetition of the first, is this. God's deity is lodged in a portion of his body, and represents that body. But since his body is infinite, his deity (I allow myself to turn deity from a quality into a concrete thing just as I use mind sometimes for the mental quality, sometimes for the concrete thing, mental processes), which represents his body, is infinite. God includes the whole universe, but his deity, though infinite, belongs to, or is lodged in, only a portion of the universe. The importance of this for the problem of theism will appear later. I repeat that when God's deity is said to represent his body, that representation is physiological; like the representation on the brain of the different portions of the body which send nervous messages to the brain. Deity does not represent the universe in the mathematical sense, in which, for example, the odd numbers represent or are an image of the whole series of numbers. Such mathematical representation would require God's deity also to be represented in his deity; and it is not so represented in the same fashion as his body is represented.

God's infinitude

The infinitude of God's deity marks the difference between him and all other empirical beings. Deity is an empirical quality, but though it is located in a portion only of the universe, which universe of Space-Time with all its finites of lower order is God's body, yet that portion is itself infinite in extent and duration. Not only is God infinite in extent and duration, but his deity is also infinite in both respects. God's body being the whole of Space-Time is omnipresent and eternal; but his deity, though not everywhere, is yet infinite in its extension, and though his time is a portion only of infinite Time his deity is, in virtue of what corresponds in deity to memory and expectation in ourselves, infinite in both directions. Thus empirical as deity is, the infinity of his distinctive character separates him from all finites. It is his deity which makes him continuous with the series of empirical characters of finites, but neither is his body' nor his ' mind ' finite.

We are finitely infinite; God is infinitely infinite

For clearness' sake I must linger a little over this important and difficult matter; for in one sense our minds and all finite things are infinite as well. We are, however, finitely infinite; while deity is infinitely infinite. We are finite because our minds, which are extended both in space and time, are limited pieces of Space-Time. We are infinite because we are in relation to all Space-Time and to all things in it. Our minds are infinite in so far as from our point of view, our place or date, we mirror the whole universe; we are corn-present with everything in that universe. I need not repeat at length what has been said more than once. Though only a limited range of distinct things comes within our view, they are fringed with their relations to what is beyond them, and are but islands rising out of an infinite circumambient ocean. The whole of which they are parts may shrink in our apprehension into a vague object of feeling or be conceived more definitely as infinite. Still it is there.

But this infinite world of Space-Time with its finite things engendered within it finds access to our minds only through our bodies and thence to our brains, and is cognised through our neuromental processes and the combinations of them. Our minds consist of our mental processes, which are also neural ones. If we follow a dangerous method of language, or of thinking, and fancy that the objects we know are the content ' of our minds we may be led into the belief that, since our minds contain representations of all things in the universe, our minds are infinite, in the same way as God's deity. If, however, we recollect that our minds are nothing but the processes of mind and have no contents but their process-characters we shall avoid this danger. We shall then understand how our minds can be finite in extent and duration and yet be compresent with and correspond to an infinite world.

We may distinguish two sorts of infinity, which I will call internal and external. An inch is internally infinite in respect of the number of its parts and corresponds to an infinite line of which it forms only a part. But it is itself finite in length. In the same way our minds, though finite in space-time, may be infinite in respect of their correspondence with the whole of things in Space-Time.

We said that our minds represented our bodies, because to speak generally the various parts of our body were connected neurally with their corresponding places in the cortex. External objects excite our minds through first impinging on our organs of sense. As such representations of our body, our mind is finite. But through that body it is brought into relation with the infinite world. Thus though finite in extent of space and time we are

136

internally infinite. We are so as pieces of Space and Time. But also within the brain there is room for multitudinous combinations initiated from within and enjoyed as imaginations and thoughts, and, for all I know, these are infinitely numerous in their possibilities of combination. We have at least enough of them to comprehend the universe as a whole so far as such apprehension is open to our powers.[9] It is sufficient for our purposes of argument that our minds as spatiotemporal substances are -like all spatio-temporal extents internally infinite. Externally we are finite.

But there is nothing whatever outside the body of God, and his deity represents the whole of his body, and all the lower ranges of finites are for him organic sensa.' The spatio-temporal organ of his deity is not only internally but externally infinite. Deity, unlike mind, is infinitely infinite.

Thus when we are said to represent the universe in our apprehensions we must be careful to distinguish this sense of representation, which in truth signifies only the fact of compresence, from the physiological sense in which the brain is said to represent the body, the sense in which I have used the term in this chapter,. in which the mind represents the bodily organism in which it is placed. Failing to make this distinction we should conclude as Leibniz did that the monad, since it represents the whole by standing in relation to every part of it, is in itself infinite and eternal. The mind is thus removed from the limitations of Time and Space. From our point of view, the mind exists both in time and space; and if it is true that Time is nothing without Space, it is difficult to understand speculatively how an eternal existence of the mind could be possible without that specialised complex of space which experience tells us is the basis of mind. If convincing experiment should in the future demonstrate the persistence of mind without its body which here subserves it, I should have to admit that the doctrine of this work would require radical alteration and, so far as I can judge at present, destruction. But this is not the only word which I should wish to say on so tender and, to many persons so precious, a belief.[10]

God as actual

We are now led to a qualification of the greatest importance. The picture which has been drawn of the infinite God is a concession to our figurative or mythological tendency and to the habit of the religious consciousness to embody its conception of God in an individual shape. Its sole value lies in its indication of the relation that must be understood upon the lines traced by experience to subsist between deity and mind. This is adequate for finite gods, supposing the stage of deity to have been reached. But the infinite God is purely ideal or conceptual. The individual so sketched is not asserted to exist; the sketch merely gives body and shape, by a sort of anticipation, to the actual infinite God whom, on the basis of experience, speculation declares to exist. As actual, God does not possess the quality of deity but is the universe as tending to that quality. This nisus in the universe, though not present to sense, is yet present to reflection upon experience. Only in this sense of straining towards deity can there be an infinite actual God. For, again following the lines of experience, we can see that if the quality of deity were actually attained in the empirical development of the world in Time, we should have not one infinite being possessing deity but many (at least potentially many) finite ones. Beyond these finite gods or angels there would be in turn a new empirical quality looming into view, which for them would be deity—that is, would be for them what deity is for us. Just as when mind emerges it is the distinctive quality of many finite individuals with minds, so when deity actually emerges it would be the distinctive quality of many finite Individuals. If the possessor of deity were an existent individual he must be finite and not infinite. Thus there is no actual infinite being with the quality of deity; but there is an actual infinite, the whole universe, with a nisus to deity; and this is the God of the religious consciousness, though that consciousness habitually forecasts the divinity of its object as actually realised in an individual form.

God and other infinities

The reason why the universe as possessing deity is purely ideal is found in the contrast between God so described and other empirical infinites. God is not the only infinite. We have, in the first place, the infinite Space-Time itself which is a priori, and besides this we have infinites which are generated within Space-Time and are empirical. Instances are infinite lines in Space and infinite numbers. These are empirical determinations of categorial characters and belong to the class of existents with purely primary qualities. Hitherto in the preceding chapters we have confined ourselves to finites, but it now remains briefly to discuss these empirical infinites, which are always less than the a priori infinity of Space-Time itself. God is no exception to this statement, for though his body is the whole universe, his deity (and deity is what distinguishes him) is lodged in an infinite portion

139

only of this whole infinitude. Empirical infinites with primary qualities were touched upon in a preceding chapter, and in view of this very question how far they were ideal and how far real.[11] Along with the empirical infinites go the beings which are infinitely small.

Unqualitied infinities actual

In both cases there is an ideal or conceptual element involved as well as a sensible or, to speak more properly, an intuited one. Neither the infinitely great nor the infinitely small is presented to intuition without the help of reflective concepts. But since concepts are as real as percepts their presence does not destroy the actual reality of the thing into which they enter. I do not propose to discuss the status of the various kinds of infinite numbers and to consider how far, if at all, any of them are to be treated as on a level with the conceptual creations of mathematics such as imaginaries or n-dimensional Spaces.' [12] I am speaking of such empirical infinites as infinite lines or the number of, say, the infinite system of integers. It might be thought that such infinites cannot be more than ideal because it is impossible to possess them completed. There seems, however, no reason to doubt the actuality of infinite lines, nor of the number of the integers, whether number is defined extensionally or, as we have preferred, intensionally. For infinite number is the number belonging to classes containing infinite members. The fact that an infinite system cannot be completed is irrelevant to its actuality. For infinity means only that the infinite system can be represented in the mathematical sense by a part of itself; and it is indifferent that we cannot in intuition complete an infinite line. To suppose that the infinitely great must be completed is to eliminate Time from its nature; just as to suppose that the infinitely small is an indivisible self-subsistent entity or infinitesimal is to eliminate Time from its nature. Infinites, whether of division or of composition, are actual, just because of the element in them which makes them conceptual for us. Points and instants are not fixed minima but the elements of things, and their characteristic is that we can never come to a stop with them. Hence it was said before that points and instants, or more properly point-instants, are real and actual just because they are ideal. If we could take them in at once they would not be continuous with one another. The same thing holds of empirical infinites. Lines are actual and infinite and can be selected from Space, and infinite numbers, or at least some of them, from actual Space-Time.

but not qualitied infinites

Now these infinites are without quality. God as the possessor of deity, on the other hand, is a qualitied infinite, and we learn from experience that quality is borne by finite complexes of space-time. There may be actual infinites with none but primary qualities, for these are not qualities at all, and the entities in question are infinite portions of the infinite Space or Time. But the qualified infinite is not merely ideal as implying, like all infinites, a conceptual element, but it is ideal because it is not actual. At any level of existence there is a claimant to be a qualitied infinite, and that claimant is not actual. It is a projected picture of an actual infinite, in which that quality is being engendered but has not actually come to birth.

141

The qualitied infinite, if the quality could be actually realised, would present overwhelming difficulties, when we ask if it is subject to the categories. God's body, being the whole universe of Space-Time, is the source of the categories but not itself subject to them. Since his deity is realised in a portion only of the universe, it might be thought that deity at any rate, which is equivalent to some complex of mind, might be subject to the categories, and be a true individual substance. It is not however an individual, for an individual is the union of particular and universal. And realised deity is not universal, since, representing as it does the whole, it admits of no repetition, which is vital to a universal.[13] We can only say that, like Space-Time itself, it is singular. Neither is it a substance, for the same reason. Representing the whole in the physiological sense, it admits no relation to other substances, but is the whole of Space-Time on a reduced scale. In this breakdown of the attempt to apply to it the categories (for the same considerations can be advanced in the case of the other categories as well) it betrays its merely ideal character of a picture and nothing more. The picture is not the less eminently worth drawing. Only nothing actual corresponds to it. We have an individual forecasted which is not a real individual. The actual reality which has deity is the world of empiricals filling up all Space-Time and tending towards a higher quality. Deity is a nisus and not an accomplishment. This, as we shall note, is what prevents the conception from being wholly theistical. Finite gods, on the other hand, are of course subject to the categories.

Finite Gods and infinite God.

Two different questions accordingly may be asked as to the existence of deity, to which different answers must be given. The first is, do finite beings exist with deity or are there finite gods? The answer is we do not know. If Time has by now actually brought them forth, they do exist; if not, their existence belongs to the future. If they do exist ("millions of spirits walk the earth ") they are not recognisable in any form of material existence known to us; and material existence they must have; though conceivably there may be such material bodies, containing also life and mind as the basis of deity, in regions of the universe beyond our ken.

That is a scholastic and trivial question. The other question admits an answer. Does infinite deity exist? The answer is that the world in its infinity tends towards infinite deity, or is pregnant with it, but that infinite deity does not exist; and we may now add that if it did, God—the actual world possessing infinite deity—would cease to be infinite God and break up into a multiplicity of finite gods, which would be merely a higher race of creatures than ourselves with a God beyond.

Infinite deity then embodies the conception of the infinite world in its straining after deity. But the attainment of deity makes deity finite. Deity is an empirical quality like mind or life. Before there was mind the universe was straining towards infinite mind. But there is no existent infinite mind, but only many finite minds. Deity is subject to the same law as other empirical qualities, and is but the next member of the series. At first a presage, in the lapse of time the quality comes to actual existence, animates a new race of creatures, and is succeeded by a still higher quality. God as an actual existent is always becoming deity but never attains it. He is the ideal God in embryo. The ideal when fulfilled ceases to be God, and yet it gives shape and character to our conception of the actual God, and always tends to usurp its place in our fancy.

How can a variable God be the whole universe?

I may pause for a moment to anticipate a possible objection to this notion of a variable God, which is, as it were, projected in front of each successive level of existents. Since God's deity is different for plants and men and angels, and varies with the lapse of time, how can we declare him to be the whole universe? Must not God be different at each level? I answer that the variation lies in the empirical development within the universe, and therefore not in God's totality but, first of all, in his deity, and secondly, and in correspondence therewith, in the orders of existents within his body which have as yet been reached. It is still one Space-Time within which grows up deity in its successive phases, and within which the body of God varies in its internal composition. Yet God's body is at any stage the whole Space-Time, of which the finites that enter into God's body are but specialised complexes. Only certain existents, qualitied or unqualitied, are at any one moment actual or present. The rest are past or future, but they are included as past or future in total Space-Time as it is in any one moment of its history. They are only not actual. It is thus always the one universe of Space-Time which is God's body, but it varies in its empirical constitution and its deity.[14] For we are not to think of the matrix, Space-Time,

144

as something which grows bigger in extent with the lapse of Time; its Space is always full and it grows older through internal rearrangements, in which new orders of empirical finites are engendered. No matter therefore what quality the deity of God may be, his body is always the whole Space-Time.

Blending of the finite gods and infinite deity

Thus the conception of finite gods and that of infinite God are different conceptions in metaphysics. In the one we are transporting ourselves in thought to the next order of finites; in the other we think of the whole world as tending towards deity or godhead. But in the inevitable blending of speculation and pictorial mythology the two conceptions may be confused. This occurs, for instance, wherever God is conceived merely as the chief in the hierarchy of gods and not different in quality from them. For as we have seen, in speculation, either there is an infinite God, which is an ideal, and there are then no angels or finite deities; or if there are finite gods, the infinite or supreme ideal has ceased to be God. Polytheism represents the attempt to secure deity in finite forms, and it is not unnatural that in this imagination the divine quality should also be construed in terms of our humanity and the gods be conceived as transcendent human beings. Polytheism seeks to do justice to the claim of religion and speculation for a higher quality of existent. But it misses the conception of a God who is in his body coextensive with the whole world. In some polytheisms, like that of the Greeks, this defect is made good by recognising a rule of necessity or fate to which even Zeus is subject. Here we have the totality of things in its infinite quality. I have not knowledge enough to say how far in other polytheisms a corresponding element is to be found. But if the contention of certain anthropologists is sound,[15] there is in savage theologies a stage of pre-animism which precedes the belief in more or less human spirits or ghosts, resident in trees or stones and corresponding in their definiteness to what we have called finite gods or angels. The sense of something mysteriously spiritual, not definite but vaguely animating the world, would be, if these contentions are sound, the imaginative presage of what our speculation calls the ideal infinite deity, expressed in the forms natural to the mind for which deity as the next empirical quality would seem to be a vague abstraction.

It remains to observe that the conception of an infinite world contains nothing which does not follow the lines of experience. The nisus in the world which drives it, because of Time, to the generation of fresh empirical qualities is a verifiable fact. Its extension from mind to deity is an application of analogy, but an analogy which is no more than an extension of what can be traced as existent already. But the notion depends undoubtedly on the hypothesis which has inspired hitherto our whole interpretation of things. We have still to ask whether the existence of God required by the hypothesis is verified, not in sense but in the religious emotion. To this I proceed in the next chapter, delaying for a moment over two incidental topics.

The world-soul

Philosophy has often used the conception of a world-soul, and it might seem that we had saddled the world with a superfluity of souls. For Time has been described as the soul of Space-Time, with Space for its body. And deity also performs to God's body the office of soul and God's body is the whole world. In truth the world is considered differently in the two conceptions. The world whose soul is Time is the world which precedes quality. The world for which deity is the soul is this same Space-Time but with qualitied finites evolved within it up to the level for which deity is the next quality in advance. If the ideal God could be actual, and his deity realised, deity would truly be the soul of the world in strict analogy with the human soul or the colour of things to which it has been compared, lodged like our soul or like colour in a portion of the body whose soul it is. We should only have to remember that the world-soul so conceived is a variable quality, according to the level for which it is the next in the hierarchy of qualities. But it is never realised and remains prophetic only—in the immortal phrase, "the soul of the wide world dreaming of things to come." [16] There is thus no true world-soul, but only a soul of Space-Time and a nisus in the world to deity. Soul and body are distinctions within finite things. When we take Space-Time as a whole in its purely spatio-temporal character, its soul is coextensive with its body. When we take the world of things with qualities, its soul is only ideal not actual.

Whether we think of Time or deity, in either case we may use the designation of a world-soul, but in either case with a qualification which is different in the two cases.

Comparison with the notion of an Absolute Spirit

Before leaving this purely metaphysical discussion we may however profitably compare the conception of empirical deity with that of the Absolute Spirit of the current doctrine of idealism. According to that doctrine, as we have seen more than once, finites though real are not real in their own right but are real appearances of the one Absolute. The God of religion does not escape from this, description and is in turn a real appearance but not ultimately real. All these appearances are contained within the Absolute but, as in it, are transformed. At the same time it is declared of the Absolute itself that it is spirit.

Now as to the first half of this statement it is not necessary to repeat at length the results of earlier discussions. Finites, though partial, are real in their own right and are not affected by their being only parts of the whole. For in the end all finites are pieces of Space-Time with that distinctive complexity of spatio-temporal structure which makes them the bearers of their distinctive empirical qualities. The finites are not lost in the whole but constitute it, and all the while are (if only as spatio-temporal complexes) in continuous connection with the whole. The finite things may through their interactions change or be destroyed or modify each other; but in this process it is their empirical characters which vary. Their reality is not affected at any moment. They are what they are. Nor, as we have urged, is there contradiction in finitude nor in the categories that describe and are constitutive of .it. The measure of what is self-consistent is the nature of Space-Time itself, which for our view is the only absolute. We have avoided the designation of absolute, because it suggests mistakenly the unreality of what is relative, and prefer to speak of total Space-Time, a designation which indicates the ultimate homogeneity of the infinite whole with the finite parts.

Still, though the parts are not transformed in the whole, the conception of transformation when understood in a certain sense is legitimate and corresponds to facts. Finites of a lower order are combined to produce a complex which carries a quality of a higher order. Thus physiological complexes of a sufficient complexity carry mind or consciousness. They may be said to be 'transformed' in the consciousness they carry. This is the empirical fact. But in the complex which thus acquires a new quality the parts retain their proper character and are not altered. The physiological elements remain physiological. So does the complex of them; though since it is also psychical, it is not merely physiological but something empirically new. All the chemical substances which exist in the organic body perform their chemical functions. The water in our bodies remains water still. It is the physico-chemical constellation which carries life. Thus even when we go beyond bare spatio-temporal forms which are the basis of all finites and consider things with their empirical qualities of colour, life, and the rest, we see that the parts are used up to produce something different from them and transcending them, but, used up as they are, they are not altered or superseded but subserve. In this special sense there is 'transformation' of the parts in building up a higher existence, but the parts remain what they were.

In the same way a complex of parts which are of the nature of mind becomes the bearer of a quality of deity higher than mind or spirit. In this sense there is transformation of lower quality into deity. But neither is this deity spirit; nor is deity a property of the Absolute as such. Deity is located only in a portion of the infinite whole of Space-Time, and therefore God, though infinite both in respect of his body and his deity, is only in respect of his body coextensive with the absolute whole of Space-Time, while his deity is empirical and belongs only to a part of the Absolute. Thus the Absolute is not deity as if it were permeated with that quality, any more than the human organism is mind, but only that part of the organism has mind which is equivalent to it. Hence even if we could think of spirit as the highest quality in the universe— which we cannot, unless it means something not merely different in degree but in kind from the human spirit—we still could not declare the Absolute to be this spirit but only to contain it as an empirical quality of an infinite part of itself. And we have already seen how the realisation of such a quality means the appearance in the world of finite deities, so that infinite deity is but an ideal. But while on the one hand deity, that is God's mind, does not belong to the Absolute, in God's body which is the whole of Space-Time and is absolute the finites are not submerged nor transformed; they are constituent portions of the Absolute. Thus, where we are dealing with what is absolute or total, the parts are neither lost nor are they transformed; where we are dealing with transformation, we are referring to what is not absolute but empirical.

Thus it is true, as absolute idealism contends, that God is (at least in respect of his deity) on the same footing as finites and if they are appearances so is he, though an infinite appearance. But both God and finites are appearances only in the proper interpretation of that term, as parts of the thing to which they belong, and in which they are not submerged but retained. It still remains that neither is God a spirit, nor far less is the whole or Absolute which includes spirit itself spirit; nor is it deity but includes deity. Yet the fact that finites of a lower quality subserve a higher quality gives an intelligible meaning in accordance with experienced fact to the notion of transformation of finites which, as I think, absolute idealism maintains in the perverted sense of forfeiture or alteration. The well-attested fact that the lower life subserves in the course of time the higher is perverted into the erroneous doctrine that there is a higher something or Absolute in which all lower life is submerged and transformed, and this Absolute is spirit, which is not even the highest empirical quality. Dowered with this empirical quality the Absolute claims to be above the empirical, but would be itself empirical. This result is to my mind the inevitable outcome of the procedure, which I need not again criticise, of taking the measure of consistency and contradiction from our thoughts instead of from things themselves, of pronouncing Space and Time to be contradictory; whereas it is only obedience to the nature of the one "mother" and "nurse of all becoming" which determines consistency and freedom from contradiction.

Notes

[5] Bk. III. ch. ii. A, vol. ii. p. 43, note I.

[6] For physiological bodies with minds are finite. An infinite mind would require for its body the whole universe (see later) and would not then be one mind subsisting along with others but inclusive of them all, and would thus come under the suggestion of the next paragraph. There may indeed be an infinite part of the universe, e.g. a line. But this would not be the bearer of mind. In other words either God's mind is really a mind and then it is finite; or if it is infinite, it must either be an all-inclusive mind (which is merely Time), or not mind at all but deity.

[7] *Prolegomena to Ethics*, sect. 184; taken from the table of contents, p. xxi.

[8] "Frances, when a little one, had been told by her parents that ' in God we live and move and have our being': and then was overheard one day, when she was five years old, explaining to her younger brother that God had a stomach ever so big—everything in the whole world was inside it." *The Dawn of Religion*, by Edith E. Read Mumford (London, 1915), p. 32.

[9] To illustrate this qualification. If it is true that our enjoyment of the past is a past enjoyment, as has been maintained in a previous chapter (Bk. I. ch. iii.), must our minds not then, it may be asked, be eternal? This would be so if we had memory of all the past and anticipation of all the future. But I do not remember the death of Julius Caesar, but only think of it as a past event. The past which I have not been present at, and the future at which I shall not be present, shrink into a thought of past and future time, just as I think of the whole of Space without being sensible of all its parts.

[10] Later, ch. iii. pp. 4.23 ff.

[11] Bk. II. ch. ix. vol. i. pp. 324 ff.

[12] Touched upon in Bk. I. ch. v. vol. i. pp. 158 ff.

[13] It is of course a 'concrete universal '; but that conception has been already examined (Bk. II. ch. iii. vol. i. pp. 233 ff.).

[14] Cp. the same topic discussed in another connection, Bk. II. ch. x. vol. i. p..339.

[15] R. R. Marett, *The Threshold of Religion* (London, 1909), ch. i.

[16] Perhaps from this point of view, though it reverses the Leibnizian order of things, we may be more inclined to find a justification for his conception of God as a transcendent monad, usually regarded as the part of his system which is most open to cavil, than if we consider only its obscurity and inconsistency.

The Pandeist Connection

By Poffo Ortiz

Poffo Ortiz is an author, artist, poet, philosopher, teacher and theological innovator, with an extensive, self-taught education in: Philosophy, Psychology, Biology, Science, History, Mythology, Metaphysics, Religion and the Occult. Specializing in biblical history and comparative religion, he espouses a passionate, comprehensive, integrated philosophy, derived from a deep understanding of these subjects and experiences that range from counseling and evangelism, to acting, directing and designing special make-up effects for television and film.

An outspoken leader and educator in the philosophical realm of Pantheism, he is the creator and founder of a burgeoning new movement: "Biopantheism", an ethics-based, biologically-focused, codification of Pantheism, with a comprehensive ontology that includes a speculative, Pandeistic explanation for the origins of the Universe and practical, real-world applications involving ecological awareness, sustainable living, environmentalism, wildlife conservation, and animal rights activism.

If you are unfamiliar with the term "Pandeism," it is essentially Pantheism, with a logical explanation for the origins and purpose of our existence, that centers around an infinite, unknowable, primordial intelligence or consciousness, that set everything in motion and instigated the Big Bang, by annihilating Itself and "becoming" the physical Universe.

This infinite Being now exists only as the forces of Nature; the indomitable "Life Principle" that I have come to call the "Omnia" which, over eons of time, is now reconstituting and manifesting Itself in collective, intellectual form, through conscious, energy/matter (all bacteria, plants, fungi & animals), and coming into personal self-awareness and cognizance, presently and locally, through us— this is the heart of what I believe.

Pandeism is not Theism, or anything close to what Christians, Jews or Muslims believe (except in the most mystical and unorthodox traditions). And just as with Pantheism, there is no anthropomorphic deity present... only the spontaneous, self-organizing, perpetual, internal/external forces and powers that govern and sustain our world (those who are non-spiritual would simply label these as the "Laws of Nature").

If you've read any of my previous works, you should know me by now and what I stand for. I care about reason, logic and common sense. I seek to dispel the archaic myths of the past and unite people under one banner: REALITY <–that, is my religion. That, is what I preach. The marriage of science and spirituality with a sober and acute awareness, reverence, respect, and appreciation for the natural world.

In terms of the Abrahamic faiths, we already know that no such deity exists or has ever existed in the history of our Universe, but the relevant point is, we HAD a beginning... there was a start of the natural processes that gave rise to all conscious Life. Life IS moving toward greater complexity and self-awareness and this is not coming from outside, but from within... from creation Itself. And this is where Biopan steps in to speculate and articulate what others have already understood for quite some time.

To any and all who are reading, can we stop for a moment and just contemplate, really contemplate what it means when we say: "God is both immanent AND emergent"? Within this reality, there is only the Universe Itself and the vital "essence" or driving "Life Principle" inherent in Nature.

What existed before time and space is unknowable, but by observing reality and studying biology and the current path we are on evolutionarily speaking (first, toward greater complexity and self-organization, then toward unity and coherence in terms of consciousness), we can extrapolate what the Cosmos is actually doing: expanding and contracting, moving out of chaos and multiplicity and back toward singularity and oneness, etc.

What is the main difference between Pantheism and Pandeism? Well, for starters Pandeism deals primarily with origins. It posits that at a point before the Big Bang, before time and space as we know it, an infinite, all-powerful, unknowable, indescribable Being, annihilated Itself and became the physical Universe that we now inhabit. Whereas Pantheism on the other hand, acknowledges the *essence* or divine quality of that Universe and involves our current relationship with It.

It is not Theism, nor is it Deism in any traditional sense, it only deals with our ineffable origins, the source of all that we now see and experience and the reason why it came to be so (be aware, these are some of the most profound subjects anyone could ever discuss). When you question or contemplate who made this god (the problem of infinite regression), you must remember Einstein's Law of Conservation.

The answer is that It simply exists outside of time and has always existed and always will in some form or another. We live *in* time, experiencing existence in a linear illusion that is broken up into the ideas of past, present and future, pushed and pulled along by survival and natural laws like entropy, so we cannot comprehend It with our rational minds, due to the (temporary) illusion of time.

But the "Deus" in Pandeism never actually *lived* per se, in our reality. It was only (and is only), potential energy... and that energy could be likened to an infinite Mind, capable of thinking anything, but not capable of actually *experiencing* anything tangible... until, It took the form and shape of one of Its own imaginings. Hence, It chose to destroy Itself in terms of self-awareness, in order to experience something beyond what It was (or what It is right now, outside of time).

You see, the only way an infinite, all-knowing, all-powerful, eternal Being could "do" anything, or learn something new and actually enjoy it, would be to forget that It is all-powerful, annihilate Its own awareness, and scatter Itself into trillions and trillions of Life forms, then gradually find Its way back, in order to experience something novel. And that's what we are; the discombobulated, incoherent body of God, working our way back toward wholeness as we evolve and progress.

Right now, it is non-existent as a cohesive, conscious, singular Being, even if It was at one point (before the Big Bang), although It is thoroughly entangled and entrenched immanently and almost subliminally, throughout all of creation, manifesting in and through us at all times, pushing us to evolve and adapt and survive and grow and shift and change in relation to our environments. God wants to experience Itself subjectively, and yet simultaneously It also wants to return to pure, non-manifest, potential energy.

Everything exists, because this is what Omnia *wanted* on some level... but I also believe on another level, that It desires to return to singularity. So Nature and reality are caught between both a push and a pull from both directions (infinite past and infinite future), which are really just the same place, since the model is cyclical. That being said, I absolutely believe that we should still do everything in our power to minimize suffering... and I see this as a significant part of the process of becoming whole and complete again once more.

We should not therefore, neglect or abandon Omnia's first wish and intention to manifest as matter (the fundamental force of Dark Matter), but we should also be cognizant of Its inherent desire to fly apart and become nothing once again (the fundamental force of Dark Energy), since this IS the ultimate goal of existence. Or better put, the ultimate destiny and *destination* to unite, but only in terms of awareness/consciousness.

So as much as It longs for (and is inclined to), move back toward singularity, It wants just as much to experience everything that It is currently experiencing, or It would not have annihilated Itself to form all the space/time and energy/matter that exists currently and has existed for the last 14 billion years.

In terms of the sacred pattern of the Torus, we are in the funnel, going outward or inward, however you choose to look at it, the white point of light in the center is the Singularity, i.e. "God." As we expand and spread out into a trillion different

158

emanations and manifestations; stars, planets, galaxies and so on, we also begin to develop and evolve into highly complex, organized, structured beings with sentience and conscious awareness of ourselves and the Whole.

In time, humans will collectively evolve to the point where we are no longer forced to kill and ingest other organisms to sustain ourselves, but will eventually be able to draw our energy and fuel directly from the earth, from the sun, and from the atmosphere—similar to the way in which a conductor draws electricity from the ionosphere or the magnetic field of the earth, etc.

As we become more and more coherent, we also become less and less physical, less and less animalistic and primal... until eventually, we no longer inhabit bodies, we upload our individual or collective consciousness to a universal computer, or we simply project our awareness into the Universe and learn to manifest in whatever forms we choose, eventually uniting and combining again as one cohesive, conscious whole...

Only to begin again and start the whole process anew in another form with no memory of the former. It is an endless cycle that moves and transforms infinitely and perpetually. Incidentally, this is a perfect explanation for the basis of "Cosmic" Multiverse theory (I have my own emerging interpretation of how the experience of life on Earth actually constitutes a subjective, perception-based form of Multiverse in relation to the individual as well, but we'll save that for another time).

Now in truth, when it comes to Pandeism, all of this is irrelevant to us in a practical, everyday sense... as this cosmological and theological "speculation" is only necessary in order to maintain a complete ontological model that includes our origins and the birth of the physical Universe. It is not however, a prerequisite that you believe this, only that you understand it and remain open to its validity as an authentic and accurate theory.

Likewise, since the future extrapolation will take billions of years to occur, it does not hold precedence in relation to personal, day-to-day life. What IS relevant however, is that we understand all of this scientifically, and in so doing, apply what it suggests to our own lives in terms of our morality, our ethics, how we treat one another and the planet.

Several years ago, I co-authored a book on this very subject with several highly esteemed scientists, philosophers, mystics, theologians and critical thinkers and it did quite well. If anyone would like to read more about this theory, you can find links to purchase the book at PandeismAnthology.com.

Multiverse Theory is a speculation postulated by theoretical physicists because they have no scientific explanation to account for the First Cause. Pandeism however, is the most logical explanation for the First Cause. Let me explain. No one knows what initiated the Big Bang, scientists theorize and come up with all kinds of concepts like a multiverse, etc., but that's because they have no idea.

They also discount "God" and rightly so, but that's only because they are viewing Divinity from a traditional Theistic perspective... e.g., a perfect, personal, intelligent being that is distinct and separate from the Universe, etc. Theists equally make the mistake of oversimplifying the idea and projecting a personal, anthropomorphic creator-deity with volition, discretion and will; a perfect being that knows everything and can foresee everything and can do anything, etc.

This is incorrect as well and goes against all known logic and reason. The Pandeist explanation is the only viable solution, as it accounts for why the Universe was initially created, why there is evil and suffering, and why all living organisms are moving towards greater self-awareness, complexity, cohesion and unity.

Keep in mind, all of this IS speculative, it's just that this is probably the only feasible answer based on what has actually transpired... i.e., how the Universe has coalesced into these pockets of energy and matter (galaxies and star systems), that eventually give rise to living organisms and conscious Life. Some, like British Eastern Mystic Alan Watts, have rightly stated that we are the "apertures of the Universe" and the *means* by which the Universe becomes conscious of Itself... but what exactly does this mean?

Well, it all starts with Pandeism. As stated, "Pandeism" is a theological doctrine that combines aspects of Deism with Pantheism. It holds that the creator deity *became* the physical Universe at the beginning of time and ceased to exist as a separate, conscious entity.

What makes me think that the Universe was a conscious, coherent entity at one time? Simple, because we are conscious... and so are the trillions of other Life forms that exist on this planet and no doubt exist throughout the galaxies and star systems.

We know that the Omnia was conscious and will be once again, because everything that exists, has the *potential* to become conscious and self-aware... this is what all energy/matter instinctively does; It organizes Itself into environments and ecosystems that eventually give birth to, and harbor, complex Life.

We know we are the Omnia becoming coherent and whole again, because that is the path of evolutionary biology. It may take millions of years, encompassing multiple pathways and threads, with thousands of starts and stops and hundreds of variant branches, but this IS exactly what is occurring.

Keep in mind, the process is not a linear one... it manifests in an infinite variety of forms and shapes and it happens in what would seem to be a completely random, arbitrary way (in outward appearance), yet according to whatever beneficial mutations and traits that are most successful within each species in relation to their environments...

Rewarding whatever bacterium, plant, fungi and animal, that are most able to adapt and survive under whatever conditions they happen to find themselves in. And this is the process of Evolution, via Natural Selection, which includes Variation, Inheritance, Adaptation and Time.

Why has It done all of this? Well, have you ever had a thought or an experience and then forgot that specific thought and the memory of the experience? It's the same thing with the Universe/Omnia. It cycles through existence for the sake of the experience itself.

The Universe IS expanding and accelerating outward in every direction and will eventually fold in on Itself and condense and "crunch" back into Singularity, with all the accumulated knowledge and experience It has acquired, to then exist for an unknown amount of time (outside of time), as the God of myth and legend, only to expand outward and do it all again in a different way once this time of unity and cohesion is no longer desired.

We know this, because we can see it in the Toroidal energy pattern. We know that the Omnia was conscious, because consciousness exists, so logic dictates that the potential for all consciousness had to have already been contained within the Singularity that existed before the Big Bang.

We also know this is the teleological intent, because that is literally what has happened and what is happening now, in terms of physics and the evolution of all biological Life. When I speak of the god of myth and legend, I mean the personal, conscious and coherent god with agency, discretion, volition, and causal intent (i.e. the god all Theists mistakenly believe exists now).

Right now It is not conscious in a cohesive way, because right now "God" is the Universe... which has no particular will or coherent mind, but It had to have a conscious will at some point, otherwise nothing would exist. There would have been no Big Bang and no physical Universe, had there not been an "intention" at the first. This is what is known as the "First Cause."

There is no reason to shy away from this concept, though at first glance it may reek of religious ideology, it is actually the most rational and viable explanation. Don't be afraid of the Deistic god, It is real and It is us. Just as with Pantheism and Panentheism, in Pandeism, you have other subsets, such as Panendeism. Personally, I would never subscribe to the concept of Panendeism, because just like Panentheism, it is also another form of Theism.

Essentially positing that in addition to the Universe being the physical manifestation of the Divine, God also lives "outside" of the physical Universe in some transcendent realm, or that there is an *aspect* of Divinity that is transcendent or "beyond" Nature... which I do not believe, because it would imply that God is exceedingly evil (or at best, a neglectful, negligent deity), due to the existence of so much suffering and evil in our world.

As stated earlier, Pandeism deals more with origins. Specifically, what initiated the Big Bang, which no scientist or astrophysicist can give a definitive answer to (even though they'll postulate impressively and speculate with Multiverse Theory and quantum fluctuations, etc).

Pandeism actually gives a logical, rational explanation, which admittedly, is speculative itself... but it also accounts for the many strange anomalies and apparent supernatural and paranormal phenomena that have occurred and been reported and witnessed and experienced throughout the history of our species.

The Pandeist model accounts for all of the many seemingly strange and unusual metaphysical phenomena that humans have experienced throughout all cultures, by positing that the fundamental "essence" of God (i.e. the ability to create and reshape matter based on thought), is also *imbued* within the fabric of our reality, and remains an ever-present aspect of Nature.

And since Nature is what makes up and permeates the physical world, it then stands to reason that ANY aspect or element within the Universe, can be subject to glitches, tweaks, alterations and deviations from the established pattern or mode, of the standard operating system expressed through the sleeping body of Omnia, which is Nature.

And this occurs as we, the first intellectual precursors of a conscious Divinity, interact with

164

and manipulate Nature, using our own latent psychic powers of intuition and intention... and this can take place whether we know we are doing it or not; whether it is a conscious and deliberate extension of our will, or just an unconscious wish or desire for something to occur that meets a deeply held emotional need (i.e., answered prayer).

In this way, the Pandeist perspective rationally accounts for any and all paranormal activity and every apparent *deviation* from the set laws of Nature. In other words, a real and tangible "glitch" in the Matrix is possible, because of our own heightened awareness of the divine potential we *already* inherently possess.

This is the true meaning of "Transcendence" and the actual scientific basis for what is known in New Age circles as: Ascension, in Eastern Mysticism as: Enlightenment, and in ancient and esoteric lore as: Apotheosis. In modern terminology, it is referred to as: Self-Realization, Self-Actualization, Awakening the Sleeping Giant Within, and so on.

So, Pandeism is essentially Pantheism; the theological notion or awareness that equates the Universe or the totality of Nature with God, combined with the added theoretical, speculation or belief, that God also *became* the physical Universe at the moment of the Big Bang.

It views God as the Universe, not in a conscious form intellectually speaking, but as a latent, autonomic, instinctive, all-encompassing, living system... that contains within It, all the potential for *apparent* supernatural phenomena, and in my ontology, represents the very *reason* all of Nature is perpetually becoming self-aware through conscious Life forms like us. This is what constitutes the theory of Pandeism.

Taoist/Pandeist Alarm Clock

By John Ross, Jr.

HOMO sapiens sapiens may sit and sport at chess
'til their alarm

Clock... *Drops* and charms ...then...*Rocks.*

IT cushion-ticks *and* tocks: all *jade-eared* as tabled
by the yellow tides.

THEY wholly know their checkered Truth, those
majestic seconds by China's-told-times.

WE never quite comprehend their cost of a Rook, a
Pawn, or a dethroned Lady-Star Empress.

BUT let me tell you about the royal—younger *duo*,
the high prince *Tao* and his *Sister Pan-deist* Tall.

THEY'RE check-mates, on a checker board and
double-squared: the ones enshrined within
us...*dialing...dialing* ever a call.

INVITING us as royals all!

Simple Pandeism

By Amy Perry

It's easy
To overcomplicate
Things.
When discussing
The origins
Of the Universe
It's pretty easy
To feel
Overwhelmed,
Insignificant,
Out of place.
But you are
Just where you
Need to be.
Soaking it all in,
Absorbing experiences
Like the roots
Drink the rain.
Your eyes are
The vehicle
For universal
Understanding.
The sensory
Manifestations
You gather
Culminating into
Humanity's story,
Earth's poetry,
And Deus' art.
Feel it all, enflamed.
Write your story,
So it can be
All of our
Stories.

Stage Dramas

By Amy Perry

The Grand Architect,
A playwright of the age,
Hoisted us to play our parts
On a manifested stage.

Spinning and turning we go,
Learning tricks and cunning speech.
Cutting through scene after scene,
Ignorant how the ending will reach.

The audience and actors will blend
All into one dizzying show,
Watching each other while performing the part,
Nobody more or less in the know.

Still, the show must go on,
Though we know not the end.
We bicker over the final scenes,
Oblivious to a play we attend.

Though there's so much uncertainty,
We do know in spades
That death is a constant,
Where we either ascend or we fade.

We spend so much time
Worrying about the ending of the play,
We tend not to enjoy
The absurdity of every day.

Everyone just wandering around
Upon this divine stage.
With a blanket of stars above
And the death of every sage.

Upon men's bones,
We crowd and clutter
And make ourselves a home,
Safe behind shutters,

Keeping out one and the other,
From the truth that we don't know
What's to happen, once and for all,
After we exit the show.

Is Pandeism a Sufficient Explanation for the Universe?

By Steven Schramm

Steve is an author, speaker, and Bible teacher with a heart for exploring God's Word and God's world. Steve was raised in church and became a Christian at just four years old. After having been a Christian for over 20 years, he began taking his faith more seriously after a brief battle of doubt in the validity of the Christian Story. After a thorough evaluation of the evidence and changing his mind about quite a few things, Steve came out of that season of doubt with an even stronger conviction that his belief in Jesus Christ as Creator, Sustainer, and Savior of the world held true. Now, he trains other Christians to become confident, passionate servants of Jesus, so they can grow in their walk with God and share their faith more persuasively. Aside from his ministry, he works full-time as IT and marketing professional and resides in Statesville, NC with his wife and four children. Browse his website, https://www.steveschramm.com/, for faith-affirming books, articles, podcasts, and videos that point others toward the truth and beauty of the Christian Story.

Not long ago, I shared an article on my Twitter timeline from a popular apologetics blog on the topic of deism. I was most intrigued by the response I received from another user account, simply labeled "Pandeism":

"No accounting for Pandeism. Good; for Pandeism fully accounts for all theistic propositions as manifestations of the underlying unconscious."

I have to be honest—until this point, I had never heard of Pandeism! And here I was receiving a tweet from Pandeism itself! I have, of course, been exposed both to deistic and pantheistic belief systems, and have not found the arguments for either very convincing.

But, in the world we live in, people have ideas and ideas have consequences. Maybe this idea, a combination of two implausible ideas, actually has some weight to it? Perhaps in this sense, two wrongs *do* make a right?

An objective critique of Pandeism is, therefore, in order. We can do this by *internally* critiquing a worldview; that is, following it to its logical conclusion, and determining whether this is consistent with our experience.

What is Pandeism?

Pandeism is best explained as the marrying of two worldviews as discussed earlier: pantheism and deism.

In the pantheistic worldview, the universe (and everything in it) is god. This is not a theistic worldview in the sense of there being one true Creator God, as taught by Christianity, Judaism, and Islam. On this view, you are god, I am god; the washing machine is god! As such, this god is not personal, and neither is he anthropomorphic.

In the deistic worldview, god is also not personal. He is thought to be some sort of divine, galactic clock-maker who wound up his creation in the beginning and has essentially let it go, to follow its natural course. In other words, there is no interference with the creation at all—no answered prayer, no divine intervention, no miracles, etc.

In the pandeistic worldview, we find a mysteriously impersonal god who indeed created, but in doing so, lost consciousness and became the universe.[1] So the creation of the universe by this god was actually accomplished in the becoming of the universe itself. Though we will unpack this later, the fundamental flaw in each of these worldviews seems to be a misdefinition of God.

Another fundamental problem, which again we will explore later, is the absence of an objective moral standard in these worldviews. In other words, any moral reasoning seems not only unnecessary but simply impossible. As mentioned, pantheism brings with it the idea that all is god—which would mean that Hitler and Stalin were, at one time, part of god.

Where is the Proof?

In light of what we know about these worldviews, one must simply ask, "where is the proof?" This question is asked of the Christian God all the time, and therefore I think it is fair to level it against any other belief system that claims to be superior.

Though its tenets may have roots stemming back further than I have been able to trace, it appears that the term "Pandeism" was first coined in the present meaning in 1859 by Moritz Lazarus and Heymann Steinthal.

This worldview necessarily maintains that there has never been and never will be any "special revelation," such as we find in the Bible. The natural revelation is all we have, and thus, we must use our own logic and human reason to conclude what is true about the nature of the universe.

The inherent contradiction here is that without any special revelation, we have no standard against which to measure what is true. Therefore, I think we can draw a preliminary conclusion that Pandeism could not be true in any logically possible world (i.e., a world consistent with the law of non-contradiction, at minimum).

Consider this: fundamental to acquiring knowledge is the concept of truth. God has told us in his revelation (the Bible) about his nature–we know he cannot lie, cannot contradict himself, is all-knowing, etc. So when we see "laws" operating in nature that are consistent with what he has revealed about himself, we have no reason to doubt the claim, and we also gain a piece of evidence working in our favor. The PanDeist could argue that when god became the universe, these laws which reflect his nature were established. But, this explanation is only plausible if we know something about that god. In other words, it would be borrowing from the Christian definition of God to simply assume that god is a logical, perfect being without any other special revelation. Those characteristics are often assumed of a "god-like" being, but what fuels those assumptions if not the Christian definition of God? If this view is true, the pandeistic god, in its becoming the universe and choosing not to interfere with the affairs of mankind, has actually eliminated itself from one's rational affirmation of its existence by not providing any information about its nature.

An Argument from Silence?

It appears, then, that one could arrive at the conclusion of the pandeistic god only by making arbitrary assumptions about its nature. Absent any special revelation, one must argue from the deafening silence of the universe.

One of my favorite lines of Scripture is "the heavens declare the glory of God" (Psalm 19:1). But it is only because of Psalm 19:1 that we know the heavens declare the glory of God!

Even before the completion of the biblical canon, God specially revealed himself to his creation using manifestations in nature (e.g., Moses' burning bush), theophanic expression (e.g., his appearance to Abraham), and in the person of Jesus. But merely starting with the universe, one could arrive at any number of conclusions, and could never be sure that his set of conclusions was the correct interpretation of the evidence. Moreover, in a world where there is no objective morality, no sin, and no consequences, what exactly is the purpose of life itself, let alone knowing or caring if there is a creator? More on that below.

It seems to me that, at first glance, the notion of Pandeism itself is a philosophical argument from silence, and has little to no philosophical, scientific, or empirically verifiable evidence against which to validate its claims.

Impersonality of the Creator

Perhaps one of the biggest difficulties for Pandeism to overcome is the impersonality of the god who allegedly created. Fundamental to the Christian God is his personal nature—it answers the "Why are we here?" question that has plagued the mind of man since the beginning of time.

Throughout the centuries, gods upon gods have been proposed to account for this. India alone has over 330 million different "gods," some of which indeed demand exclusive worship and claim responsibility for human nature as we know it and experience it.

I am starting with the basic premise that in order for a worldview to be coherent, it must make sense of our experience. That is, it must correspond to reality.

Is Pandeism Congruent to Our Experience?

Knowing what we know about the world and about ourselves, does Pandeism make sense? Does it comport nicely with what we see when we make new discoveries and experience the world around us?

Let's look at this from a few different angles: A universal beginning. Pandeism teaches big bang cosmology. And actually, if big bang cosmology were true, provides nice justification for it! Pandeists believe that the big bang is the result of the translation of Creator to Universe. Considering the energy required by the big bang, it would make sense to have come from an all-powerful god. In effect, this is similar to the Cosmological Argument for God esteemed by many thoughtful Christians who hold an old age view.

To quote the Institute for Pandeism Studies (hereafter referred to as "the Institute"),

> "Like deism, Pandeism accepts scientific evidence of things such as the big bang and evolution by natural selection as accurate indicators of the mechanism by which the Universe achieved its current form."

The argument breaks down on this point. In order for Pandeism to be true, it is entirely dependent upon the scientific "evidence" of both

175

big bang cosmology and evolution, both of which have been refuted scientifically, philosophically, and biblically.

The Institute continues,

> "Pandeism is notable for explicitly accepting, and even revering, concepts such as chemical abiogenesis and evolution by natural selection, including human evolution from a common ancestor shared with modern apes."

I have considerable doubt that big bang cosmology is accurate in its current form, and evidence is mounting higher and higher that evolution is entirely unable to account for our experience. I submit to you that Pandeism also goes down with the ship. A finished creation. According to the Bible, God has finished creating (Genesis 2:2). This means that there is no new matter or material created. Interestingly enough, we see this concept in the sciences as well. What's here is here– it can be restructured, reshaped, or reformed, but the ultimate creating is done.

This is not consistent with Pandeism, although they may claim it to be. According to the Institute, the creative act itself was that of god becoming the universe, and from there god just left it to be. But since Pandeism reveres abiogenesis, the irrational teaching that life can (and did) arise naturally from non-life, there is no reason to believe that this god has not finished creating, which denies the best science we have. Consistent laws. Though we will hone in on this later, it is instructive to point out that the pandeistic god cannot account for the uniformity of nature. There would have to be inherent aspects of this god which would make it be consistent from one day to the next.

This god would have to explain why we have laws such as gravity, and it would have to explain why we expect the future to be reasonably similar to the past. The pandeist would actually use this as positive evidence for his god—essentially arguing, "Since the universe is orderly, the Deus (the "official" name for the deistic/pandeistic god) must have been orderly."

But this no different than the materialist saying, "Since the universe is orderly, it must be the nature of matter." In both cases, it begs the question of "why?" The reason we can consistently attribute the orderliness of nature to the biblical God is that he has told us about his nature in his Word, and his Word is self-attesting and fully consistent with our experience.[2]

Logical accuracy

In the same way that the pandeistic god must account for the uniformity of nature, it must also account for the laws of logic and for the ability of humanity to interact and understand things rationally. Ironically enough, advocates for Pandeism insist that it is the very use of logic and reason that makes it the superior view. The problem is that there is no reason to believe that the pandeistic god was logical and/or rational other than to assume that he was before becoming the universe.

This presents a huge problem for the pandeist, who holds the view that his god is, in fact, lacking in vital knowledge! According to the Institute,

> "And so our Creator was necessarily lacking in vital knowledge, that being the knowledge of facing and overcoming limitation itself. Can a

177

being that is alone in existence experience fear, much less conquer fear through courage? Can it overcome grief, anger, despair, and experience comfort, contentment, triumph? It can do so only through the existence as a Universe which may come to be populated by beings capable of having these feelings, with no portion of the Creator reserved outside the Creation to assuage these beings to any degree. And so, the lack of such knowledge would virtually compel the Creator to undertake the sacrifice necessary to obtain it, to exist for billions of years as our Universe, as all things in it, as all of us within it."

So the conundrum stands: (1) Human logic and reason are the vehicles through which one will ultimately come to know the pandeistic god, but (2) since the pandeistic god is necessarily lacking in vital knowledge, we have no reason to assume that it is responsible for logical reasoning.

Thus we are left with the same problem as above—the pandeist must argue in a circle in order to arrive at his conclusion, all the while being unable to make sense of his own argument. Ethical reasoning. Here we find one last area where Pandeism seems to fall short of our experience. We know that we humans operate under a system of ethical law, and the biblical God tells us exactly what that is (Romans 2:15). The Pandeist holds quite a unique view.

According to the Institute,

"The moral basis of Pandeism is somewhat ambiguous, depending on the view of the purpose of the Deus. One possibility is that, since the Deus created our Universe with no conception of right and wrong, we may exist to teach the Deus these things, and should develop and abide by concepts of right and wrong for the purpose of providing the Deus with our understanding of them. Another possibility arises for those who believe that we will continue to share in the experience of the Deus when our Universe returns to being the Deus. If we share in the experience of the Deus, and the Deus shares in our experience, then each person ultimately shares in every others' experience. If that is so, then whatever harm we do to one another may be experienced by all in the return to the Deus, and we should strive to minimize the suffering that we inflict on others now, in order to preserve ourselves from sharing in that suffering later."

But this does not provide a satisfactory explanation of our experience. On this view, morality is merely something that the Deus wishes to understand and/or experience. But if there were an all-powerful creator, should one not assume that he already understand the reason for our moral impulses? And insofar as our experience tells us things are objectively right or wrong, what justification can the Deus provide for that? One could rightly argue that a sense of objective morality is core and central to the human condition –how 3 could the god responsible for our creation not know and understand this?

This brings us to the next overarching problem:

The Human Condition Unexplained

Quite obviously, we live in a fallen and broken world. Societies rise up one against another, and we often make choices that fundamentally contradict the choices we wish we had made. There is a name for this human condition, and it is called sin

It is necessary at this point to revisit a statement made by the Institute:

> "And so our Creator was necessarily lacking in vital knowledge, that being the knowledge of facing and overcoming limitation itself. Can a being that is alone in existence experience fear, much less conquer fear through courage? Can it overcome grief, anger, despair, and experience comfort, contentment, triumph? It can do so only through the existence as a Universe which may come to be populated by beings capable of having these feelings, with no portion of the Creator reserved outside the Creation to assuage these beings to any degree. And so, the lack of such knowledge would virtually compel the Creator to undertake the sacrifice necessary to obtain it, to exist for billions of years as our Universe, as all things in it, as all of us within it."

There are human feelings and emotions described here that, according to the Institute, the creator desired to experience—so much so that he sacrificed himself in order to obtain it.

There are many problems with this view:
1. This still offers no explanation for moral issues. Why be good or bad, and how should they be defined? How did they even develop?
2. How would the creator know anything about these feelings and experiences at all, let alone not be able to experience them?
3. The "sacrifice" seems like a selfish sacrifice—it is merely the quest for knowledge at the costly expense of other lifeforms.
4. There is no real concept of "love" in the pandeist's universe. Love is based on our choice to unconditionally accept others and sacrifice for their sake . The pandeist has no basis for this emotion.

The Bible explains that as humans, we are made in the image of God. Given the biblical revelation, this makes sense out of our being rational, intelligent, moral, and emotional beings.

The Bible explains that when humanity sinned against him, we were exiled from paradise, and the world (including humanity) began a downward spiral of brokenness, which is our experience today. We love one another because we were initially created to do so and later commanded to do so, and we sin against one another because one man and one woman thought they knew better than God.

A natural reading of the Bible by a heart and mind ready to receive its truth will explain the human condition perfectly. Pandeism just cannot account for our human experience and condition.

Borrowing from the Christian God?

When we examine the claims of the kind of god that pandeists worship, we run into a serious problem: we discover attributes, but no basis for them. Let me be more specific. The pandeist would have us to believe that their god is rational. However, there seems to be no rational proof for this claim!

The god of Pandeism suffers from the same problem every other invented god does: their creators borrow attributes and concepts from the real God.

Here's what I mean:

Speculation vs. Revelation

We addressed this briefly earlier on, but one of the biggest issues here is that there is no special revelation from the Deus. By special revelation I mean there is no Bible, Quran, Book of Mormon, etc. that Pandeism appeals to. The conclusion of his existence is based entirely on inference from general

revelation. The problem with this is that there is no way to gain an accurate understanding of what the pandeistic god is like.

Now, that does not mean that just any special revelation is true. After all, the Bible was written by human's right—wasn't it just the writers' imaginations at work? That is where the hard work of testing the truth claims of a worldview comes in, which is a different issue. Good reason, spiritual understanding, and discernment leads a person to believe that the Bible is true. But Pandeism has an altogether different problem: there is no claim to a special revelation from their god. Therefore, we can't know anything about him! We can test the Bible, the Quran, and the Book of Mormon—we can't test silence! The pandeist might say that we can test nature and nature is the special revelation of the Deus, but again, on what basis can that be said? The whole project is an exercise is question-begging.

Pandeism and Life's Four Big Questions

Here is where the rubber meets the road. For a worldview to be coherent, it must provide a sufficient explanation for the "big four" questions of life—origin, meaning, morality, and destiny—to sum it up in the prose of Ravi Zacharias.
Let's see how Pandeism fares:

1. **Origin.** Pandeism *does* provide a story of origins. However, there is no way to

182

authenticate the truth of this story. The reason being that the Deus did not make this claim. If there were a "bible" from the Deus that offered an explanation of origins with claims that could be either falsified or verified, we could make a judgment about origins. Unfortunately, there is not, so we cannot.

2. **Meaning.** As we have discussed, there is no personal relationship to be had with the Deus. The only explanation offered is that the Deus wanted to take part in experiencing the emotions that humans feel, which it was unable to do. But, how could it have even known about those emotions in the first place? No explanation is given for the human condition. Therefore, there simply is no reasonable meaning to life in the pandeistic universe.

3. **Morality.** Again, the Deus is amoral. It does not claim to be the ultimate standard of morality, and if anything, some pandeists claim it created in order to learn about morality from humans! But this is not a satisfactory explanation. Pandeism cannot explain why humanity is sinful, wicked, and broken. It also cannot explain why there should be "good" in the world. Pandeism is bankrupt from a moral perspective.

4. **Destiny.** Pandeism seems to be somewhat silent on this matter. I only found one reference in pandeistic literature to "destiny," and it claimed that the universe would someday return back into the Deus, where it would then learn about all that it experienced during its time as the universe. But, this offers no explanation for the true destiny of mankind, other than simply "returning to the dust."

The beauty of creaturely free will is that you and I are welcome to believe any explanation that we find satisfactory. I just do not find that Pandeism meets the criteria necessary to answer the biggest questions held by all of humanity.

Conclusion

In summary, I am forced to conclude due to the lack of evidence that Pandeism cannot be considered as a viable explanation for the universe.

My strongest objections to it could be summarized as follows:

1. Pandeism's strong and necessary tie to naturalism's best scientific theories is an immediate disqualifier.
2. Its failure to offer satisfactory explanations for the meaning of life and objective morality we all affirm in practice makes it unworthy of consideration.
3. Even if some of its claims could be proven likely, they do not offer alternative explanations for the facts proven to be true that we find in the Bible.
4. Finally, any "evidence" for the pandeistic universe must be fundamentally speculative, since we've no special revelation to examine.

Hopefully, this has been a helpful and insightful look at Pandeism. Though I have been careful to maintain integrity, I am not perfect, and recognize my shortcomings.

Nevertheless, I am ultimately calling on all pandeists to repent before the one true God and open their minds to consider that the God of the Bible is the best and only explanation for the world we see around us. I would be happy to share more

with you personally about the truth and beauty of
the Christian worldview.

Notes

1 A reviewer of this piece raised the following question to
the author: "If it's [the PanDeistic God] impersonal, how
could it have a consciousness to lose? To be conscious is to
be a "person." This is a good question, and one I will leave
to the reader's consideration.
2 In other words, there are arguments from within the
biblical text itself which suggest it is divinely authoritative,
such a fulfilled prophecy, remarkable coherence,
unparalleled historical accuracy, etc.
3   https://uncommondescent.com/intelligent-
design/michael-ruse-update-morality-is-just-an-aid-to-
survival-and-reproduction/

It, My *Yin-Yang* Tao

By John Ross, Jr.

IT is never *this*...yet...always seems like *that!*

IT can't be nursed by vowels, a busted clock, or your Universe hat.

IT can't swear on clarification, *nor* offer a knowing proof.

IT means exactly *this*; and never, ever *that*, yet perched upon our being's roof.

IT is NOT...*IS*. Oh no!

IT is not there, nor upstairs, our attic flat.

IT is never, ever...our tether-leashed puppy hound?

IT *always*...IS...yet never, ever near to clip our basement's rat?

IT best be our birth, our murky, mysterious Lao-Tzu Cat.

Tao-Te-Ching: **Chapter Five**

By John Ross, Jr.

THE *Tao* doesn't take to forming teams;

HE gives rise to both the Noble and the Foul.

SHE welcomes both saints and sinners.

THE *Tao* is like a bellows:

HE is unfilled yet, ever infinitely full.

THE more you consume *him*, the more *she* harvests;

The more you talk of them, the less you understand.

Hold on to the center of the Two Babes.

WAIT, expect, silence ... *rest...pause* for both of *them:*

They're One.

My Journey to Pandeism

By Daniel Torridon

Daniel Torridon is a former Jehovah's Witness who, after finding that belief no longer sustainable, began an exploration of theological models resulting in a gravitation towards Pandeism. This experience is recounted here, in an essay derived from Daniel's podcasts, *The Freedom to Rethink God—My Journey to Pandeism* (Transcript of OnionUnlimited podcast episode 034), and *Why I Swapped Christianity for Pandeism* (Transcript of OnionUnlimited podcast episode 035), available online at:
`https://onionunlimited.com/the-freedom-to-rethink-god-my-journey-to-pandeism/`
   and
`https://onionunlimited.com/why-i-swapped-christianity-for-pandeism/`
   the respective audio for these can be found at:
`https://rss.com/podcasts/onionunlimited/325014/`
   and
`https://rss.com/podcasts/onionunlimited/325719/`

Part I.
The Freedom to Rethink God—
My Journey to Pandeism

One of the great things I find about no longer being one of Jehovah's Witnesses is that I'm free to explore deep, spiritual, philosophical questions and find my own answers as opposed to being told what the answer is and being expected to just accept it because it's supposedly "the truth". For example, the question of how the Universe and everything in it, including ourselves, came into being.

As a Jehovah's Witness you're pointed to Genesis chapters 1 and 2—to be taken very literally—and if, for any reason, it doesn't sit well with you, or resonate with you, tough! You just have to accept it, and believe it, because that's what the Bible says and that's what the governing body says it means. There's no room whatsoever for variance in thought and you can't look elsewhere for your answers other than the Bible and the governing body's current interpretation. Once you've joined the cult, questioning is over. It's complete information control from thereon in.

But when you leave Jehovah's Witnesses all that changes. You can actually *think* about a subject and look wherever you want for ideas. You can, if you wish, adopt those ideas wholesale or you can pick and mix ideas and create your own unique philosophical understanding. No longer is there anyone telling you what you can and can't think. You genuinely have an open mind and the opportunity to search for, and find, answers that you never had before.

The other thing you can do is *change* your mind or revise your philosophies as and when you receive new data, or a chosen belief is no longer working for you. As a Jehovah's Witness, you would have to "wait on Jehovah"—in other words, wait for the governing body to change their mind about what is true—before you could have a different viewpoint, and even then, there would be no guarantee that their "new light" would be something that you would instinctively believe.

As a Jehovah's Witness, I previously accepted and believed, the Watch Tower's interpretation for creation, namely that God created the Universe by means of his "dynamic energy", and that he literally created the various elements on earth—the sea, the land, the plants, the animals, and, ultimately, humans, but in 2006, at the pinnacle of my questioning everything, I read a short book by the writer Scott Adams. Adams, if you're not familiar with him, is the creator of the Dilbert comic strips, but he wrote this book called *God's Debris* in which he tells the story of a young delivery guy who delivers a parcel to an old man, and before leaving, the old man says something profound which initiates a deep conversation between the two. The book is basically a transcript of their discussion. In it, they discuss God, and the old man postulates that there was one thing that an eternal, all-knowing God did not know—that is, what would it be like to *not* exist—and in trying to find the answer to this elusive question, God literally blew himself up thinking. The result of the explosion, or Big Bang, was our Universe—hence the title of the book—we are "God's debris".

This idea of a God that fully invested himself into the creation of the Universe really resonated with me, and it was an idea that stuck with me over the years, but, of course, I was a Jehovah's Witness and I was expected to think within the bounds of Watch Tower theology, and so this idea of a God destroying himself in order to create the Universe was something I couldn't, at the time, fully embrace, and why would I? To do so would be to effectively annihilate my long-held belief of a transcendent, ever-present God from my life, a God who, it seemed to me, was guiding and protecting me like some kind of father figure. Nevertheless, I tried to reconcile the two ideas, thinking that maybe Jehovah *did* blow himself up to some degree in the process of turning at least some of his energy into matter, but being that he had infinite energy it essentially made no difference to him in the long run. However, there were always questions in the back of my mind about God and creation, and the answers given by Jehovah's Witnesses just never sat right with me.

For example, the idea that God created two perfect humans and placed them in a paradisaic garden only to then test them with a 50/50 chance of them failing the test. Why would he do that? Being all-knowing, surely he would know they would fail the test and introduce death to the entire human race. Why subject billions of people to that? Jehovah's Witnesses would, of course, answer that it was a test of free will—that it elevated them above animals that only live by instinct—dignifying Adam and Eve with the choice as to whether to obey God or not, but was it *really* a choice? They really only had one viable option—do what God said. If they didn't choose God's prescribed option for them then the outcome would be death, but not to give them the choice—to live or die—Jehovah's Witnesses would argue, would make them like robots and that's not what God wanted. God wanted them to be like him with free will, but that didn't sit right with me either because the Genesis account makes it very clear that they were punished for becoming "like God". They simply weren't allowed to make their own minds when it came to what was "right" or "wrong", "good" or "evil". Everything was preset and they had to jump through the hoops or die.

Then, also, why allow them to be tempted by the serpent? Jehovah's Witnesses blame the whole temptation fiasco on the Devil, but surely God was ultimately responsible for that because he allowed it to happen as an intrinsic part of his purpose to test creation. No Devil, no temptation, it would be unlikely Adam and Eve would have sinned—easy test, game over. It seemed to me that the Devil was effectively working for God!

The Genesis account, as far as I was concerned, had numerous holes in it and the answers Jehovah's Witnesses gave just raised more questions.

In the book *What Does the Bible Really Teach?* the illustration is used of a student questioning a teacher on a maths problem. The teacher hands the floor to the student and allows the student to prove him wrong. Of course, the student is unable to do this and the class then knows for sure that the teacher was right all along. This is used to illustrate how Satan challenged God, but when you think about it, it really is an appalling illustration. Watch Tower is likening the Devil challenging God—with the result being death and destruction to billions of humans—to a simple maths question. There really is no comparison, and it always struck me that a God who would allow humanity to be exposed en masse to sin and death, purely to prove that he was right, would not be the kind of person I would especially want to worship. Yet, there I was, believing in a God that was supposedly looking favourably upon *me*, guiding and protecting *me*, answering *my* prayers—even mundane ones such as finding a suitable parking spot—while apparently turning a blind eye to the slaughter of six million Jews at the hands of Hitler, or more closer to home, the epidemic of child abuse within the Watch Tower organisation itself, just to prove whether God was right or not. Being told that God doesn't *cause* bad things, but only *allows* them, did very little to improve my opinion of him. Why would a loving

God stand on the sidelines with his arms folded, non-intervening, when he presumably has the power to end it with a click of his fingers? I mean, if I had that power, that's definitely what I would do, so does that make me more moral than God?

As I say, as a Jehovah's Witness, I had no choice but to accept Jehovah existed and to do the mental gymnastics necessary to make him a loving God with good reasons for allowing wickedness, but once I left the cult, I was free to re-evaluate things— even the existence of God himself. Would I maintain a belief in God or would I, like many who leave Jehovah's Witnesses, become an atheist? I could never see that happening, and to be honest, there was a part of me that didn't want to give up on God because I liked the idea of someone watching out for me, but honesty and integrity and the search for truth was the order of the day for me, and so I did begin to question whether God actually existed or not.

The question of why God does not intervene in human affairs ultimately led me to believe that he was simply not there, but I struggled with the idea of a Universe existing without an initial, conscious cause, and so for a while, I adopted the Pandeistic view presented in *God's Debris*, namely that God *did* exist at some point, but chose to invest his whole self into the creation of the Universe, and in doing so, ceased to exist as a singularity—but, I found I missed God. I missed the idea of someone watching on, guiding and protecting me, answering my prayers, and so I set about thinking of a solution. How could I effectively have it both ways? How could I have a Universe that was the product of God *becoming* it, therefore not being responsible for human atrocities, while still maintaining a level of transcendency and presence in my life? Was that possible?

The answer I initially came up with was to think of things from a dualistic point of view—a God who, on a *temporal* level, ceased to exist as a result of becoming the physical Universe, but on a non-*temporal* plane continued to exist in eternity, but that didn't really solve the problem of evil in the world. Again, why would this eternal God, from his eternal vantage point, not intervene and prevent crimes such as genocide, abuse, and so forth? At first, I toyed with the idea of a Source Consciousness that was not God in the traditional sense—more of an awareness principle, but indifferent to humanity's plight, a force rather than a personality, not someone I could blame—an "it" not a "he"—but nevertheless something I could still connect to through prayer and meditation, but this idea felt convoluted. It lacked the simplicity that I believe is intrinsic to truth, and so I returned to the purely Pandeistic view, that there was a Source that *became* the Universe and, in doing so, ceased to exist as a singular entity.

However, in choosing the Pandeistic model, I also adopted Roger Penrose's Conformal Cyclic Cosmology theory, where the fateful end of one Universe is identical to the Big Bang of the next. In fact, in essence, this allows even the *same* Universe in terms of its matter to experience a never-ending cycle of deaths and rebirths—like the Hindu notion of the serpent eating its tail. Then, I got to thinking that at that moment where the Universe collapses and then re-expands, that is the moment where everything returns to Source. Now that idea felt right and answered most, if not all, of my questions. So, during the lifetime of any current Universe, God—or Source—as a singular entity, simply does not exist, having transformed himself into the actual Universe, but at the point of collapse and re-expansion, Source Consciousness exists again—if only for a moment.

So, now, I subscribe to a Universe without a transcendent God. This is it. We are "God's debris"—fragmented instances of Source Consciousness if you will, and ultimately our Universe will come to an end. Time and space will come to an end, as everything returns to the singularity, and at that moment all conscious experiences, good and evil, become known by Source. Then there is another Big Bang—if Source chooses to create again—and the process starts over, each time Source becoming more and more knowledgeable from the experiences that we have lived.

This general idea is not new. I just made reference to Hindu philosophy. This idea of the Universe undergoing cyclic deaths and rebirths is present in Hindu sacred literature and although not widely accepted in Western scientific circles, there is some evidence presented by Roger Penrose to the effect that the Universe is indeed cyclic and goes through these periods of death and rebirth. It is, as I say, a very Hindu concept. While I don't intend to subscribe to the entire Hindu religion with its 33 million deities—all manifestations of Brahman, the Ultimate Reality—I do feel that the Hindu sacred literature has much to offer in understanding the principle of a Source Creator and the cyclic nature of the Universe, and this is definitely something that I will be continuing to investigate.

As it stands now, I would not class myself entirely as an atheist insofar as I do believe a God— or a Source—*did* exist at some point, even though he no longer does as a singular entity. However, my current view of Source is definitely not the same as my previous view of Jehovah, a god, the God, in the traditional Biblical sense. I now view the initial Source as much more of an indescribable, eternal, energy source than an actual person, although I do feel it may have possessed consciousness, which it then passed on to us.

I feel it's acceptable to refer to the Universe, including ourselves, as a Whole, as "God". That works for me. We are the "I Am". That realisation, of course, places the responsibility squarely on us as humans to do the right thing, the moral thing, with no excuses or rationale that a God will ultimately step in and sort out our mess. We have to look within ourselves and see what is beneficial, not just for us but for everyone and everything that exists—and what is beneficial, I believe, can be classed as "good".

:----:

I do believe that there is fundamentally only one conscious awareness that runs through all sentient beings in the Universe and that if I was you, or you were me, we would essentially feel no different. Strip away the unique experiences that make us who we are, and pure awareness would feel exactly the same regardless of the physical body we were in. The billions of humans that have ever lived are the way Source experiences everything that can be experienced, temporally, in space and time— even if it is waiting for the collapse of the current Universe to benefit from that knowledge.

With no actual "God", at least not in the traditional sense, religion, of course, becomes unnecessary. There is, however, I believe, a connective force that flows through the entire

Universe—a residue of Source energy—which we, as humans, can connect to via prayer or, more specifically, meditation, and even manifest our own reality. Therefore, I will also be looking deeper into meditation, again no doubt drawing on Hindu philosophy. To all intents and purposes, I guess I am an atheist in terms of no longer believing in an interventional God, a god that demands worship, but I remain spiritual, seeking truth and connection with the greater Whole.

Now I'm no longer one of Jehovah's Witnesses, I can look for my answers anywhere I want without fear of criticism or retribution.

Part II.
Why I Swapped Christianity for Pandeism

In response to my post entitled The Freedom to Rethink God—My Journey to Pandeism: What can I say? Wow! I never expected to receive so many emotive comments on this subject. Most of them have been from Christians who have expressed that I have now lost everything—God, my salvation, my eternal life even. Some commenters have been a bit vague and just told me "Jesus is Lord" for some reason. I'm not really sure how that helps anything, but I honestly never thought that declaring myself a Pandeist would result in so many comments and direct messages, not all particularly positive, but it has.

So, let me just explain something. I don't know what the truth is about God, creation, the Universe, consciousness, life and death, and so forth. I have absolutely zero evidence that a Pandeistic viewpoint relates to reality in any way, shape, or form, but I've adopted it because it feels right to me. It answers a number of questions I've contemplated for many years and does so in what, I feel, is a quite elegant way. In my mind, Pandeism is a minimalistic philosophy—it doesn't require me to belong to a religion, or worshipping anyone or anything—but it provides scope for there being an initial Cause, and coupled with the concept of a cyclic Universe, allows for human consciousness to return to something, and start over. It gives me an initial "God"—although I prefer the term "Source"—that started things off, one who set out the laws of nature at the beginning but it also explains why he (or it) doesn't appear to intervene in the Universe—namely, he no longer exists. Simple. His *becoming* the Universe, and everything in it, including us, makes a great deal of sense to me. I know with some certainty that the Universe is real. I know *I* exist, that I am conscious, and while this "knowing" may not be how things actually are, it feels real and it gives me a foundation to build and live my life on. Whereas, a transcendent, intervening God, does not. I simply see no evidence at all of that on a day-to-day basis, and it really adds nothing to my life. Granted, if I joined a religion it would provide me with a social aspect, a group to share my spiritual thoughts and feelings with, but I feel I can do that anyway. I have great, spiritual conversations almost every day with people.

Just to map out my reasoning a little—

So, there is theism. Theism is essentially the belief that there *is* a God, or gods, who created the Universe and who continues to intervene in it by means of miracles, supernatural revelations, and so forth. Now, I personally have never seen a miracle. I've seen things that seem unexplainable, but nothing I could say was an actual miracle. I've never seen anyone convincingly healed, or raised from the dead for example, and those who claim to speak for God—supernatural revelation—how do I know? *Anyone* could claim to have a revelation from God. I could. It doesn't mean it's real. For me to remain a theist, as I was for 50 years, would require a personal experience of God, and it would have to be so overwhelmingly convincing that I couldn't deny it.

Now, as a Jehovah's Witness, and as one of the "anointed", I felt I was "born again" and I experienced what I felt at the time was the indwelling of the holy spirit which lasted for some 15 years, but to be clear, I did not view this experience in the way that a typical Jehovah's Witness thinks of it. For example, I didn't believe in the 144,000 doctrine. I actually identified as a "born again Christian", just trapped in a cult. I used to listen to Christian music in private. I frequented Christian bookshops, and chat rooms, and I had many a conversation with other Christians of many denominations or none. I do still believe I had a spiritual experience in 2004, but I no longer think of it so narrowly as being a *Christian* experience. I believe it was a spiritual awakening, and that I interpreted it at the time within the religious framework I was familiar with at the time, but all that said, that does not mean that God exists. What it means is that in 2004 I had a spiritual experience. I was engaged in much prayer and Bible reading at the time and I felt my spirituality ascend a level. That's it. It may be that I was connecting to a Universal force of some kind—a residue of an initial spirit being, or Source,—or I may have just been imagining things. The experience felt was very real. I felt connected to "all that is", but as time's gone on I've realized that simply feeling "the spirit" or whatever doesn't in itself mean that Christianity, or any other religion for that, is wholesale "the truth". It just doesn't.

To be fair, my experience of religion has been a bad one. I was a Jehovah's Witness for 50 years, during which time I felt spiritually suppressed, suffocated, to be honest. I was told what to believe by a governing body who claimed to be appointed by Jesus as God's only channel of truth on earth. I was never allowed to question what was presented as "the truth" and I was even mentally abused when I did dare to question. Now, that put me right off Jehovah's Witnesses *and religion in general*. I did look elsewhere, within Christianity, but to be honest, I wasn't that impressed. Everywhere I looked there were men, leaders, claiming to have found "the truth", claiming to speak for God, with no perceptible credentials. You were just expected to accept it. In fact, most, not all, but most were quite arrogant in their outlook—they were right, everyone else was wrong—and then there were the threats, believe or spend an eternity in hell. It just felt completely wrong to me. So did the Bible. Everywhere I turned, people had a different interpretation of what the Bible meant. I could find no real evidence that the Bible was 100% inspired by God. I found contradictions in it. I found sections that I found morally repugnant, such as God killing 70,000 Israelites because King David dared to count how many soldiers he had in his army. I found accounts that condoned genocide, the rape and pillaging of non-Israelite nations, slavery, abuse. It just didn't feel right.

Granted, I do find some Universal truths in the Bible. I'm not saying it's completely useless, but I just feel nowadays it's unnecessary. For example, Jesus' teaching that we should love others as we love ourselves—that's great, I mean, it really is, but it's not exactly unique, is it?—and I could have figured that out myself. In fact, I don't think the Bible has anything to offer that I couldn't just, with a bit of thought, work out for myself. Basically, be nice to people—that's it. In fact, the Bible is actually used as a weapon. Just think of the millions of people that have been abused or even killed "in the name of God" or "in the name of Jesus", using the Bible as their authority. The same goes for other holy books. Basically, I came to the conclusion, that I didn't need the Bible, or any other book, to live a moral, kind, unselfish life, and I certainly didn't need to belong to a religion—Jehovah's Witnesses, mainstream Christianity, or any other. In fact, I honestly do believe I'm a better person now than when I belonged to a religion. I'm certainly more honest now because I don't feel a need to pretend anymore—to pretend to believe things that I don't, simply because I'm told my salvation depends on it.

So, for me, theism is currently out of the question. I cannot see, for the life of me, a God who is present in the Universe, and I see no religion out there—and trust me I've looked at many, many religions—that teaches "the truth". What I do see is very much falsehood, which is way easier to identify than truth and through a process of elimination, I've eliminated every religion, cult, sect, denomination that I've investigated, but in doing so, I've been careful not to immediately "throw the baby out with the bathwater". Accepting that God may not exist *now*, does not in itself lead me to the conclusion that he has *never* existed, and this is where Pandeism comes in.

Deism, to start with, is the belief in a Creator, which I find completely plausible, but a Creator that does not intervene in his creation. That, for me, seems to fit the facts I can see. I certainly see no evidence of intervention in the Universe, but I needed to reconcile in my mind why God would not intervene. It seemed strange to me that God would set things in motion and then just stand by watching the good, bad, and ugly take place in his creation. Why does he not intervene when he observes, for example, atrocities taking place? There could be any number of reasons. Maybe he doesn't care to intervene. Maybe he doesn't have the ability to intervene. Or, maybe, and this is just one option among many, maybe he doesn't exist anymore. That, to me, makes so much more sense— and why doesn't he exist? Where did God go? He became the Universe. He became us.

Now, if I was alone in thinking these things, I could understand why people would accuse me of being crazy. Of course, that wouldn't mean I was wrong, but I'm not even alone. Pandeism is an accepted belief by many people. It's not new. It goes back at least as far as monotheism. It bears many similarities to Hindu philosophy, which dates back possibly as far as 2300 BC, and the more I study science, quantum physics and so forth, the more I find thoughts and ideas that fit into this Pandeistic worldview. Above all, and this is really important, it works for me. It's a spiritual framework that my enquiring mind feels settled with. Nevertheless, all that said and done, I accept that Pandeism may simply not be true. It may not be, but that doesn't make Christianity true, or Islam, or Judaism, or any other religion that I'm constantly being told is the only truth—and it's okay, that's okay. It's my life. These are my beliefs. It's all good.

When religious types come onto my Twitter feed and start telling me I'm "going to hell for giving up on Jesus", or that my Pandeistic views are just a "reboot of paganism" as if I should be embarrassed by that, or that I've "lost everything—God, my salvation, my eternal life", this does nothing to make me think those people have the truth, absolutely nothing. In fact, it completely turns me off, because I spent 50 years being forced to believe things by men who claimed to be God's only channel of truth on earth.

I have met some Christians who are humble, not forceful, but on the whole, in my quest for truth, I've been subjected to many a religious type who comes across as extremely arrogant. They are right, everyone else is wrong, and if you don't believe you're going to be tortured forever in hell, or lose your eternal life, or die a horrific death at Armageddon. None of this does anything to warm me to the Christian God of the Bible. It may be true. Maybe God really is that cruel. Maybe there is no choice. Maybe it is a case of "do what God says or die". If that's true, then I'm sorry, but no. I won't be forced by means of threats to worship a God like that. No way.

So, as it stands now, with Pandeism, I have a working model of how the Universe came into being. I also have a simple explanation as to *why* God permits evil—it's not that he can't or won't deal with it, it's that he no longer exists. I have the Universe. I have me. I have my consciousness. I have my love for other people and I honestly don't mind if this is it—and if it turns out that there was no Source to start the Universe off—if atheism is a more realistic model—then I'm okay with that too. Or if any religious person out there can convince me that they have "the truth" without being arrogant or hurling around threats for my non-compliance, I'm open to that too, but for now, I still pray, I still meditate, I still feel I have a purpose in life. I still feel spiritual—whatever that means—and I don't feel I need a religion. My thoughts are my own. I share them with others but I don't claim to have "the truth", and I don't expect anyone to believe what I believe. I claim no authority whatsoever in these matters and above all, I remain open-minded and ready to learn.

The Idea of God

Dr. Paul Carus

A self-described "atheist who loved God," Dr. Paul Carus was a theologian and philosopher who made numerous contributions to the theological categorizations at play in the field. He believed that religions were evolving towards an emergent "cosmic religion of universal truth." A native of Germany, Carus earned his PhD from the University at Tübingen in 1876 before making his way to Chicago, Illinois. There he developed a panpsychistic philosophy of 'panbiotism,' proclaiming: "everything is fraught with life; it contains life; it has the ability to live." His most pandeistic idea is, perhaps, entheism, developed in his 1896 article, *The Idea of God*, which follows.

THE word God is one of the most wonderful expressions in our language. Its etymology has long been a puzzle to philologists. Its history is shrouded in obscurity. And although it is mostly employed in a vague and ambiguous sense, the meaning of the word, its scope and contents have exercised the greatest influence upon the development of humanity.

I. THE NATURE OF IDEAS.

A word consists of two things: First, a sound, and second, an idea. The sound is used as a symbol of the idea. The sound is the body and the idea is the soul and life of the word. A word without an idea is "as sounding brass or a tinkling cymbal," and an idea which is not embodied in the sound of a word is like the evanescent spectre of a wraith haunting our diseased imagination, too volatile for a real existence.

Sounds are vibrations of air which we perceive by the ear as a revelation of something that appeals to us,—of something that tells upon us and communicates with us.

Everything around us is productive of sounds. Let the air stir, and it will gently blow in the zephyr or howl in the storm. The trees, moved by the winds, rustle. The wood in our cottages or houses when exposed to a change in temperature creaks and warps with an odd noise. Every bird has its peculiar song and every animal has its cry, which is modulated according to the situation, expressive of all kinds of sentiment and desire. But whatever communication the songs of birds and the cries of animals convey, they do not express ideas and are at the same time more or less inarticulate.

Man is the only animal whose language is articulate, and expressive of ideas. Man's language thus becomes *speech*.

Ideas are the life-blood of what is human in man; they nourish his intellectual and emotional faculties. Without ideas, no thought, and without thought man would be a brute. Ideas make, of his conduct, ethics, and, of his perception, science.

What then is an idea and what is its history and development?

The word *idea* is derived from the Greek εἶδος, a picture or image. Plato was the first to use it in a philosophical sense. He was aware of the importance and reality of ideas, he attributed to them an existence independent of ourselves and even considered *them* as the prototypes of things.

The ideas in our brains are not, as has been supposed by many philosophers, of transcendental origin. They have been developed by a slow process of interaction between man and his surroundings, between the subject thinking these ideas, and the objects of which these ideas are images.

The *ideal* and the *real* thus stand in a certain opposition. The ideal world (in the proper and original sense of the word, which means pertaining to ideas) is a new creation, a kind of higher nature in the domain of reality. But it must be understood from the beginning that, as *the real* and *the ideal* are not contradictions, they do not exclude each other. The ideal is just as real as any objective thing is, but its reality is of another kind; it is a sublimated reality which is erected on the domain of vegetative animal life as an intellectual empire of a grander growth and with higher, nobler aims.

Our ideas are we ourselves; they form the reasoning and thinking man, and the empire of ideas is humanity. The ideal element raises man above the animal and makes him the master of the earth. Yet, it is nothing supernatural or transcendental; it is a sublimation of the natural reflexes produced in us by our reaction upon surrounding objects.

The history of the ideas which make up our individual existence is older than we ourselves. It commenced long before our birth, for it is the history of humanity. And the history of humanity is even older than humanity; for the history of humanity begins with the first living protoplasm upon earth. All the struggles and efforts of our ancestral amoebas are preserved in *us* and form a part of our present existence.

The mechanical means by which nature attains to the ideal life as represented on earth in humanity, is the development of certain forms of organic structures. The living matter of protoplasm suffers a slow combustion resulting from a combination of oxygen with particles of its substance. It attracts new substance for the continuation of the combustion, and covering itself under the influence of surrounding conditions with a membrane, the protoplasm forms cells, which grow and divide into new cells. The form of life which these cells acquire, continues the same in all the cells into which they divide. Every struggle which is experienced, every effort which is made, has a certain effect upon the form of life; it leaves a trace which somehow molds the living substance, and is in some way, however dimly, recorded. All the activity of our ancestors is thus registered in the structures of our body, and thus our ideas become a great store of intellectual energy gathered through innumerable generations.

This truth of the unity of life on earth admonishes us to be careful in all we say and do—nay even in what we think. Our actions, our words and our thoughts will live after us, and it will take a certain and equivalent amount of good thoughts to counteract the evil effect of bad thoughts. Every bad action, word or thought retards, every good one enhances the future of humanity in working out superior forms of life-structures exhibiting nobler souls and thinking grander ideas.

Not all ideas are images of reality. Many of them are mirages or visionary phantasms which our lively imagination shapes from the hazy mists of error and illusion. The birth of such bugbears in the human mind has always been attended with all sorts of evil consequences. The errors in our minds are worse than illness in our body; as Marcus Aurelius says: "Dost thou think that a false opinion has less power than the bile in the jaundiced, or the poison in him who is bitten by a mad dog?"

It is my object in this essay to investigate whether the idea of God is a truth, or an hallucination of the human mind.

The idea of God is the grandest thought which in ages past humanity ventured to think. Shall we faithfully retain it as a sacred inheritance, or shall we discard it as as a fallacy of former times? Perhaps we may be able to do both, to keep what is good and true, and to rid our minds of what is false and detrimental in the conception of God. Perhaps there is a grand truth at the bottom of this idea, but it is mixed with injurious errors; if so, we shall purify it, and the idea of God will be greater, sublimer and more awe-inspiring to future generations than it ever was to our ancestors.

II. THE ETYMOLOGY OF THE WORD GOD.

The word "God" is of Teutonic origin. Accordingly, it is an offshoot of pagan thought and not Christian or Jewish. The word "God" was used among our forefathers, although in a neuter gender and not as a proper name [...] long before Ulfilas preached the gospel to the Goths and long before Pope Leo III. sent his missionaries to the Anglo-Saxons; and it was used in distinction from the gods whom the Teutons called Ases.

The Ases were Wodan and Hertha, Thor or Donar, Ziu, Fro and Freia, Baldur, Loki and others. They were looked upon as powerful and active presences, each of them having a distinct character. But these gods were mortal like men and were going to die on the great doomsday of the world.

Above these gods ruled Alfadur, who was the real God, who, it was hoped, would restore the world from its ruin, and who would from the ashes of its conflagration create a new earth and a new heaven.

The popular etymology connects the word *God* with the adjective *good*. Both words are spelt alike in Anglo-Saxon; but this is a poor evidence, which must be dropped because the other Teutonic languages indicate that the words *God* and *good* have no etymological relation whatever. They must have been derived from different roots.

Besides it would be an unparalleled exception in folk lore to characterize the nature of a deity as goodness. It is quite a modern idea to reverence a god for his beneficence and it is therefore not probable that the old Teutons should have been so different from other nations.

Not much more plausible is the derivation of the word God from Odhin or Wodan, who in some German dialects was also called Godhin. If this derivation were correct, it would be strange that the word God is used in its different forms as *Got* in old German, *Guth* in Gothic, *God* in Dutch and Anglo-Saxon, *Gudh* or *Godh* in Icelandic, *Gud* in Swedish and Danish. These variations show no correspondence to, or relation with, the different forms of the name *Wodan*, which is *Wôdan* in Saxon, *Wuotan* in Old High German, *Wêda* in Friesish, and *Odhinn* in Icelandic.

The Persian word *khodâ*, lord, master, has been suggested as a clue to the name of God, but this word is only preserved in the Zend *quadata* and the Hindoo *khudâ*. If it existed in the Teutonic languages, it was early lost, which leaves little probability that the term God originated from this root.

The same objection can be made to another derivation from the Sanskrit *Gudha*, secret.

Some philologists connect the Gothic *Guth* (*God*) with the Gothic verb *guthan* (German *giessen*, to pour forth), and suggest that according to this etymology the original meaning of God may be that of a source from which all life springs. This etymology however is as little satisfactory as that from good, or that from Wodhan. It is artificial and improbable.

Yet the word *guthan* has a specified meaning. Like its Greek analogue χέειν (to shed, to pour) it means to spend, to offer, to bring sacrifice. "The root *ghu*," says Kluge in his latest (4th) edition of the "Etymologisches Worterbuch der deutschen Sprache," p. 119, "corresponding to Sanscrit *hu* means to invoke the Gods, (participle *huta*). God in its original neuter word-form is 'the being invoked.' In the Veda, Indra has the usual appellative puruhflta which means 'the much invoked.'" Thus "God" would signify in its etymological meaning that being who is or who is to be worshipped, who is or is to be sacrificed to, who receives or should receive offerings.

*   *   *

Our etymologists who had so much trouble at home, encounter less difficulty with the names of God in other languages. The root of the Latin, *deus*, Greek θεός, akin to the Persian *deva*, and to the Greek, Ζεύς, (Διός,) and the Latin, *dies*, day; *diespiter* or *Diupiter*, *Jupiter*, (viz.: father of the day,) means bright, radiant, light.

The Persian *Ormuzd* (Ahura-Mazda) means 'the wise lord'; and it is significant of Hindoo piety that Brahma means 'prayer, devotion.' Other Indian names of God are *Brahamapati*, lord of prayer, *Prajapati*, lord of creatures, *Visva karman*, all-doer.

The Hebrew, *El*, *Eli*, and *Elohim* (the same as the Mohammedan *Alla*) means the strong or the mighty one. Elohim is a plural form, but it does not therefore, as has been supposed, denote a plurality of gods. Elohim is always used as a singular form and has its verb following in the singular. The Hebrew use the plural form as a singular, to denote abstracts. Elohim accordingly should be translated godhead or deity.

The other old Hebrew name *Zebaoth* is likewise such a plural form, derived from *Zabha* star. It means the godhead of the starry heavens.

The name *Jehovah* was introduced, according to Scriptures, by Moses. The ancient Jews derived it from *hajah*, "to be, or to live," so that it would mean "the Eternal One." This conception has been embodied in the old Mosaic words with which Jehovah characterises himself "I am that I am," and has thus become so popular with us that we involuntarily identify the ideas Godhood and Eternity, recognising in Eternity the most characteristic divine feature.

The word *Jehovah* does not possess its own vowels. This was brought about by the Mosaic injunction: "Thou shalt not use the name of thy God in vain." By a slight change of meaning, the verb "to use in vain" signified, a few centuries after Moses, "to use." The ancient Jews now interpreted the law in the sense: "Thou shalt not use the name of thy God at all." Wherever the name *Jhvh* appeared the Jews said Adonaj, i.e. my Lord. In the original Hebrew texts the consonants only were written and when long afterwards the vowels were added by the rabbis, they placed the vowels of adonaj—viz. (i) *sh'va*, (2) *o*, and (3) *a*—under the consonants *J, h, v, h,* so as to read J' hovah.

The etymology of *Jahveh* from *hajah*, "to be," although it was current among the ancient Jews, is now, mainly for linguistic reasons, rejected as untenable. The similarities of sound that have been discovered in the Roman *Jovis* (genitive of *Jupiter*) and the Egyptian *Iao* or *I-ha-ho*[1] with *Javeh* are incidental. What, then, is the original significance of the name?

Professor Cornill recognises in the Biblical description of Jahveh a thunder-god, and derives the name from an old Semitic verb, *havah*, to fall, which in Arabic has still preserved its original meaning. The word accordingly means "he who makes fall," or "he who overthrows," viz., with thunderbolts. Jahveh was, according to Professor Cornill, the deity who resided on Mount Sinai, manifesting himself in thunder-storms. This agrees well with the Biblical tradition that Moses adopted the name while staying in the desert with Jethro, the priest of Midian, whose influence upon Moses appears to have been very great.[2]

The early Christians, ignorant of the fact that the word Jehovah was a combination of the consonants of *Jahveh* and the vowels of *ădonaj*, pronounced it as it was spelt and thus gave currency to this absurd formation of the word, which since then has often been repeated by human lips in devout prayer and adoration.

III. GOD AN ABSTRACT IDEA.

A clergyman and a lawyer once became engaged in a hot dispute concerning the nature of God; the former said that God exists, and promised to prove it from the order of the universe and the wonders of creation, while the latter said that God does not exist, and he also agreed to prove his statement by the absurdity of such an idea. A personal God, he declared, is an impossibility and a self-contradiction. A merchant who was listening to their arguments, was called upon to decide. The lawyer as well as the clergyman were good customers of his, and the merchant had upon other occasions privately assented to either view. Now he was caught in a difficult dilemma, and for fear he might lose the patronage of either, he said: "I should say that the truth lies exactly in the middle."

Perhaps this man is right after all; the truth lies in the middle. Only it is a pity that the middle between 'yes' and 'no' cannot be found by a simple calculation of the extreme and mean ratio. If we know that the truth does indeed lie in the middle between 'yes' and 'no,' this solution offers a new problem, viz., in what sense does God exist and in what sense does God not exist?

In the attempt at answering this question we do not mean to shirk the truth. We do not intend to make concessions to either party, but shall go to the bottom of the problem.

We can expect to reach a final decision only by the application of radical thoroughness. This method places us between the two parties as an umpire; but there is little hope that we shall please either, for our verdict will most likely be that both are in the wrong.

The history of the idea of God is lost in dark antiquity. In historic ages we find it connected with all that is great and sublime, and it has at the same time served as a pretext for committing crimes of oppression and injustice. The idea of God is the cornerstone of the Platonic, Aristotelean, and of the Neo-Platonic philosophies. Warriors used the word as a battle cry, martyrs died with it on their lips, and millions of people were comforted in misery by the thought of God. All of them thought of God as a great person, the creator of the world or a good philanthropic master of our fates.

Ideas are either concrete or abstract. We call them concrete, if they are images of things. A chair, a table, a tree, a dog, are concrete ideas; they are generalizations of all the chairs, tables, trees and dogs we have ever seen. Abstract ideas are of a later growth. Whiteness, goodness, courage, virtue, are abstracts. We notice the whiteness of the snow, the whiteness of a lily and of many other objects. The color red being often observed, is recognized again as soon as our eye meets with a red object. Thus it happens that the notion of red which we acquired by seeing red blood, the red dawn of the morning, red roses, etc., forms an independent conception in our mind, as undoubtedly it is also localized in certain relatively independent cells of our brain which are excited as often as red is perceived.

Abstract ideas were considered in olden times as real things. The Greeks thought of virtue or ἀρετή, as a beautiful virtuous woman, and as the gender follows the sex, ἀρετή, is feminine. Gender in all our modern languages is a remnant of this personal view of ideas. The English language is most advanced in development, for it has gotten rid of this infantile mode of expression.

The idea of God, if it signifies anything, is an abstract idea and not a concrete one. Is it anymore than natural that at an early period of human development the idea of God was personified as a powerful man, a creator and ruler, the judge of right or wrong? This phase of the idea of God was just as necessary as the phase of a personification of virtue and vice. In consideration of the fact that it is

215

only a few centuries since philosophy freed itself
from the old view according to which ideas are
things, it is not to be wondered at that this phase of
a belief in a personal God has not yet passed away.
It will take some time, but it is certain that it will
pass away, and later generations will smile at the
paganism of our present ecclesiastical view as we
smile at the ingenuous belief of the ancients in the
Deities, Virtue, Wisdom and Beauty, as Arete,
Athene and Aphrodite.

We can no more doubt that the ancients
virtually believed in the real and objective existence
of such deities, and whoever from his modern
standpoint, cannot understand this psychological
state of mind, should study the religious views of a
devout Catholic from the interior of Poland or
Ireland, who believes in all the archangels and
saints without having the slightest doubt that they
are live presences hovering somewhere above him
in the air.

Even more cultured people of the present time
believe in the personal existence of abstracts, and
those who believe will easily find occasion to
communicate with them. I received a few days ago a
letter from a well educated American clergyman
who professes to believe in good and evil angels,
messengers from heaven and creators of discord.
Who, under the evidence of such facts, can doubt
that the ancients literally believed in their
mythological deities?

The prologue to the Reformation was a contest
between the schoolmen as to whether ideas were
things or *names*. This contest was decided in favor
of those who declared that ideas had an objective
existence, that they were real things. The
Nominalists, who said that ideas are names, were
worsted and persecuted, but by and by their views

developed a philosophy which was consummated and perfected in the eighteenth century by one of the greatest thinkers of all times, by Immanuel Kant.

Kant wrote a book, "The Critique of Pure Reason," in which he explains that our concepts are representations of things, our ideas are noumena or thoughts, and our concepts do not possess reality in the sense which we usually attribute to reality; they are ideal, i.e., they are concepts. Of reality Kant says, as an explanation of the term in the narrower sense in which he uses it: "We can be conscious of nothing as real, except a sensation (*Wahrnehmung*) and the empirical progression from it to other possible sensations. For phenomena as mere conceptions (*Vorstellungen*) are real only by sensation. And sensation is, in fact, nothing but the reality of an empirical conception, that is a phenomenon. To call a phenomenon a real thing prior to sensation, means either that we must meet with this phenomenon in the progress of experience or it means nothing at all."

Shall we ever meet in our experience with God as a phenomenon? Certainly not. God is according to Kant no phenomenon, but a noumenon, a thought, an idea, and it is undoubtedly an abstract idea. Kant boldly drew the last consequence of Nominalism, he declared ideas to be names and God he called a noumenon, a thought of our mind.

Did Kant state that God does not exist? By no means; he simple proved—and he proved it beyond a doubt, by arguments which have been accepted even by orthodox Theology—that God is a noumenon. But at the same time he declared in his "Critique of Practical Reason," that God is a Noumenon *which we must of necessity conceive*;

217

God's existence cannot be proved, but the idea of God, he said, is a *postulate* of practical reason.

In Kant the development of the idea of God reached its climax. The battle about it is long since decided, and yet such is the complexity of the subject that now a century after Kant the general confusion is not yet cleared up. Philosophers of lesser penetration are fighting in the dark, the zealous iconoclasts on the one side, and ingenuous pagans under the modern name of orthodox Christians on the other. The hazy mist of their misconceptions concerning the nature of ideas, which surrounds both parties, will perhaps settle under the influence of a brighter morning and then they will see that they have been fighting about a word, and that, in their quarrel about the name, they quite forgot the idea of the word.

IV. THE CONCEPTIONS OF GOD.

The idea of God is so variously defined that we make bold to say that every single individual has a conception of his own. There are no two alike, and the idea of God among different persons is indicative of their character, for every man creates his God in his own image.

There was a brave officer in the Austrian army under Prince Eugene. When once in his presence the problem of God's existence was discussed, he clapped his hand on his sword and said: "Gentlemen, I stand up for God with my sword, I challenge whoever denies him and, so help me God, I'll conquer him. I hope that God will stand up for me, too, on the day of judgment."

The God of this gallant man is, like unto himself, a gentleman, who, I hope, will not disappoint the expectation of his friend on the day of judgment.

Although we have seen that God is an abstract idea and a noumenon, this idea nevertheless possesses for the life of every individual a powerful reality. *Every* idea possesses in the realm of the human mind a reality. One idea influences the others, and such a central idea as that of God is generally dominant over our whole conduct and exercises a directive agency in the development of our lives.

The conceptions of God have been grouped according to fundamental characteristics under certain headings. We speak of Polytheism, of Pantheism, of Monotheism, of Theism, of Deism, and of Atheism.

The oldest view of civilized mankind is Polytheism, or the belief in many gods. Polytheism is the religion of the ancient Greeks in Homer's time, and of the Hindoos about 1000 B. C. Polytheism conceives of ideas as personages, it fancies to hear a thunderer in the thunder and a divine driver in the chariot of the sun. Polytheism is preceded by a state which Max Muller calls Henotheism (single-godedness) a view which deifies single things, such as have a mysterious influence upon ourselves, springs, rivers, mountains, trees, etc. Henotheism is based on the conception so natural with mankind in its childhood, that our environment is alive like ourselves—not only alive in the broader sense of possessing self-motion, but in the narrower sense of being psychically animated. This henotheism must be distinguished from fetishism, which is a worship of idols. Fetishism is common among savage tribes and characterizes a degeneration of the religious sentiment, while henotheism, in spite of many similarities to fetishism, must be regarded as the promising dawn of a brighter morning.

Polytheism is alive still. The belief in saints and martyrs, madonnas, angels and devils, is only an ecclesiastic Polytheism, a true paganism in Christian disguise.

Polytheism naturally develops into Monotheism. All the diverse gods are recognized as one and the. same. And this 'one and the same' is considered as the almighty author of the phenomena in the world. Monotheism, accordingly, is the belief that there is but one God, and this one God is a personal deity with passions and emotion like ourselves.

Monotheism is not exclusively a Jewish or Christian idea. In Grecian history its time was shortly before and during the prime of Athens. It prevailed among the Israelites from Moses to Christ, and it was but natural that in such a time all interest was absorbed by the idea of God and that the loftiest emotions took the shape of worship.

During the period of monotheism, God became the main problem of philosophy. Dionysius, the ruler of Syracuse, asked one of the sages of Greece "What is God?," and the philosopher requested one day for consideration. On the next day he demanded two days more. He shut himself up in his room and was engaged in deep meditation. When the term had elapsed, he wished for another respite, and this time of three days more. Dionysius grew impatient, but the philosopher declared that the longer he pondered upon the subject, the obscurer and the profounder a mystery it seemed to become.

The Christian church adopted monotheism, although it accepted at the same time the Indian Trinity of the godhead.

Monotheism developed naturally out of a preceding Polytheism, and in the course of time the problem of Monotheism 'what is God?' was answered by bold philosophers: God is no person like ourselves, God is the world and the world is God. This view which identified the All and God is called Pantheism.

Monotheism is dualistic, as it believes in a God above nature. Pantheism is the beginning of Monism. The system of Spinoza is Pantheism, and the poetic and philosophic grandeur of his view exerted its power like a magic charm upon humanity.

Monotheism was greatly affected by the strong influence of Pantheism. A deity above nature, a supernatural God in the old sense had become impossible. Theology had to change some fundamental conceptions of its personal God, and the result was a differentiation into two views, *Theism* and *Deism*. Deism was the belief of the enlightened eighteenth century, of a Voltaire and a Rousseau in France, of a Shaftesbury in England, and of a Lessing in Germany.

The deist believes in a personal God as the creator of the world; but the deistic God is different from that of Monotheism. Since miracles become impossible, he no longer interferes with the laws of nature.

Theism is the more orthodox view. Theism only purifies the idea of God from the crudest anthropomorphic traits and declares that God as the creator of the world exists in his works as well as distinct from them. Natural laws and miracles are both the expression of his will; as a monarch may issue general laws and special orders.

In all fundamental points the God of Theism and of Deism remains the same as that of

Monotheism. All three views consider God a transcendental and supernatural person, although we may fairly acknowledge that the systems which are presented under the name of Theism are often philosophically more elaborated than others.

Atheism was formed in opposition to all these views. The transition from Theism to Atheism is Agnosticism, which teaches that there is something unknowable in or behind nature, and this unknowable is God, or, as Agnostics say, 'the cause and source of all phenomena.'

Atheism is the most modern conception of God but hardly the last one. Atheism cannot stand, for it is no positive view; it is negative and exists only as a criticism of the other conceptions. Atheism does not declare what it believes, but what should not be believed. It was developed from Pantheism, and is an outcome of the materialistic philosophy. Atheism rejects the idea of considering the universe as God, since materialism maintains that the universe consists of matter only, and matter cannot be an object of reverence or worship. Pantheism, the Atheists declare, leads astray, and conveys, if it means anything at all, the phantastic conception of a world-soul; and such a view is just as false as monotheism or polytheism.

And certainly atheism is right in so far as it criticizes all the previous views of God and finds them to be wanting. Have we, then, to be content with this view and rest satisfied in this negative result?

V. DEFINITION OF THE IDEA OF GOD.

Let us see, whether there is any truth at all in the idea of God, and whether, as Atheism declares, the belief in God was merely a heavy dream of humanity, the nightmare of a childish imagination.

God is an abstract and we have learned that abstract ideas are none the less true and real, although they are no concrete things such as chairs, tables, trees and dogs.

The idea of goodness or virtue does not exist as a beautiful woman in the shape of a spirit-being, but so long as there live and aspire virtuous men and women, virtue exists and is no mere illusion or product of imagination. Virtue exists in the virtuous and the idea of virtue is a live presence which should not be blotted out from the ideal domain of the human mind.

Is it not exactly the same with the idea of God? Certainly, a supernatural being, all-wise and almighty, all-present and eternal, and at the same time limited to the personal existence of an ego like a mortal man—such a deity does not exist. But as virtue exists in the virtuous, is there nothing divine in nature and in man in which the presence of God can be found as an actual reality? Surely God exists as certain as virtue and other abstract ideas exist; but God will remain a mystery as long as our minds are fettered with the pagan notion that God is a concrete thing or a phenomenon. We shall understand God better if we take God to be what Kant calls a noumenon, an idea.

The content of this idea has been denned differently. God was called by Matthew Arnold "the power, not ourselves, that makes for righteousness." But why does Arnold exclude ourselves from God? Is there nothing divine in us? We should correct Arnold's expression into "the power that makes for righteousness, which is manifest in nature as well as in humanity *and* ourselves."

J. R. Seeley finds God in the Unity of Nature, in the harmonious order to which every one has to conform under the penalty of penance.

It would lead me too far here, if I were to advance my objections to Matthew Arnold's as well as to Seeley's conception. Both are the most progressive theologians I could take hold of, but both are not yet fully free from the monotheistic conception and the idea of a supernatural deity.

Seeley speaks of the Laws of Nature as being God's laws. But God is to him the broader concept, "since God includes nature." A God who is within nature but also outside nature, remains after all supernatural. Nature is, so to say, God's activity. That part of God which is supposed to be outside of nature, would be inactive. It would be redundant and being without efficacy, it would be non-existent.

The same must be said in much stronger words about Fiske's view, who sees in the 'dramatic tendency of the universe' a multiform manifestation of 'the Infinite power.' Fiske rejects the Theism of Paley, but goes so far as to attribute to his own God psychical attributes, although disclaiming the word anthropomorphic.

Yet all these views mark a progress; all are at least not quite unsuccessful efforts to establish a positive statement of what the idea of God will be in the future.

*   *   *

If we could make of the innumerable God-ideas in the minds of men a composite photograph, such as Galton made of certain classes of faces, we should find in all of them one feature most prominently present: God is to everybody who believes in a God the ultimate authority in conformity to which he regulates his conduct. In accord with this fact, we may say that everyone who somehow regulates his actions, recognises such an authority, or in other words, believes in a God.

There are Gods of all kind, and many of these deities would with a wider range of knowledge soon be recognised as demons of evil. To one that which affords pleasure is God, while another one perhaps worships the golden calf of the money power of the marts. But to him who has rent the veil of Maya, who has recognised the illusion of individual existence, who knows that he is a part of that soul-life which appears upon earth in humanity, that he is a phase of this life, that his soul with its mentality, intelligence, and aspirations has been transmitted to him from the generations of the past and will continue in future generations, who knows that his brother-man, to the same extent as his ideas and ideals are the same, also possesses the same soul, that his brother is an *alter ego*, another himself, of whom the Buddhists say *tat twan asi* (i.e. that art thou),—to him who has recognised this and who acts accordingly, a man who by resigning his sham individuality enters the nirvana of immortal life: to him God is that power which makes morality possible, God is the sum total of all the conditions which have produced man as a living, thinking, and aspiring being, God is the authority whom man must obey in order to live and to progress, in whom man has to trust for the preservation of his soul beyond the grave.

Says Goethe:

"There is a Universe, also, within,
And hence the good old custom did begin

That everyone on the best of what he knows
The name of God, yea of *his* God, bestows.
With Heaven and earth he'll Him endue,
Fears Him, if possible, loves Him too."

"Im Innern ist ein Universum auch;
Daher der Völker löblicher Gebrauch,
Dass jeglicher das Beste, was er kennt,
Er Gott, ja seinen Gott benennt,
Ihm Himmel und Erden übergiebt,
Ihn fürchtet, und wo möglich liebt."

It is true and very well expressed that we first fear our God, and obey him because we fear him. But if he be the right God we shall learn to love him. We must try to love him, for if we do love him, obedience will be easy; says the apostle St. John: "For this is the love of God that we keep his commandments, and his commandments are not grievous."

Goethe's poem makes the impression that God is a mere subjective picture of our imagination. But that was neither Goethe's view, as I understand him, nor is it the view of God maintained here. God is a real objective existence and our God-idea can be a more or less perfect representation of God. Similarly the law of gravitation is a thought-construction of our mind, a subjective representation, an idea, but it de scribes real facts; gravitation itself is a reality.

*   *   *

Having spoken of the veil of Maya, I feel urged to add a few words about Buddhism. Buddhism was the first great revelation of the illusive existence of the ego,[3] but Buddhism failed to solve the religious problem of mankind because it represented the resignation of the ego as an annihilation. Buddhism became pessimism. It was the great work of Christianity to emphasise that the recognition of the sham existence of the ego is actually a recognition of immortality.

That which is real and permanent in an individual is the humanity of his soul. The language of man is the expression of a common life, and in the same way all the mental structures of a human soul are traces of a common activity. Soul-life is communal; it originated by communication and exists in the communism of social exchange. Man's soul is the mental intercourse of mankind incorporated in an individual organism, and while the individual organism will die, the soul continues to live. There is no death in the sense of extermination. All our ancestors live in us, their souls are with us and will remain with us even unto the end of the world. And so we shall live even though the body die.

It appears to be of great importance to understand rightly the positive aspect of soul-life. The negative aspect depresses without elevating; the positive aspect elevates without depressing. The negative aspect destroys man's activity, the positive raises it upon a higher level. The former leads to stagnation, the latter to progress, the former is a peculiar kind of atheism: the authority for the regulation of conduct leads to the annihilation of life; the latter is based upon a belief in God as that power which is the life of our life.

Science will in its further progress more and more enlighten and deepen our views of God, but no critique of science can ever destroy this conception, for it describes God as certain facts of

227

nature that can be investigated, that can be verified by experience and formulated with scientific exactness. These facts of nature exist as sure as we ourselves exist. These facts are the principle of the cosmic development of solar systems in the starry heavens and also of organised life upon earth; these facts are the cause of man's progress and the basis of ethics. They are the ultimate authority from which all the rules have been derived that are called ethical precepts or moral commands, and with which to remain in conformity is the highest ideal of man. We may call these facts the ethical life of nature or the moral law of the universe, but in so far as they are the authority in obedience to which we regulate our conduct they are God.

This conception of God contains all that is true in the old views and is at the same time free from any supernaturalism and anthropomorphism. It is indeed the old conception of God, only purified by critique, for we cannot better and more concisely describe the nature of God than with the words of the apostle as being He, in whom we live and move and have our being.

This conception of God is not the iconoclasm of the infidel, it is the purest and holiest faith of the believer. Yet at the same time it is not the superstition of the credulous fanatic, of the bigot, it is the outcome of the most radical freethought and of unflinching criticism.

This view of God is more than an idea, it is an ideal. An ideal is an idea that is an aim for our aspiration. An ideal is a living idea, i.e., an idea which can constantly be more and more realised and always admits of still greater perfection.[4]

*   *   *

The solution of the problem of God, in this sense, will be satisfactory only to few—to those few who take an impartial view of the subject and who are not embittered by the prevailing strife and hatred of parties.

Those engaged in the strife either will denounce me as an atheist, because I say 'God is not a person like ourselves,' or the opposite party will decry me as a reactionary believer and an inconsistent thinker, because I say ' there is some truth in our old religious views, but it is mixed with errors.'

I shall answer to the former that concerning the idea of God I have rejected the pagan and superstitious conceptions only, viz., anthropomorphism and supernaturalism; I have retained all that is true, and great, and beautiful. If the purification of our ideals is atheism, let us embrace the name and be proud of it.

I shall answer to the latter that the iconoclast lacks in radical thoroughness and consistency. If the idea of God is an empty dream which we must expel from our minds, why not expel all ideas and all ideals? They are just as much and just as little real. And if virtue, duty, hope, scientific formulae, and artistic conceptions have no reality, then, the sublimated reality of an ideal existence is naught, and the only possible reality is animal life. From this point of view a denial of the existence of God would with consistency lead us also to a denial of an integral, or a logarithm, or a differential. An integral is just as little a concrete object as is God. And the idea of God is just as important in the real life of human activity, human thought and emotion, as the idea of honesty is in the mercantile world, that of courage among warriors, or that of truth in science.

It follows from this that we would do better to use the word God in the neuter sense, saying that *it* is the moral life in nature. This may seem objectionable to many and yet it is a truism which was known thousands of years ago. God is neither man nor woman; yet he is manliness in man and womanhood in woman. If we speak of God in the personal form as *he*, this is a usage of our language not different from that of speaking of the sun as *he*, and the moon as *she*. There is no necessity for discarding this usage, if we are conscious of the simile, which is very appropriate when accepted in this sense. Christ did so; he spoke of God as his father. Men are the children of God inasmuch as humanity is a product of the ethical life of nature. When Christ was asked where that father is and how he happened to know him, he answered: "I and the father are one." Man is the incarnation of the ethical life of nature. Man and God are one. Christ acknowledges the fact, and my whole essay tends to prove the truth that true humanity is divinity, and divinity is no unknowable being in wonderland, divinity is true humanity, divinity is the ethical life in nature and the ideal of perfection in man.

VI. ENTHEISM THE MONISTIC CONCEPTION OF GOD.

Our view of God is not theism, not pantheism and not atheism. It does not teach that God is a person above the world, nor does it identify God with nature, nor does it deny God's existence altogether. If our view must be labeled and registered among the different 'isms,' I must form a new word and call it *Entheism*, which clearly denotes the conception of a monistic God, who is immanent, not transcendent, who is in many respects different from and superior to nature, yet pervades all nature.

Entheism being at variance with Theism, Pantheism and Atheism in many respects, nevertheless agrees with these views in others; for to some extent they all contain some truth. Entheism agrees with Theism in so far as it recognizes an actual power in nature that makes for righteousness, not only *in* ourselves but *also beyond* ourselves. It agrees with Pantheism in so far as its God is a law of Nature. We may call it the highest law of nature which is exactly as omnipresent in the Universe as is for instance the law of gravitation. Accordingly its God is the Cosmos itself, the All, or the totality of the world as an orderly unity. Entheism agrees even with Atheism in so far as it unreservedly accepts the criticisms of the latter on supernaturalism and anthropomorphism. Atheism, it must be confessed, has achieved most for the purification of the conception of God.

One serious question arises: Whether this idea of God may fitly become an object of worship? My answer is:

If worship is taken in the usual sense as an act of adoration, or a submissive cult of self-humiliation, I do not propose to worship God. However, if worship is to signify what it does according to its etymology (Anglo-Saxon *weordhscipe*), considering and bearing in mind the worth of something or of somebody, I do propose to *worthship* God. We should fully appreciate his import for our lives, and for those who shall live after us. Such a worship is one "in spirit and in truth," as is recommended by Christ. It will keep us in harmony with humanity as well as with the cosmical order of the universe. It will not disparage us, but elevate man as the first born son of nature and the legitimate child of God.

The same holds good of prayer. If prayer is a supplication with kneeling down in abject self-humiliation, it is detestable. But if prayer is a severe self-criticism, a moral atonement for trespasses committed and also the strengthening of our moral sense for avoiding errors in the future, if prayer thus keeps us in unity with God as the moral life of the world, prayer is recommendable.

God—as an object of worship and prayer, as a power who can be influenced by our devotion so as to favor us in this life or in a hereafter,—is an idol, and such a conception of God is pagan, for it is only sublimated fetishism. There is but one worship of God "in spirit and in truth" and that is to do his will. There is but one kind of prayer which is not heathenish, and that prayer is the self-discipline by which we prepare ourselves to do his will. And what else is God's will than the moral prescripts about which there is scarcely any dissent and in which almost all religions and philosophies agree.

Sometimes it may appear that we shall reap great advantages by a violation of these moral laws and that the just will suffer while the sinner is prospering. But although the immoral man may injure or even ruin his righteous neighbor, one thing is sure, and always has remained true, that in the end a violation of the moral laws will never pay. Those who are immoral and act immorally (i.e. those who do not do the will of God) must perish at last. There is no escape from this, for only what harmonizes with the All and what concurs with the order of the Cosmos can survive. A lie may occasionally be profitable, but truth only can stand for good. The immoral man has built on sand and only the house of the moral man stands on a rock.

When the rain descends, and the floods come, and the winds blow and beat upon that house, it will not fall, for it is based upon a solid foundation.

If God is an abstract, and not a concrete thing or a person as our forefathers imagined, would it not be better to discard the *word* God altogether and to retain what is explained as the idea of God under such a name as "Morality," or "the Good," or "the Ethical Law," or "the Natural Aspiration for the Ideal?"—Certainly it is advisable to do away with the word God wherever its use is ambiguous. Science can dispense with it, for when science has to deal with what we have defined as the idea of God, a scientific expression, such as is wanted for the occasion, would be preferable. Similarly in Chemistry, the words "salt" and "water" may be used; but their proper terms are ClNa and H_2O.

But if the word God is to be canceled in the domain of science, it need not be thrown aside altogether. It would be ridiculous to dispose of the words salt and water in the same way and substitute in their places H_2O and ClNa. The word God is not a scientific term; it is an expression which for centuries has been connected with the holiest emotions and the most pious apprehensions of humanity. It is a poetic term and an expression of sentiment. Whether such a word is to be discarded from our languages is not a matter which can be decided by philologists. Words if they are expressive have a tenacious life, and ideas if they are true are immortal. If the word God is strongly expressive of what the idea of God in its best sense can mean, it will live in spite of the explanations of atheism. However, if the word God is inseparably interwoven with the errors which, we know, have been connected with the idea of God, it will die, and no power on earth will be able to raise it from the dead. *Our* duty is to eliminate the false notions and to point out the truth which it contains; but *history* will decide its fate.

I know that my view does not agree with many rites and customs of churches and sects; but I am glad to say it well agrees with Christ's view, who abolished prayer in the sense of begging, and substituted for it a prayer in which Christians no longer ask that *their* will, but that *God's* will be done.[5]

A peculiar lesson is involved in the fact that Buddhism, the greatest non-Christian religion, which is distinguished for inculcating the noblest moral maxims, such as love of enemies, chastity, sincerity of heart, and charity toward all suffering creatures, knows nothing about God. Unfriendly critics have on that account branded Buddhists as atheists, and yet they face the same facts of life and have derived therefrom the same rules of ethical conduct. The main difference between Christians and Buddhists consists in the employment of different systems of comprehending and symbolising the facts of experience. Both religions, Christianity as well as Buddhism, recognise an authority for moral conduct. The former call it Christ, the latter Buddha. Christ reveals to Christians the will of God; Buddha teaches men enlightenment. There is this difference: that Christ appears as the son of God, and therefore his teachings must be accepted as revealed truth, while Buddha is a man, who after a diligent search at last obtained the highest wisdom, that will deliver mankind from evil. In Christianity the sonship of Christ vouches for the truth of Christ's message, while in Buddhism Buddha's enlightenment constitutes his Buddhahood. Now Buddha teaches that enlightenment is the same, and that all

Buddhas teach the same religion, which consists in the abandonment of the vanity of selfhood, of all hatred and envy, and of lust, implying at the same time a far-reaching and unbounded love, which refuses none, not even those who hate and despise us, compassion with all those that suffer, and holiness. Enlightenment is a living recognition of the truth seen in its moral application to practical life, and truth is a summarised statement of facts, or rather the laws pervading the facts and constituting a comprehensive aspect of their eternality. And this essence of Buddhahood, the eternal laws, the recognition of which constitute enlightenment, has been formulated by the later Buddhists under the name of Amitabha, which means illimitable light, and is conceived as eternal, immutable, and omnipresent. It is the *Sambhôga Kâya* (the body of bliss) among the three personalities of Buddha, the other two being the *Nirmâna-Kâya*, the apparitional body of Buddha the teacher, and the *Dharma-Kâya*, the body of the law, which is Buddha's religion in its historical development.[6]

The facts are the same in Buddhism and in Christianity; the modes only of formulating them in symbolical expressions varies. Both religions recognise an authority of conduct which, in a word, we may call "the ethical law of the universe, as manifested in the evolution of life."

If God manifests himself in the "ethical life of nature," and if ethical life means growth and progress, God is not identical with nature nor is he a psychical principle in nature, a kind of world-soul which animates the universe, as the soul, according to the dualistic view, resides in the body. God is not a being, not mind, not a spirit; he is higher than any being, and higher than any person; he is superpersonal. If the cosmos were the handiwork of a world-creator, this world-creator would still be the subject of Amitâbha, of the superpersonal God;[7] for in creating the world, he would have to conform to him, and in pointing out to man the way of salvation, he could only teach him the eternal truths, from which the unalterable moral injunctions are derived.

This God can, just as well as the law of gravitation, be made an object of our observation and study. God as a law of natural life is recognised in evolution and as a power he is felt in the lives of every single individual as well as in the history of nations. God fought with the small number of Greeks against the numerous hosts of Persians, for in the hearts of the Greeks throbbed love of freedom and noble aspirations for high ideals. God revealed himself in the songs of David and in the dramas of Shakespeare. God lived in the sermon of Luther and in the writings of Lessing. He is a power in the history of mankind irresistible in its manifestations. "In God we trust" for our national development in the United States, and God must be the guiding star, also, of our personal destinies—"the divinity that shapes our ends, roughhew them how we will."

God bursts forth in the flowers and fresh verdure of spring; He inspires all noble emotions of men, the poetry of the poet, and the inquiries of the scientist. Yea, God lives in our very tribulations and afflictions, as mainly through them our nobler nature is aroused. *Per crucem ad lucem.* The cross teaches us the most impressive moral lesson.

Wherever man's self disappears in duty, wherever the authority of conduct, that speaks to us in the experiences of life, has taken possession of the soul, wherever passions, vanity, and egotism

yield to self discipline, truth, and love, wherever
there is an aspiration onwards to a nobler morality
and a higher conception of life, there is God. In this
sense we join in the beautiful song:

> 'Nearer my God to thee,
>   Nearer to thee,
> E'en though it be a cross
>   That raiseth me!
> Still all my song shall be
> Nearer my God to thee,
>   Nearer to thee.

> 'Onward our march must be,
>   Faithful and true!
> Nobler humanity
>   Will us imbue.
> No pain nor trouble shun
> Sternly our duty done,
>   Faithful and true!

> "Let us all brothers be,
>   Who lovingly
> Join hands in sympathy
>   God before thee.
> This is the way to thee.
> Thus we rise constantly,
>   Nearer to thee."

Notes

1 Suggested by Schiller in his article *Die Sendung Mosis*.

2 Professor Cornill is one of the very best authorities on Hebrew literature. See his fascinating book, *The Prophets of Israel*. Sketches from Old Testament History. The Open Court Publishing Co. 1895.

3 See *Homilies of Science*, the article "Enter into Nirvana," p. 121, and "The Religion of Resignation," p. 143.

4 For further explanations of the author's views of the conception of God, see *Fundamental Problems*, pp. 49, 151-153, and also in the appendix of the second edition of the same book, pp. 261 and 322. *The Soul of Man*, pp. 367-369 and 437-446. *The Ethical Problem*, pp. 20-22. *Homilies of Science*, the chapters on God and World, pp. 75-120.

5 See *Religion of Science*, pp. 88-89, and *The Open Court*, No. 439, p. 4786.

6 Compare *The Gospel of Buddha*, pp. 225 et seq.

7 See *The Religion of Science*, Second Edition, pp. 22, 111 et seqq.; *Primer of Philosophy*, pp. 147, 199-203.

Why I Am Not A Pandeist

Celeste Foley

Celeste Foley is the author of *GOD-centric, GOD-centric Interior Spiritual Disciplines*, and *GOOD-centric Exterior Spiritual Disciplines* as well as the Oz behind the Life of Significant Soil[1] and Freelance Monkette[2] websites. Raised Roman Catholic, she admits to having flirted with Pan*en*deism; however, she never even winked at Pandeism. Now, she considers herself a DeFacto Atheist or, when her implicit bias is in roaring form, a Possibilian[3] desperately searching for a way to believe in a good God while still honoring her push from Aldous Huxley: "Facts do not cease to exist because they are ignored." *(Complete Essays 2, 1926-29)*

INTRODUCTION

"Is God willing to prevent evil, but not able?
Then he is not omnipotent.
Is he able, but not willing? Then he is malevolent.
Is he both able and willing? Then whence cometh evil?
Is he neither able nor willing? Then why call him God?"
~ Epicurus

In 1927, Bertrand Russell challenged the veracity of Christianity. In 2020, I will challenge the veracity or, at least, the attractiveness of Pandeism. If you listen carefully, you will hear Senator Lloyd Bentsen's voice: "I knew Bertrand Russell. Bertrand Russell was a friend of mine. Ms. Foley, you're no Bertrand Russell." That is true, Senator Bentsen's ghost; nevertheless, I write in deference to Mr. Russell's "Why I Am Not a Christian."

How serendipitous that Knujon Mapson's invitation arrived for the "natural spirituality" edition of *PANDEISM: An Anthology* for nature was the starting and ending point of my relationship with God. At the outset, I would make to make explicit my biases formerly known as implicit: God would be the Creator of all that is; God would be singular; and God would be good ~ always, not just occasionally. I believed in a Creator God: if God merely stumbled upon an eternally existing universe, then what would make god God? I was a monotheist; but, I could throw monotheism out the window as long as however many gods that be were *good*. Question: Why would someone worship a non-good God? Answer: cowardice[4] or a resonant not-goodness.[5] I believe in standing up for goodness. If God does not, then phooey on God. I could not throw goodness out the window. Slightly rewording Meister Eckhart: "Goodness is something so noble that if God could turn aside from it, I could keep the goodness and let God go."[6] And so I did.

I wanted God to be good. For two decades, I believed that God was good. For two decades, I tried to believe that God was good. Now, I don't believe that there is a good God; but, I would love to be proven wrong. *Good?* Good for whom? Good measured by what means? Good for and measured by the creation to whom a Creator God would hold a fiduciary responsibility, especially to sentient beings in creation. When I was young, creation meant the Earth, perhaps other planets in our solar system, and any life forms throughout the Milky Way.

My mind was not yet overwhelmed by multiverses and holograms. In my preferred multiverse, St. Isaac of Syria would be correct: "In love did God bring the world into existence; in love is God going to bring it to that wondrous transformed state, and in love will the world be swallowed up in the great mystery of the one who has performed all these things; in love will the whole course of the governance of creation be finally comprised." In our actual universe, as best I can perceive it,[7] I think St. Isaac of Syria was overly optimistic: The Big Bang was a magnificent but not particularly loving event. Creation is wondrous; but, also, stricken with onerous diseases and natural disasters. The Big Crunch or Freeze or Rip will swallow up the world in a manner decidedly devoid of love.

Natural evil slayed my belief in a good God and any attraction I may have had for Pantheism or Pandeism.

WHAT IS A PANDEIST?

"Pandeism is another belief that states that God is identical to the universe, but God no longer exists in a way where He can be contacted; therefore, this theory can only be proven to exist by reason. Pandeism views the entire universe as being from God and now the universe is the entirety of God, but the universe at some point in time will fold back into one single being which is God Himself that created all. "
~ Allan R. Fuller, Thought: The Only Reality

O God-in-which-I-no-longer-believe, how do we understand thee? Let me count the ways: countless theisms which suggest that you created and actively intervene in while remaining separate from the universe; Deism which suggests that you created but do not intervene in the universe from which you are separate; Pantheism which suggests that you are the universe and always have been; Pandeism which suggests that you created the universe and chose to become one with it; Panentheism which suggests that you are the universe and always have been but you are also more than the universe; and Panendeism which suggests that you created the universe and chose to become one with it but not entirely.

Being a good-freak, I instinctively ruled out ways of understanding God that inferred that God was not always good and, yes, I was comfortable holding God to human moral standards. Why would a good God create a system where up was down and left was right and evil was good? If God were always good, then all theisms with their interventionist deities were out: God could intervene to save babies dying from miserable diseases but usually can't be bothered to do so? Not my God. Deism's God who wound up the clock and walked away seemed too cold and remote to be a good God. Also ruled out of contention were Pantheism and Pandeism wherein God is the embodiment of the universe ~ a universe which God both created and in which would *be* natural disasters and diseases. My God could be breathtaking sunsets, majestic mountains, and daisies in Spring; but, not tsunamis, cyclones, Ebola, brain-eating amoebas, or schizophrenia. [BTW: Pandeist Creator God, why do natural disasters and gut-wrenching diseases exist at all? Bad plan.]

On the other hand, Panendeism briefly lured me with its siren song; but, only because I was highly motivated to find a way for God to be good and all to be right in my world. Panendeists believe that somehow God is the universe; but, also greater than the universe which isn't much of a stretch for someone raised to believe in a Trinity. Pandeism and Pantheism's "I am the universe" God had been cast aside because I could only hold allegiance to an always good God and the universe is significantly amoral. With that extra *en*, Pan*en*deism afforded a syllable of wiggle room in which I performed acrobatic logical contortions to make space for God's perpetual goodness. I devised a God who admittedly did create an amoral universe; but, also gave us in that universe the tools for goodness thereby anointing us as the means by which goodness would be created. I believed that God called us to use our free will to attend to the good in the universe and to create good in the universe. I even developed my version of heaven ~ convergence:

"You and I exist in a space-time reference which allows for only intimations of immortality. We must make good through the reality that is ours. Our eternal God exists in part in a different space-time reference. God exists in our space-time and outside of our space-time. When we touch God, we break through our space-time to outside of our space-time. When we touch God in convergence, we touch eternity. Our eternal existence is contingent on our living in and out God's love during our time of temporal historicity. We become real within our space-time; we become eternal in God's space-time. We determine how much of our life will be lived in convergence with God. We choose whether or not or to what extent we will live in and live out God's love, goodness, and fairness. We live eternally to the extent that our choices converge with God." (*GOD-centric*, Ch. 10)

Not a shabby effort; but, a blindfolded one as I will further address in "Defects In My Theodicy."

Synopsis:

Theory of God	Results from the Goodness Test
Theism	FAIL: God created natural evil & does not always or even usually intervene to stop it
Deism	FAIL: God created natural evil & just calmly observes as it plays out
Pantheism	FAIL: God is natural evil & does not always or even usually intervene to stop itself
Pandeism	FAIL: God created natural evil & is natural evil
Panentheism	FAIL: God is natural evil & more & does not always or even usually intervene to stop itself
Panendeism	FAIL+: God created natural evil & is natural evil & more & wants us to do the heavy lifting

THE EXISTENCE OF GOD

"You know, of course, that the Catholic Church has laid it down as a dogma that the existence of God can be proved by the unaided reason... Therefore they laid it down that the existence of God can be proved by the unaided reason, and they had to set up what they considered were arguments to prove it."
~ Bertrand Russell, <u>Why I Am Not a Christian</u>

Raised Roman Catholic, my first grapplings with God-questions were influenced by St. Thomas Aquinas's *Summa Theologica* that offered five logical proofs for the existence of God which, with the possible exception of Gradation,[8] would support Pandeism: The Argument from Motion sets up God as the Unmoved Mover and The Argument from Efficient Cause sets up God as the First Cause which are pretty much self-explanatory and the same thing. The Argument from Necessary Being suggests that since nothing can come from nothing, God must be eternal [*or the process of the universe is which would deflate the Arguments from Motion, Efficient Cause, and Necessary Being*]. The Argument from Gradation argues that biological beings gradually increase in goodness and complexity naturally leading to a perfect being of the highest good, God [*which would be more convincing if God were always good or, at least, good more often than the finest human being*]. The Argument from Design is basically what is now referred to as Intelligent Design: The order of the universe is too perfectly constituted for it to be the result of mere chance; therefore, an Intentional, Intelligent Designer must exist behind the curtain [*the vastness of the universe and the chance of multiverses weaken this argument: there was plenty of opportunity for the magic mix to come together and why all that wasted space-time?*].

Whatever its motivation, I was grateful that the Roman Catholic Church offered something more than "just believe or else" and encouraged the use of the mind. The unforeseen consequence of this attempt by the Church to marry reason and God was that I continued to try to marry reason and God beyond the words of Aquinas. Over the years, I have become progressively more freethinking: "Freethinkers are those who are willing to use their minds without prejudice and without fearing to understand things that clash with their own customs, privileges, or beliefs. This state of mind is not common, but it is essential for right thinking."9 If you have not done so already, please join me.

Since this is a tribute to Bertrand Russell, not Thomas Aquinas, I will follow the structure of the five arguments for the existence of God that Russell set forth in "Why I Am Not a Christian."

The First Cause Argument

"There is no reason why the world could not have come into being without a cause; nor, on the other hand, is there any reason why it should not have always existed... The idea that things must have a beginning is really due to the poverty of our imagination. Therefore, perhaps, I need not waste any more time upon the argument about the First Cause."
~ Bertrand Russell, Why I Am Not a Christian

I will follow Mr. Russell's lead and forgo further discussion on this argument; however, I will share this funny quote from physicist Michio Kaku that astutely reflects both The First Cause

Argument and Pandeism: "In the beginning God said, the four-dimensional divergence of an antisymmetric, second rank tensor equals zero, and there was light, and it was good."

The Natural Law Argument

"If you say, as more orthodox theologians do, that in all the laws which God issues He had a reason for giving those laws rather than others—the reason, of course, being to create the best universe, although you would never think it to look at it—if there was a reason for the laws which God gave, then God Himself was subject to law, and therefore you do not get any advantage by introducing God as an intermediary."
~ Bertrand Russell, *Why I Am Not a Christian*

Natural confused me more than once during my Catholic upbringing: both *natural theology* and *natural law* were misconstrued by my tender ears. The Catholic Church emphasizes natural theology over revealed theology. While natural theology actually refers to a belief system based on reason and ordinary experience in contrast to a revealed theology based on scripture, I conflated the word *natural* with St. Bernard of Clairvaux's maxim: "Trees and stones will teach you that which you can never learn from masters" and decided that God could be best understood by understanding God's creation. I also mistakenly understood the main point of Aquinas' natural law to be that the nature of nature reflected the nature of God. If God were creation, as Pandeists assert, then I would have been on the right path from a precociously early age. Unfortunately, that path contained too many ugly realities for me to ascribe it to a good God.

Apparently, *natural* confused Bertrand Russell, too. While natural law was not one of St. Thomas Aquinas' arguments for the existence of God, he did broach the topic at length in *Summa Theologica* as an argument for the basis of moral law. The theory of natural law claims that standards of morality are derived from the nature of the world and the nature of human beings that were established by God. Evidently, Aquinas had not met many human beings because he put forth that "the rule and measure of human acts is reason." Aquinas believed that human beings were naturally reasonable which he attributed to God's so making them. Aquinas further postulated "Hence this is the first precept of law that good is to be done and ensued, and evil is to be avoided." Amen, St. Aquinas, please explain that to God. If the first precept of moral law for human beings is do good and avoid evil, shouldn't God, as the highest gradation of good, be held to the same if not a higher standard? If so, then paraphrasing Ricky Ricardo: "God, you got some 'splainin' to do!" Why, if you are the highest gradation of good, create a world rife with disease, cruel modes of death, and natural disasters that destroy lives indiscriminately? If you are a good God, then you should have been more loving toward your creation.

As you, gentle reader, have no doubt noticed: I am not inclined to think of God in impersonal terms. If God created us, then God holds a fiduciary duty to us: "We call him Father and not in derision, although we would detest and denounce any earthly father who would inflict upon his child a thousandth part of the pains and miseries and cruelties which our God deals out to His children every day, and has dealt out to them daily during all the centuries since the crime of creating Adam was committed."[10] If God were relieved of fiduciary responsibility to creation, then I might just appreciate God as the wildly Byzantine mind behind cosmology, quantum mechanics, and platypuses. However, I can appreciate but neither love nor worship the laws of physics, motion, exponents, or traffic. Is there a difference between appreciating truth or standing in awe of the starry skies and loving God? Does M-theory elicit your devotion? Nikola Tesla said: "What one man calls God, another calls the laws of physics." I call the law of physics, "the law of physics." For me, God would need to offer a value-add like goodness to gain more from me than wonder at the complexity of it all.

The Argument From Design

"When you come to look into this argument from design, it is a most astonishing thing that people can believe that this world, with all the things that are in it, with all its defects, should be the best that omnipotence and omniscience has been able to produce in millions of years."
~ *Bertrand Russell, Why I Am Not a Christian*

"As a fraction of the lifespan of the universe as measured from the beginning to the evaporation of the last black hole, life as we know it is only possible for one-thousandth of a billion billion billionth, billion billion billionth, billion billion billionth, of a percent (10^{-84}). And that's why, for me, the most astonishing wonder of the universe isn't a star or a planet or a galaxy. It isn't a thing at all. It's an instant in time. And that time is now. Humans have walked the earth for just the

shortest fraction of that briefest of moments in
deep time."
~ Brian Cox, <u>Wonders of the Universe – Destiny</u>

"The universe we observe has precisely the
properties we should expect if there is, at bottom,
no design, no purpose, no evil, no good, nothing
but blind, pitiless indifference."
~ Charles Darwin, <u>The Descent of Man</u>

"The more I learn about the universe, the less
convinced I am that there's any sort of benevolent
force that has anything to do with it, at all."
~ Neil DeGrasse Tyson

"The Supreme Arrogance of Religious Thinking:
'That a carbon-based bag of mostly water on a
speck of iron-silicate dust around a boring dwarf
star in a minor galaxy in an underpopulated local
group of galaxies in an unfashionable suburb of a
supercluster would look up at the sky and declare
'it was all made so I could exist.'"
~ Peter Walker

Five quotes. You think I have an issue with the
Argument From Design? I do. It, along with my
slightly mistaken notion of natural law, shattered
my belief in an always good God. As a child, the
Argument from Design had appeal to me in
moments of reverie gazing at the stars or losing
myself in the ocean's rhythm; but, not so much
when I watched victims of natural disasters struggle
on the nightly news or animals eat each other on
Mutual of Omaha's Wild Kingdom.[11] The Roman
Catholic Church is quite fond of categorization:
natural vs. revealed theology, venial vs. mortal sin,
moral vs. natural evil. According to the Church,

moral evil is caused by human activity while natural evil is caused by nature itself and is beyond human control [*think: all those diseases and disasters about which I keep whining*]. In short, the blame for moral sin falls on humans if you believe in free will and the blame for natural sin falls on God if you believe that God created nature or if you are a Pandeist who believes that God both created and is nature. If you don't believe in free will, then the blame for moral sin would also fall on God unless you don't believe in God either in which case please pass the wine.

The problem of natural evil demands this question: If God is only sometimes good and I am only sometimes good, then why should I worship God? Frankly, I would never have created a world plagued with disease, earthquakes, tornadoes, and floods. Should I be venerated? I think not. Should God be held to a higher standard than me? I think so. It is inconceivable to me that God could not have created a world without natural evil. Even if we do gain secondary benefits from suffering, do we really need so much of it to learn the lesson? A better creation with less suffering caused by indiscriminate natural disasters and disease certainly seems possible if designed by a good God.

The Moral Arguments for Deity

"One is often told that it is a very wrong thing to attack religion, because religion makes men virtuous. So I am told; I have not noticed it."
~ *Bertrand Russell, Why I Am Not a Christian*

The Moral Argument for Deity is less Catholic than catholic (universal): "Worldwide, Many See Belief in God as Essential to Morality."[12] The facts do not support this claim: With few exceptions, more secular nations are less crime-ridden than more religious nations and more secular states in the United States are less crime-ridden than more religious states.[13] A cursory glance at human history will reveal that many of the most heinous events were sparked by believers of some deity or justified by quoting a supposedly sacred text: holy wars, inquisitions, slavery, subjugation of women, religiously inspired acts of terrorism, burning of witches, honor killings, and more.

Asking a believer to describe their deity is an insightful Rorschach test into the nature of that believer's own soul. You will find as Ralph Waldo Emerson noted: "The god of the cannibals will be a cannibal, of the crusaders a crusader, and of the merchants a merchant." The God of believers who want to kill their enemies would kill its enemies or command the killing of its enemies. The God of believers who want to burn witches would burn witches. The God of Pandeists would be accepting of both good and evil in an amoral universe. The God of Celeste Foley would be always loving, good, and fair. Morality has less to do with an actual deity than with the qualities the believer projects onto that deity.

That said, I do long for the days when I believed in the loving, good, and fair God of my projections. When I believed that love, goodness, and fairness actually resonated with a Supreme-Eternal-External-Referent; then, the case I could make for centering in and acting on them was much more compelling: "Living in and out God's love, goodness, and fairness will mystically converge you with God in eternity" sounds so much more persuasive than "Gee, it's a nice thing to do and benefits the whole which, in turn, benefits you" ~

an argument which would barely nudge the previously morally unmotivated. I stand with Albert Einstein: "If people are good only because they fear punishment, and hope for reward, then we are a sorry lot indeed." Indeed.

The Argument for the Remedying of Injustice

"In the part of this universe that we know there is great injustice, and often the good suffer, and often the wicked prosper, and one hardly knows which of those is the more annoying; but if you are going to have justice in the universe as a whole you have to suppose a future life to redress the balance of life here on earth. So they say that there must be a God, and there must be heaven and hell in order that in the long run there may be justice. That is a very curious argument."
~ *Bertrand Russell, Why I Am Not a Christian*

So, God created a universe riddled with injustice where the good suffer and the wicked prosper all so God can save the day after we die? God sounds like one of those wayward firefighters who sets the blaze so they can put it out and be praised as a hero(ine) ~ only we can actually know if the blaze has been extinguished. A justice-remedying afterlife is improbable conjecture: Why would a God sinister enough to set up this unjust world be just in another life? Is God just playing games? Would that game-playing God be a good God? If God were loving, good, and fair, wouldn't our striving to be so too be challenging enough?

THE CHARACTER OF GOD

"God is the map whereby we locate the setting of our life. That God is the water in which we launch our life raft. That God is the real thing from which and toward which we receive our being and identify ourselves. It follows that the kind of God at work in your life will determine the shape and quality and risk at the center of your existence. It matters who God is."
~ *Walter Brueggeman,* <u>Sermons</u>

Raised in the post-Vatican II Roman Catholicism of the 1970's in the United States, I was never plagued with trying to reconcile God's goodness with biblical accounts. Thankfully, s*ola scriptura* was not our bag. The low-hanging fruit of the flood and hell would have put an end to my faith in a good God during early childhood. Whenever bible stories implied that God was not good or fair or loving, I simply didn't believe them. For me, the character of God was Aquinas' perfect highest good. I assumed that the character of my God was the character of all Gods. I was wrong.

If Pandeism were true, then God's character would be amoral reflecting the amoral universe that God both created and *is*. If we believe in God, then I think that Walter Brueggemann was on the mark: I don't want to locate my life in or receive my being from or identify myself with the amorality that Pandeism infers to be God. I don't want amorality at the center of my existence. If there were an amoral Pandeist and/or Creator God, then I would embrace morality and oppose God whenever necessary.

The Moral Problem

*"No religion has ever given a picture of deity
which men could have imitated without the
grossest immorality."*
*~ George Santayana, <u>Little Essays, No. 24</u>,
"Pathetic Notions of God"*

The Christian God delivered Robert Green Ingersoll
to agnosticism: "This God withheld the rain, caused
the famine, saw the fierce eyes of hunger ~ the
wasted forms, the white lips, saw mothers eating
babes, and remained ferocious as famine." (*Why I
Am Agnostic*) What moral example does the
Pandeist God provide? The Pandeist God both
created and includes in its being natural evil.
Natural evil is my nemesis. I so wanted to believe in
a good God despite natural evil that I developed the
following theodicy:

> "The theodicy that evil and suffering were
> necessary for spiritual growth gave me
> considerable pause. Yes, it was true that
> valuable lessons in compassion, self-sacrifice,
> and interdependency were born of suffering.
> Socially, natural disasters invited disparate
> groups to come together to face a shared
> challenge. Individually, overcoming obstacles
> built character and strengthened us for further
> challenges ahead. If all suffering were karmic or
> just, then we would be far less likely to grow
> spiritually from it because, instead of feeling
> compassion, we may just feel smug knowing the
> suffering person deserved it. Unjust suffering
> taught us important lessons that just suffering
> might not. I had learned important lessons from
> suffering but only because I had survived my

suffering and was capable of learning. There was the rub. The people who died during a natural disaster did not benefit by learning valuable lessons in compassion, self-sacrifice, and interdependency. Babies who suffered did not benefit by learning valuable lessons in compassion, self-sacrifice, and interdependency. Severely and profoundly developmentally disabled people did not benefit by learning valuable lessons in compassion, self-sacrifice, and interdependency. Actively psychotic people did not benefit by learning valuable lessons in compassion, self-sacrifice, and interdependency. The animals that suffered or died did not benefit by learning valuable lessons in compassion, self-sacrifice, and interdependency. I sat with this for some time. I could not figure out how God could care for each one of us individually and still allow the suffering of babies and mentally challenged people and animals who could not benefit from their suffering. I could not understand how someone who died in a natural disaster grew spiritually from the experience. In my commitment to face a fact though it slay me, I came to a conclusion that troubled me very much at first: I decided that God did not care about us individually.

After the initial shock wore off, this idea began to trouble me less. I had grown uncomfortable with individual salvation because it seemed like a lot of supposedly religious people were more concerned in reaping rewards and seeing 'other' people suffer than pursuing, loving, and living out God. I felt like heaven and hell were impediments to people's purely loving God for the sake of loving God. As long as you were concerned for your personal salvation, you were not really focused on God. I had been intrigued by the Eastern Orthodox concept of deification and the Hindu goal of Brahman and Atman uniting once the Veil of Maya had been lifted.

The point of convergence was the goal, not a personal salvation. The death of a baby in a flood did not help that baby grow spiritually but it did invite others to grow and at the point of convergence that baby was one with all of us and with God. We were all in this together. Convergence celebrated our interconnectedness and properly valued our personal salvation in the context of our loving relationship with others. If we had not moved beyond our self-concern, we had not yet moved to God and we were not yet saved. When we reached out in love to others as agents of God's love, we converged with God and that was our salvation. Convergence. I was so happy to have found it because had I not the problem of natural evil would have bested my belief in a good God.

My belief was not quite bested; however, I will admit to you that the problem of natural evil remains the weakest link in my faith in God. If I was unwilling to build my foundation on a religion that suggested bad things about God, how could I build a foundation on a God that established a natural order that led to evil? Well, I could interpret natural evil as necessary for inviting convergent spiritual growth since the impersonal and undeserved quality of natural evil invited the love of neighbor in a way that a deserved evil would not. Okay, but how did inviting convergent spiritual growth through the atrocity of natural evil differ from God's somehow inviting spiritual growth through the atrocities ascribed to God in the Bible and other holy books? The best response I could come up with is this one: Natural evil invites the movement of love in the world. When we hear about the victims of disease, we donate money to help find a cure. When we hear about the victims of natural disasters, we send money and supplies and travel to the site to help in any way we can. On the other hand, when we hear of God's supposedly threatening parents with the death and cannibalization of their children or ordering the genocide of an entire people including babies and livestock or killing sons for burning the wrong incense, we just think badly of God. We come to fear God rather than love God. When we hear that God condemns those who have not believed in the name of His 'one and only Son' even though many, many people were at a severe disadvantage to ever hear his Son's name, then we think God is unfair or we decide that we, too, have license not to love these 'other' people. The atrocities ascribed to God in the Bible and other holy books do not invite the movement of love in the world; so, I could logically defend my building a foundation on a God that established a natural order that led to evil while refusing to build my foundation on a religion that ascribed atrocities to God." (*GOD-centric*, Ch. 5)

Defects In My Theodicy

"There are two ways to be fooled. One is to believe what isn't true; the other is to refuse to believe what is true."
~ Søren Kierkegaard

In *GOD-centric* (2011), I tried mightily to shield the character of the [Pandeist] Creator God of the natural world from the obvious blight of natural evil. In *GOOD-centric* (2016), I recognized, owned, and confessed my failure to face the truth in the sub-chapter, "From GOD-centric to GOOD-centric":

> "Long before I wrote GOD-centric, I developed my 'God Statement' which first articulated my fervent, yet decidedly non-religion-specific belief in an eternally good and fair God of love. My 'God Statement' also revealed the thread that would lead to my faith's unraveling: *If God were not good and fair, then I would have no interest in knowing or pleasing God.* This thread was exposed again in *GOD-centric*: *If God were not good, I would not love God. End of story; quest over. To love a bad God, to kowtow to a tyrant, was to be a coward.* (Ch. 5)

No coward soul was mine or so I thought. During my dark night of the soul, my mantra had been Thomas H. Huxley's 'God give me the strength to face a fact though it slay me' but I was neither strong nor brave. Like an apologist doing back flips to justify the bible, I had been an acrobat contorting logic to try to justify natural evil. In *GOD-centric*, I acknowledged that: 'The problem of natural evil did leave me staggering. Staggering like a drunken sailor who if pinned to the sweating wall would admit to being intellectually agnostic. How can I honestly be otherwise?' (Ch. 6) but I was not courageous enough to let the fact slay me. I clutched onto an imaginary sliver of hope while spouting some nonsense about irrational versus transrational belief: 'I was willing to leap but my leaping would be transrationally beyond reason rather than irrationally against reason. Beyond reason meant that I might still be in the process of rational understanding but rational understanding still seemed possible. Against reason meant that reason had defeated faith but you were going to believe anyway.' (*GOD-centric*, Ch. 5) In what way was I still in the process of rationally understanding natural evil? Thomas's grandson, Aldous Huxley, provided the push that I needed: 'Facts do not cease to exist because they are ignored.' (*Complete Essays 2*, 1926-1929) Natural evil slayed my faith in an eternally good and fair God of love.

Why had I been unwilling to face the truth? Because I loved God. Because I had a long and involved relationship with God. Because I felt loyalty to God who had been my rock during childhood. Because I really, really wanted God to be eternally loving, good, and fair; but, that simply is not true. If there is a God, that God is only occasionally loving, good, and fair. That fact is written in nature and in every holy book." (*GOOD-centric*, Preface)

THE EMOTIONAL FACTOR

"Oh my friends, my friends don't ask me
What your sacrifice was for
Empty chairs at empty tables
Where my friend will sing no more."

~ *"Empty Chairs at Empty Tables" from Les Miserables [Michael Ball's version]*

Human beings, along with countless other life forms, through no fault of their own, are afflicted by natural evil. If there were a Creator God, then God created natural evil. A Pandeist God would also *be* natural evil. Are you feeling warm and fuzzy about God yet? Would it help if you thought that this same God who created and perhaps is natural evil is just playing a game with you and all whom you love to test your faith? Do you take comfort in the God-as-an-emotional-abuser model? Somehow, some mothers who lose their babies to disease or disaster think this is part of a magnificent plan and love God all the more. This makes no sense to me other than as the most desperate of justifications that should have a very short half-life: God created the disease, God created the disaster, and perhaps God failed to intervene if you believe in an intervening type of God, and now your baby is dead and the best that you can hope for is that the same sinister God that created the disease or disaster that killed your baby will turn out to be a gem after all in an afterlife. This was the best plan that a good God could devise?

Perhaps I am more like these mothers than I care to think. As the acrobatic mind behind the convergence theodicy, I, too, tried desperately to justify a good God's creating natural evil. The only difference between those mothers and me is that I did not love God all the more or all the same: "While my position on natural evil's inviting convergent spiritual growth could be defended logically in my head, my heart was not at all satisfied: 'Really, God, how could You?'" (*GOD-centric*, Ch. 5) I was willing to selflessly throw myself under God's disaster-and-disease bus: I would live in and out God's love, fairness, and goodness just so I could share mystical moments of convergence with God with nary a care about God's treatment of me. I was okay with God's not caring about me individually. What I was not readily okay with was applying this principle of self-sacrifice to the brotherhood of man. What I was not at all okay with was applying this principle of self-sacrifice to my brother ~ or mother or niece or nephew or extended family or friends. I was not okay with God's not caring about each of them individually. Emotionally, in the end, I could not reconcile, despite my near desperate motivation, natural evil with a good God. My emotional revolt stemmed not from our dying;[14] but, our suffering diseases and disasters attributable to a Creator God. Unfortunately, not believing in a good God may afford me intellectual integrity; but, it is not emotionally satisfying either: Natural disasters and disease still kill indiscriminately, non-good Pandeist God or no God.

WHAT WE MUST DO

"We want to stand upon our own feet and look fair and square at the world—its good facts, its bad facts, its beauties, and its ugliness; see the world as it is, and be not afraid of it... We ought to stand up and look the world frankly in the face. We ought to make the best we can of the world, and if it is not so good as we wish, after all it will still be better than what these others have made of it in all these ages."
~ *Bertrand Russell, Why I Am Not a Christian*

A wise woman once said: "Asking a believer to describe their deity is an insightful Rorschach test into the nature of that believer's own soul... Morality has less to do with an actual deity than with the qualities the believer projects onto that deity." (Me, *earlier this essay*) An even wiser man once said: "And if that word [God] has not much meaning for you, translate it, and speak of the depths of your life, of the source of your being, of your ultimate concern, of what you take seriously without any reservation." (Paul Tillich, *The Shaking of the Foundations*) What we must do is proclaim our ultimate concerns and project our expectation for their fulfillment onto ourselves.[15] I have declared my ultimate concerns in my books: love, goodness, and fairness. For most of my life, I projected these concerns onto God; now, I embrace them as my own. What are your ultimate concerns? What do you take seriously without reservation? Are you proud of your answer? Does it reflect the person you want to be and the legacy you want to leave? If not, then become the person you want to be and project your values onto yourself. If so, then proclaim your ultimate concerns and live them; so, your life and legacy will reflect your best self, the self you want to be.[16] Isn't that enough?

Notes

[1] An homage to natural theology and the souls who helped me on my way.

[2] A female monk without a religion, a free-thinker with a Roman Catholic operating system, trying to hold the tension and explore the possibilities between believing in a good God or just goodness.

[3] Possibilianism is a philosophy which rejects both the diverse claims of traditional theism and the positions of certainty in strong atheism in favor of a middle, exploratory ground: https://www.eagleman.com/blog/why-i-am-a-possibilian.

[4] "The dangers of believing in a God whom we cannot but regard as evil, and then, in mere terrified flattery calling Him 'good' and worshiping Him, is still greater danger." ~ C.S. Lewis, Letter to John Beversluis, July 3, 1963.

[5] "Gods always behave like the people who make them." ~ Zora Neale Hurston, *Tell My Horse: Voodoo and Life in Haiti and Jamaica*.

[6] "Truth is something so noble that if God could turn aside from it, I could keep the truth and let God go." ~ Meister Eckhart (A Modern Translation (1941) by Raymond Bernard Blakney, p. 240).

[7] The human eye can only see between 430-770 THz. Our ears can only detect sound between 20Hz-20 kHz. These ranges make up a fraction of the total sound and light frequency range. This means there is a lot going on around us that we cannot see or hear.

[8] The Argument from Gradation does not contradict Pandeism, it just lacks relevancy.

[9] Attributed to Leo Tolstoy.

[10] The Character of God as Represented in the Old and New Testaments by Mark Twain.

[11] "I cannot persuade myself that a beneficent and omnipotent God would have designedly created parasitic wasps with the express intention of their feeding within the living bodies of Caterpillars." ~ Charles Darwin, *Life and Letters*, Vol 1.

[12] Pew Research Center Global Attitudes Project: Belief in God Full Report, May 27, 2014.

[13] Secular Societies Fare Better Than Religious Societies: *Psychology Today*, October 13, 2014.

[14] "Remembering that I'll be dead soon is the most important tool I've ever encountered to help me make the big choices in life. Almost everything - all external expectations, all pride, all fear of embarrassment or failure - these things just fall away in the face of death, leaving only what is truly important... And yet, death is the destination we all share. No one has ever escaped it, and that is how it should be, because death is very likely the single best invention of life. It's life's change agent. It clears out the old to make way for the new." ~ Steve Jobs, *Commencement Address to Stanford Graduates* in 2005.

[15] "I prayed for freedom for twenty years, but received no answer until I prayed with my legs." ~ Frederick Douglass.

[16] "Live a good life. If there are gods and they are just, then they will not care how devout you have been, but will welcome you based on the virtues you have lived by. If there are gods, but unjust, then you should not want to worship them. If there are no gods, then you will be gone, but will have lived a noble life that will live on in the memories of your loved ones. I am not afraid." ~ Marcus Aurelius.

Being Alive

By Amy Perry

The arm of the galaxy
Spirals
Like the tendrils of a vine,
Green and yearning,
Slow moving yogis of the divine.
Sipping on the cusp of life, playing games,
Conscious creatures,
Children of fire,
Living on the air, flicking up flames.
The Earth eats it all -
To dust and decay
Even the strongest cannot survive
Past destruction and disarray.
Revivification, revitalization,
And evolutionary changes underway.
Until we all just play the game,
We'll think this is a cruel joke,
Until we share a recognizing wink
That the divine is in us, we might choke.
And we don't need to search or
Espouse certainties
To know certainly,
This is an amazing experience.
To even contemplate being alive,
Is a treat for life in itself, is delirium.
Get lost in the madness,
Therein lies the genius,
Make the most of the ride
Experience all that's beautiful and heinous.
Find your connection to Oneness,
Find it to Source.
You have permission to suffer
And love on your course.

"The Keeper of Sheep"

VI

By Alberto Caeiro (pseudonym of Fernando Pessoa)

Fernando Pessoa (1888—1935) published criticism, creative prose, and poetry. Pessoa created alter egos he called heteronyms, with the three main ones being Alberto Caeiro, Ricardo Reis, and Álvaro de Campos. With these heteronyms, he explored different lifestyles, regions, economic statuses, poetic styles, sexualities, and other variations. Literary critic Martin Lüdke described Pessoa's literary philosophy as a kind of Pandeism— especially as to those writings under the heteronym Alberto Caeiro. In his lifetime, he published four books in English and one in Portuguese. Pessoa was awarded with the Queen Victoria Prize in 1903 and the Antero de Quental Award in 1934. Today, the Pessoa Prize is recognized as the most important award in the area of Portuguese culture.

To think about God is to disobey God,
Since God wanted us not to know him,
Which is why he didn't reveal himself to us...

Let's be simple and calm,
Like the trees and streams,
And God will love us, making us
Us even as the trees are trees
And the streams are streams,
And will give us greenness in the spring, which is its season,
And a river to go to when we end...
And he'll give us nothing more, since to give us more would make us less us.

Pessimism and Pandeism: Philipp Mainländer on the Death of God

By Sam Woolfe

Sam Woolfe is a writer, blogger, and journalist based in London. His main areas of interest include philosophy, ethics, psychology, psychedelics, and mental health. Other than writing essays and articles, his interests include asemic writing, drawing, hiking, playing the cajon, and exploring new landscapes and cultures. You can find more of his work at www.samwoolfe.com

Philipp Mainländer (1841 – 1876) was a German poet and philosopher, born in Offenbach am Main. He was a disciple of Arthur Schopenhauer's philosophy and one of the patron saints of 19th century German pessimism (other notable figures belonging to this curious philosophical trend include Eduard von Hartmann and Julius Bahnsen). Unlike these other pessimists, though, he had quite a unique theory about why the universe came into existence. It is a theory that can be classed as a kind of pessimistic pandeism.

Pandeism refers to the idea that the creator of the universe became the universe through the act of creation, ceasing to exist as a conscious and separate entity. This theological doctrine combines elements of deism (God created the universe and its natural laws and then 'stepped back', letting things run their course, without interfering) and pantheism (God is everything, i.e. nature or the universe in its totality). Pandeism seeks to explain how the universe began and why God appears absent in it. Like deism, pandeism lacks a belief in a personal God that should be worshipped, and in line with pantheism, pandeism holds that God is immanent, all-encompassing, and impersonal but not transcendent, which is the theistic notion that God exists above and independent from the universe.

In this piece, I want to specifically focus on an intriguing myth of creation that Mainländer formulated in *The Philosophy of Redemption* (1876), which is pandeistic in nature.

Philipp Mainländer: A Patron Saint of German Pessimism

While Schopenhauer's posthumous public recognition in the 1860s helped to popularize philosophical pessimism in Germany and gain followers, his pessimism was still passionately contested and critiqued, by philosophers like Eugen Dühring. The philosophical pessimism of Schopenhauer and his followers entailed the essential belief that life is not worth living, which Mainländer certainly ascribed to, but Dühring counteracted this general belief with an optimism that we can increase the happiness of the greatest number through science and redistribution. Mainländer, like Dühring, was a socialist, but he did not think that socialism could ever do away with the problem of human suffering.

Mainländer's central work, *The Philosophy of Redemption*, stands out as one of the defining texts of philosophical pessimism in Germany in the second half of the 19th century. The philosopher Theodor Lessing has said it is "perhaps the most radical system of pessimism known to philosophical literature". Yet in spite of this, the work has still never been translated into English, although Christian Romuss, a graduate from the University of Queensland, has supposedly been working on an official translation since 2016. There does exist an incomplete and unofficial translation, which provides Anglophone readers with some of the core ideas of Mainländer's philosophy.

We can also understand his philosophy from secondary sources, including Frederick C. Beiser's *Weltschmerz: Pessimism in German Philosophy, 1860-1900*, which explores the flourishing of – and opposition to – pessimism in 19ᵗʰ century Germany. *Weltschmerz* is an interesting German term that translates to "world weariness" or "world pain" – it stands for this feeling of weariness, melancholy, and despair about the world as it is or the human condition. It is a depression related to the comparison of an ideal state with the actual state of the world; in the words of Oliver Burkeman, *weltschmerz* springs "from seeing that things could and should be better".

We can clearly see the sentiment of *weltschmerz* expressed in *The Philosophy of Redemption*, as well as in the defining works of the other influential German pessimists. The horror fiction writer Thomas Ligotti also expounds the ideas of Mainländer in *The Conspiracy Against the Human Race*, a work of non-fiction that conveys Ligotti's highly pessimistic worldview and his antinatalism (the philosophical position that assigns a negative value to birth and which calls on us to refrain from procreating). Philosophers such as Emil Cioran and Peter Wessel Zapffe have also inspired Ligotti's bleak and hopeless picture of the human condition.

Pessimistic Pandeism

In *The Conspiracy Against the Human Race*, Ligotti describes Mainländer's myth of creation as follows:

> Mainländer was confident that the Will-to-die he believed would well up in humanity had been spiritually grafted into us by a God who, in the beginning, masterminded His own quietus. It seems that existence was a horror to God. Unfortunately, God was impervious to the depredations of time. This being so, His only means to get free of Himself was by a divine form of suicide.

> God's plan to suicide himself could not work, though, as long as He existed as a unified entity outside of space-time and matter. Seeking to nullify His oneness so that He could be delivered into nothingness, he shattered Himself—Big Bang-like—into the time-bound fragments of the universe, that is, all those objects and organisms that have been accumulating here and there for billions of years. In Mainländer's philosophy, "God knew that he could change from a state of super-reality into non-being only through the development of a real world of multiformity." Employing this strategy, He excluded Himself from being. "God is dead," wrote Mainländer, "and His death was the life of the world." Once the great individuation had been initiated, the momentum of its creator's self-annihilation would continue until everything became exhausted by its own existence, which for human beings meant that the faster they learned that happiness was not as good as they thought it would be, the happier they would be to die out.

> Rather than resist our end, as Mainländer concludes, we will come to see that "the knowledge that life is worthless is the flower of

all human wisdom." Elsewhere the philosopher
states, "Life is hell, and the sweet still night of
absolute death is the annihilation of hell."

Here we see just how pessimistic Mainländer's version of pandeism is. The *will-to-die* that Ligotti refers to is Mainländer's idea that ingrained in humans is the wish for annihilation – we inherit desire wish from the pre-cosmic God, the infinite unity that had the primordial wish to stop existing. God apparently couldn't bear its existence anymore, perhaps bored with omniscience or tortured by eternity. For Mainländer, God was propelled towards suicide by the knowledge that non-being is better than being. In this gloomy creation myth, God had one single deed and that was its suicide (or deicide: the killing of a god). Everything in the universe is the remnant of this deific self-sacrifice, but rather than see the universe and human existence as precious, beautiful, and sacred vestiges of God, Mainländer thought that everything we see around us is simply part of God's decaying corpse, and driven towards a desired state of extinction.

Interestingly, this myth of divine suicide seems to correspond somewhat with the scientific concept of cosmic entropy (with entropy referring to how disordered a system is). Based on the second law of thermodynamics, cosmic entropy will always increase over time, and many physicists believe this implies the universe will eventually end in a 'heat death', in which everything is at the same temperature, a state that physicists refer to as maximum entropy. All matter decays in a heat death scenario, yet particles and radiation would still remain, so it is not clear if this would count as the complete self-annihilation that Mainländer had in mind.

We can see how Mainländer diverges from Schopenhauer since his idea of the will-to-die is the opposite of Schopenhauer's *will-to-life* (which posits that all living beings have this intrinsic and unstoppable desire to preserve their life and further propagate life through the act of procreation). Schopenhauer's pessimism arises from the fact that we endlessly pursue desires and goals with the will-to-life in mind but this striving never brings us lasting happiness. While Mainländer shares Schopenhauer's pessimism about human well-being, he differs in that the intrinsic force he believes driving humans – the *will-to-die* – is our salvation. In *The Philosophy of Redemption*, Mainländer describes the *will-to-die* – implied by his pessimistic pandeism – as follows:

> *In the heart of things, the immanent Philosopher sees in the entire cosmos only the deepest longing for complete extinction; it is as if he heard clearly the call that pierces all the celestial spheres: Redemption! Redemption! Death to our Life! and the cheering reply: you all will find extinction and will be redeemed!*

But for Mainländer the implications of his pessimistic pandeism did not mean we should patiently wait for extinction in the form of the slow and gradual decay of the universe; he genuinely believed that liberation could be found in the act of suicide. He therefore subscribed to pro-mortalism: the belief that it is always better to die and cease existing than to continue living. And so, staying true to his beliefs, he took his life at the age of 34, using a pile of his newly published magnum opus to hang himself. However, it would be simplistic to see this as being a purely 'philosophical suicide', a natural extension of his philosophical pessimism or a sober and rational decision. As a matter of fact, he had a mental breakdown soon after he had finished writing *The Philosophy of Redemption*, and prior to hanging himself, he complained to his sister about being "exhausted" and "ineffably tired". Based on his philosophical outlook and life struggles, the influence of a mood disorder like depression on his suicide is a possible and obvious explanation.

Alternative Forms of Pandeism

Mainländer's creation myth is like the Book of Genesis revamped as a cosmic horror story. But this philosopher's pandeism is unique. Other pandeists do not see God's transformation (and disappearance) into the universe in such a pessimistic way as Mainländer, who believed that God became the universe because this supreme being was aiming for non-existence. However, many alternative accounts do suppose that God became the universe due to boredom with its existence, or out of curiosity. One interesting version of pandeism can be found in the 2001 novella *God's Debris: A Thought Experiment*, written by Scott Adams, the creator of *Dilbert*, the well-known satirical comic strip.

In this novella and thought experiment, Adams lays out his theory of pandeism, stating that God annihilated himself in the Big Bang. Adams argues that an omnipotent and omniscient God would already have and know everything and:

> For that reason he would be unmotivated to do anything or create anything. There would be no purpose to act in any way whatsoever. But a

> *God who had one nagging question – what happens if I cease to exist? – might be motivated to find the answer in order to complete his knowledge...The fact that we exist is proof that God is motivated to act in some way. And since only the challenge of self-destruction could interest an omnipotent God, it stands to reason that we...are God's debris.*

A pre-cosmic and omniscient God would know everything, *except* its non-existence, and so God wanted to find out what that would be like, but of course, once the act was completed, there could be no knowledge of the change. When God became nature, nature inevitably forgot it was God. All that was left was God's amnesiac debris, which Adams defines as primordial matter and the law of probability (of course, he refers to us as God's debris because primordial matter and probability eventually led to our existence).

Alan Watts also discussed the idea of God becoming bored and – in seeking out new and interesting experiences – decided to play the game of forgetting it was God. Nonetheless, Watts was not necessarily promoting a pandeistic theory of the universe since he believed in pantheism, the idea that God was still present everywhere, and that we're all God pretending not to be God. But we can imagine how God's desire for novel experiences could equally take the form of divine suicide, perhaps because God would have the foreknowledge of eventually becoming human or some other kind of intelligence, which would offer a range of limited experiences that it was unable to experience in its previous state of absolute unity, infinitude, eternity, omniscience, omnipotence, omnipresence, and omnibenevolence. Perhaps God was interested in what it would be like to live as different incarnations.

While the concept of pandeism is not as widely known as deism and pantheism, it does, nonetheless, have a rich history. The notion of God becoming the universe, of the One being divided into the Many, and the world being formed from the substance of a dead deity is an ancient idea. Pandeism can be found in Babylonian, Norse, Chinese, and Polynesian mythologies. Many other thinkers throughout history have also adopted a pandeistic worldview, including the cosmological theorist Giordano Bruno. Furthermore, some theologians have defended the idea of pandeism, although Christian thinkers generally (and understandably) think of it as being incompatible with the core principles of Christianity. Yet perhaps no version of pandeism would be more incompatible with Christianity than Mainländer's. In fact, his pessimistic pandeism is probably antithetical to most worldviews, beliefs, and values – you would be hard-pressed to find many agreeing with Mainländer's extreme brand of pessimism.

While I don't think of Mainländer's pessimistic pandeism as a believable theory about the origin and nature of the universe, I can still appreciate it in an allegorical or metaphorical sense, as a way of describing the birth of the universe and its natural unfolding. This grim and morbidly fascinating creation myth illustrates how pessimism can go beyond the extreme, and take on cosmic proportions.

TransDeism and Divination: Reason-based Occultism and Divination

By Nick Dutch

Nick Dutch is a professional online tarot reader in Oxfordshire, England. He provides spiritual readings on love, life and career, and uses Tarot to open up to Spirit to gain the information that he needs to give clarity to those to whom he provides readings.

The word TransDeism is made up out of two words, "trans," from the word "transcendental" and "deism," referring to a non-dogmatic outlook that is based upon reason. There is something called PanEnDeism which perceives God or the Divine as being part of Nature and somehow beyond the universe. PanEnDeists, according to my research at the time, were the only kind of Deists who performed religious or spiritual exercises for the purpose of gaining spiritual experiences. These actions of a PanEnDeist were called TransDeism.

When the word Deist or Deism is used in defining a religious or spiritual perspective, it refers to something that is either spiritual but not religious (the term religious in this case meaning dogmatic), or the application of reason applied to Nature to help come to a spiritual or God-oriented belief. Deists are usually free-thinking people who accept the scientific method and the findings of science, but still have some kind of faith that it is based on reason. Deists doubt dogmatic beliefs and reserve the right to think independently and not to obey because someone has told them to do so.

Therefore, TransDeism must by inference refer to the attempt to gain some kind of strange experience that might seem to be, in some manner, spiritual, but without necessarily attributing a dogmatic, theological, spiritual or even religious explanation as to why the experience has occurred.

The word spiritual has many meanings, including self-analysis, something uplifting, or maybe something of a seemingly, but not necessarily, paranormal nature.

The New Age movement has filled the world with many new religions, but has failed in one major front. Instead of replacing social hierarchies of religious institutions with the ability of the individual be able to think freely for themselves when it comes to matters of spirituality, it has created new structures and new ways for people with a religious title to aggressively promote their spiritual interpretations and in the process do much damage to people who are either searching for a new religious path for themselves, searching for an apparent solution to one of life's many major problems, or, as in my case, searching for explanations for the apparently supernatural phenomena that I had experienced.

I agree that one of the many reasons for this could be the free market, something which has great benefits to civilization, but also makes people wish to sell, and lays down the precedent that aggressive sales techniques are permitted. This is something which can be detrimental to spiritual understanding.

If the term "TransDeism" was to separate itself from PanEnDeism, and to become a definition of a type of deistic practitioner, it could solve one of the main obstacles that is present in the New Age movement, the obstacle of dogmatism or spiritual literalism getting in the way of the personal experiential and experimental art form that is research into the spiritual, psychological, or paranormal.

During the days when I was involved in a New Age movement (nearly twenty years before writing this), there were often people who would order me to obey, to follow their tradition and indeed to worship the gods that they believed in. In short, attempting to take away from me freedom of thought and the ability to make choices. I considered that inappropriate behavior then and I still do now, especially as these New Age people rejected the dogma and Bible literalism of fundamentalist literalist Christianity only to create a new and more frightening literalism. They would not accept the performance of religious activity that was slightly different in its nature in case the Gods didn't like it and would attempt to terrify the public about times of day, phases of the moon, colours of candles, carved pieces of wood, and the like. There were even some who called science a load of rubbish, but consider the various subsections of their practices, including astrology, a hard science. It was plain to me that these attitudes weren't helping the New Age movement cause at all, weren't helping the people in the movement to grow up, certainly weren't helping anyone to get some real perspective about life, and were not really doing any good. They had replaced fundamentalist littlest Christianity with a pre-medieval aggressive superstitious evangelical New Age literalism full of dogma. Although in reflection, they were laughable people, I could see that there were some very clear dangers to their attitude, especially as they believe that they were right, that they were being scientific and that their practices, and the extrapolations and speculations that they made on the basis of a few strange experiences with the reading of a few substandard books, were correct and accurate scientific facts. Large chunks of the New Age community had become an anti-rational, anti-science movement. On top of that I also noticed that there was a tendency to not only accept personality and character flaws, but in some cases to worship them and encourage them rather than to get over them and try and progress in reasoning and logic. In some cases (but by no means all) the new religious movement had become a justification for overt racism and sectarian hatred.

Not all of the members of the New Age movement are like this, and I certainly don't wish to tar all of the New Age movement members with the same brush, but these tendencies seem to be growing in popularity amongst their communities.

Over thirty years ago now, the New Age movement preached a message of love, tolerance, self understanding, and acceptance. Over the past twenty years, the attitudes have been slowly changing, and I fear that it was for the worst. Nowadays, the group-think that I have previously noticed in the New Age movement seems to have become more heavily cemented in some sectors of their communities, and as such a need for a perspective that encourages ideological freedom, as well as the search for spiritual, religious, or apparently paranormal experience needs to become reintroduced into the movement.

You will find in this article suggested activities, an attitude to exploring the mind and the generation of seemingly spiritual experiences, but without any requirement that you believe in any supernatural being or spiritual reality at all. Much of the content of this article can be interpreted and used atheistically for the purpose of assisting and self understanding (which is a spiritual exercise in its own right, as self-understanding is to understand one's own "spirit," a word which is, at times, allegorical and can refer to one's essence or character as much as to alleged disincarnate entities), bringing about relaxation, overcoming stress and many other things. I'm not trying to give you New Age apologetics, nor am I trying to convert you.

Although some of this work does deal with such seemingly spiritual things such as astral projections, forms of clairvoyance and the like, the message of this article is not that there is a spiritual reality, but that under some strange circumstances, some strange experiences can occur. That is all.

"Results" are not promised.

Much of the ideas that are present in this book come from schools of thought that are called by some, "Magick" or "occultism," but that should not scare you as when you take out the literalist belief in any supernatural being as well as the superstitious and irrational aspects from those schools of thought, you end up with some very interesting meditation and mind-body exercises that could be useful for everyone whether they believe in any form of God concept or not.

Transdeistic Activities can be performed by people of any face, or none. I call myself a TransDeist because my opinions on spiritual, religious, or political matters will change over time, so I am defining myself by my actions, being the search for Spiritual, religious or allegedly paranormal experiences, and not by my religious or political allegiances. I will probably be a TransDeist all my life.

Aleister Crowley called "Magick" The Art and Science of change in Conformity with a will, but by this statement, he was referring to the development of a scientific attitude to life (normal boring mundane secular life) and perpetual improvement of skill. The "magic of tradition" is something he also spoke of, where practice is performed with meditation, visualization, yoga, ceremony, symbolism and the like. However, he called this other "Magick" unempirical, something that most of cultists tend to overlook. This has created probably one of the most long-lasting confusions any new age, Pagan, spiritualist and occult world. Once something is not empirical, it is inappropriate to attempt to use the language of the empirical science to describe it.

It has created a myth that occult activities are and should be regarded as a science and the other myths that results from Supernaturalistic magick are as reliable in terms of results as putting the kettle on make a cup of tea. An absurdity in its own right. It has created in the New Age, Pagan, spiritualist and occult world a precedent to legitimize the use of empiricist and scientific language when approaching allegedly supernatural phenomena and the use of the phrase "it works!" applied to activities which plainly have a very low level of success rate when performed as described.

The reasons for the success rate could be described by one single phrase: lack of understanding. If, by example, a man was told that to make a baked potato, all he had to do was to place a potato in a microwave oven, the action was executed as described, and the result was an uncooked potato, was the original statement incorrect? Well, possibly, but it is more likely that there are other factors that the person who made the statement left out, factors that maybe he didn't understand what was intellectually too weak to explain. Factors such as plugging the microwave into the electricity, making sure there was money in the electricity meter to pay for the electricity that was being used by the microwave oven, making sure the plug had a working fuse, making sure that the microwave oven was in a good state of repair and that the mains electricity current was of the right type and many other factors that we take for granted. That's all well and good, and a rather humorous example, but what about another one? What if one man was to tell another that the only way to get a good job is to get a university degree? The second man contributes one or two years getting the qualifications for university entry, goes through the head of the clearing process and eventually gets a place in a good university. After three or four years of his natural life, after having racked up a massive debt and after gaining some work experience after leaving University, he finds himself not being able to secure a good position. What has happened there? But the fact is that in order to get a good job after University, you need to have a good idea as to what you wish to do for a job, you have to already have had some experience, you need to get some of the right work experience when on summer vacation, you need to make sure that the degree is good enough for you to get to the entrance level of the job at hand. Also, that the health of both body and mind of the individual is right to go through all the processes of securing the career at hand and the social and intellectual rigors of university life. There are many other factors that are needed here, but if a position of lack of understanding is given to the would-be caretaker, he won't be able to secure a position that will give him what he needs or wanted.

Now let's take another example, let's say that an individual has some strange experiences, out of body experiences, seeing ghosts, experiencing what can only be described as prophetic dreams, having sensations that could be regarded as spiritual energy or maybe telepathic moments. Instead of looking at the phenomena objectively, he seeks to gain more knowledge of these phenomena. He seeks to have someone take away from him the unknowing and to give him some control over the phenomena so that he can achieve some particular need (e.g., a cure for an incurable disease that is preventing him from living a normal life). He reads books by people who claim to know, "spiritual" people, or occultist people. The occultist (much like most of them today) don't understand the meanings of the words that they are using and care less for the effect they have on other people and so lead the Seeker astray. Maybe they are campaigning for a cause, the promotion of a new religion, the destruction of an old religion, the adjustment of a social movement to their own will, or maybe they are just two sandwiches short of a picnic and deluded. Seeker will then find himself probably confused and hurt. Many of the books that are written by "spiritual" people are in fact written not for anyone's good apart from aligning the pocket of the author and, as such, many dishonest and unintelligent tactics are used to help brainwash the reader. Also, some books are written to look as if they are a cult manual, but are in fact motivational books for salespeople on the road. That's so the reader will just get more and more confused.

Instead of trying to find a cure for his health problem, or find the answers to why he has been having these strange experiences, he will end up believing that he is not following the right religion and may even go through an intense identity crisis.

So far, what good has the New Age world done? Sure, it may have weakened some of the power of certain major organizations, but in its place there are New Age people who take on the same role of ideologically-driven dogmatic brainwasher, do more damage, and don't promote understanding the natural world.

Surely, this has been described as an evil rather than a "good"? The New Age world has taken away from humans the ideological freedom, psychological healing, personal growth and knowledge of the Unseen World that it has worked so hard to sell to the world that it has its reason to exist.

Magic and its supernatural sense is not a science, never has been and never will be. However, there are some strange experiences that it is possible to have that dew point something, but what that is we still can't say. From my point of view, the occult experiences that I have had have allowed me to develop some weak beliefs:

1) There is more to life than just the physical.

2) Consciousness can and does seem to exist outside of the brain and body therefore there is a hypothetical possibility of survival of the Consciousness after death, but how that happens and what happened after we die, we can only speculate it best (because we don't and never will ever know) and

3) Consciousness and awareness can and do seem to stretch over time and space to a small degree (hypothetically there may be other beings

outside our physical nature, but communication with these beings is very rare, they never say anything truly useful in any physical or practical sense and it would be better to think for yourself rather that you trust them on matters pertaining to a normal life vibrancy and in very rare circumstances thoughts can be transferred from one individual to another).

A few more points I would like to add is that I managed to ascertain this without joining any religion, without going through any series of initiation, baptisms, and the like, designed by humankind and without having to wear any medallions. I sought out these things that I just called strange experiences and try to apply reason to logic to them as best I can and with a useful quantity of doubt that I have needed to help keep myself sane. One of the many meanings to trans deism by my understanding is to search for these strange experiences and certainly not describing any hard-and-fast supernaturalist explanations to them, nor promising miraculous results either.

Although I personally reject the idea that magick is a science, that should not stop you from wanting to try and improve your academic skills and skills of scientific thought. The reason for this is that you need to protect your sanity and prevent yourself from going slightly mad. Quite frankly, if you are going to expose yourself to a great quantity of ideas that come out of the new age world you have a great chance of going mad. Every human individual is to a greater or lesser degree part of or the product of some kind of political ideology. Ideas drive people and therefore you can't expect anyone to give you a totally objective interpretation of anything (and I guess that goes for me too!). One wise man once told me that people don't have ideas,

ideas have people. Humans tend to absorb information and then assume that its source was authoritative and then to follow that line of thinking, possibly and in some cases, up to the grave. This is a crying shame considering that humans believe that they are the most advanced species on the face of the planet. Surely it is a moral imperative to perpetually improve the skills of thinking that we use through education, for instance, in logic, logical fallacies and how people abuse them for their own political and ideological ends (including religious ends I might add!).

Science, itself, is not concerned with the truth, it is concerned with the search for the truth, and as such does not state that which is true, but that which seems, at the time, and under certain circumstances, to be true. The methodologies of different schools of scientific thought are many and diverse, and many academic debates rage about what is genuinely true in any particular given scientific experiment.

First, a hypothesis is created, and experiment is done to investigate that hypothesis to see if there's any validity to it, the results of the experiment become part of the search for the truth and does not fully represent the total truth of the matter.

So, when we perform an experiment ourselves, we have to be prepared to say that "under the circumstances, it appears that so and so might be the case, but I will probably never know for sure" and then as more evidence springs to light, we can amend or make prophesies and bring it to a better level of understanding with time. Unfortunately, there are many people in this world who want to present themselves as carriers of the hard and fast truth.

It is paramount that we criticize our own experiences when we are trying to become experimental occultists. Otherwise, we may find ourselves falling prey to delusions and culting ourselves up to become as bad as certain other people.

If under some circumstances, I wish to perform an experiment for fun, let's say I want to do an out of body experience. After a period of self training, I follow certain exercises that are believed to have a certain effect. And nothing happens. Can I call that experiment a complete failure? No, because something might have happened at the time of unconsciousness that might have been connected to the experiment, but I will never know. Let's say that the experiment was to go and "project" to see a certain person and convey a particular message to them, and over half a year later I meet up with that person and they relate to me that they had a certain dream in which I gave them that message, I would have more to go on one considering the phenomena at hand. But then it would be easy to have built up an all-embracing theory of astral projection based on just one particular experience and one peculiar result. So, I can neither call the experiment a success or a failure, but I can't say that for reasons outside of my knowledge, something happened there, but there is still the possibility that it occurred by chance (the more strange experiences you have the less inclined you are to consider them all to be due to chance, however, healthy skepticism can be very intellectually useful and the maintenance of your sanity is essential!).

Now, let's consider another experiment, an experiment into spirit contact. Mediumship is intellectually challenging as occult ideas go, because we have no hard and fast way of saying that spiritual beings actually exist. Sure, there are many people who believe that they do, and there is a multi-billion pounds this information and media entertainment industry based on the idea. Also there are many people who convincingly sell the idea that they have spirit guides and can communicate with the deceased. But what hard scientific evidence do we have? None at all! We have anecdotes, we do have the occasional empirical personal experiences, some of which are very dramatic (including my own!). But if we ask experimental occultists to be honest, we can't say that we know for sure whether they exist at all. All we have are beliefs and some people who say certain things "work", and that based only on anecdotes and unempirical experiences. So we are intellectually stuck, but we can still try and gain some experiences that are somehow connected to the ideas surrounding the folk myths about spiritual beings.

Let's say that you prepare yourself for training in meditation for a period of two months, slowly assembling the paraphernalia that you might need in terms of candles and "ritual artifacts" to create a religious ceremony that is part of a theological system that you were not threatened by. You go through the motions of performing the exercises, deliberately not caring whether results appear or not, just practicing the art of the meditative, spiritual, prayerful person, and then after a time, a result of sorts occurs.

What does it mean? Is it conclusive? Basically, no. The only thing that a strange experience can prove is that under some strange circumstances, some strange experiences happen and therefore there is no proof either way that the being in question has any reality at all. However, that should not stop the curious from continuing their experimentation.

It is possible to make one major intellectual mistake here, and that is to take things too literally, namely to believe that not only the spirit has objected existence, but also that the religion that you're practicing is the one and only true faith, that the God or Goddess in question is real, and that all the texts of the faith are to be considered to be trustworthy sources. This is the mistake of thought that religious people make when they have a visitation or any other kind of strange experience that has some kind of cultural connection to their faith.

Some personal experiences cannot be put down to delusion or health problems. But to maintain sanity, it is a good idea to show a strong streak of skepticism in your thinking when experiencing these things.

All of the world religions and occult practices have, at their core, altered states of consciousness. The varieties and types of altered states of mind vary greatly, and although we can gain some insight into them through academic research (e.g., brain wave frequencies), the rest of our research has to be through personal experience and through, unfortunately, researching the opinions of the various different spiritual people who have had them. Altered states of consciousness, such as those gained by meditation, become qualitatively different when there is a slight change in perception, attention or emotions. Learning to apply control of these things in various meditative states becomes part of your self-training. Do not be in a hurry to master them all, as progress is much more important than any apparent perfection that many members of the New Age world falsely claim to have. Also, it is virtually impossible to be able to maintain one's ability to reproduce the same state of mind time and time again, as with the passage of your life, your brain is always growing and developing, inserting more confounding variables into the equation on a regular daily basis.

People who try and rush to a team with some kind of supernatural skills do, in practice, drive themselves totally insane and even to the point of being a gangster to themselves and everyone else around them. So, don't! It is not a race, just another dimension to your life. The New Age world is full of people who tend to use language emphasizing quality when talking about apparent results. Sometimes this can make you feel that results of whatever type are easy and that the attainment of these altered states of consciousness will solve any life problem that you have. It won't! Try and keep all of the stuff as a hobby rather than a job, and it certainly isn't essential for this life nor the next!

Peter J. Carroll once wrote about two ways of achieving "gnosis," through both inhibitory exercises and excitory exercises. This suggests to me that one can start to enter altered states of consciousness through both slowing down and speeding up the brain's activity. So, that leads me to think about what it is that makes the altered state of consciousness. Was it the speed or some other function of the brain's activity? After playing with the strobe light mind machine for a while, I discovered that there was something called hemispheric synchronization, whereby activity on both left and right side of the brain resonates electrochemically at the same frequency. Could that be it? I played around with other concentration exercises and discovered that the mood associated with a deep mind machine session seemed similar to that of the deep concentration exercises. On top of that, practicing with the mind machine seemed to allow me to enter into those specific highly concentrated states of mind with greater ease, so keeping up with training is somehow important.

Next, I viewed some neurological documentaries which showed some strange events that occurred when a person was in a religious state of mind. The metabolic activity in the brain's organs changed to the point whereby the human individual loses to a degree a sense of self and starts to feel disassociated from the body and almost like they were one with something greater than themselves. I read more about the word gnosis and found some definition that it meant to experience a oneness with a similar concept. I thought more about the religious exercises and realized that if the religious state of mind was somehow strong or powerful enough, it could increase or reduce the rate of brainwave activity, depending on the nature of the technique deployed. It then might be able to create a sense of oneness with religious concepts such as God, Jesus, one of the four elements or any other spiritual concert. Was this the gnosis of the occultists? If so, it would make some sense that there is some kind of spectrum of altered states of consciousness that a person could train themselves into and would come under the loose category of "prayer."

Had I somehow become a believer in the power of prayer? No, but I had come to an understanding that maybe under some strange and rather hard to define circumstances, prayer did "something". Precisely what, I could not say. I did feel that I had stumbled on some kind of fact that was overlooked by both religious people and members of the New Age community, not to mention scientists.

All occult investigation is an unempirical, experimental, experiential personal art form and it does not constitute what could be called a science in the same sense as physics is a science. It shouldn't take too much intelligence to realize that using the term "science" when associated with occult matters has the capacity to promise more than it can deliver. Also, the term "body of knowledge" is likewise inappropriate, as we are dealing with subjective experiences. "Body of wisdom" would be closer to the mark, but it is not a wisdom that is universally true as some of the states of being involved in occult practices cannot be properly communicated accurately by the use of language.

Meditation is an important tool if you wish to eventually have some kind of strange experience that could be culturally (not scientifically) classified as Supernatural to any degree. It should, by my estimation, be run alongside any other tool of development that you use, such as those mentioned before and to come in this book. And again, it is a subject that becomes more and more complex and nuanced with subtleties the more of it that you do.

Does it have one singular purpose? That depends on what it is you are trying to achieve. If you think that relaxation is enough of a reason to do the exercise, then you will reach your goal very quickly, probably in a matter of months. However, did you just get a copy of this book to help learn to relax when merely drinking the right types of herbal tea or having a good social life and talking as friends would do that job more easily?

Just like with everything else in life, you might have your short-term goals, mid-term goals and long-term goals, and in order to reach the longer-term goals you may have to take yourself through different stages in order to get there. Just like if you were a person who did no physical exercise at all and wanted to be a marathon runner, you would have to start on a course of exercise to bring yourself up to a basic level of physical fitness, and then you would have to bring yourself up to a higher level of exercise, and higher still. The whole process taking a few years. Trying to rush into your first marathon run after a week's worth of jogging around the block may have some very detrimental effects on you, and you may end up being convinced that the exercise of running simply doesn't work. Try and research, generate your own program of study and exercises that you can do. Spend a period of time on each exercise before moving on.

The same is true with all forms of occultism as well as athletics. That is why a combination of both patience and perseverance is necessary. Also, you need to acknowledge that your brain and body will go through many changes as you practice. A beginner's task that you might do and gain some excellent results one year may become near impossible for you the next year. Revisit the older exercises, go back and don't feel ashamed that you are returning to the most basic exercises all over again. Practice and relearn what you used to know and enjoy the journey.

With the passage of time, and if you adjust the exercises that you do, maybe you can even gain seemingly religious experiences, even if you are an atheist.

It is my opinion that meditation is a neurological exercise more than a field goal one. It is attempting to get some kind of control over and subjective experience of the activity in the brain in a manner that is different to the waking state of mind through the use of psychological exercises.

Probably the simplest way of achieving something that can be regarded as an altered state of consciousness is a result of meditation, the use of mantra. Mantras are simply words or sounds that are repeated again and again when one is in, or trying to achieve, a meditative or hypnotic state. They can be words in your own language or another. You can (when alone at home!) mutter them to yourself out loud or just out of your breath, or if your concentration is strong enough, go over and over the mantra inside your own mind. Hold your concentration on the words or sounds without straining, make the sounds the focus of your attention seemingly automatically and try and get deeper into the state of concentration possibly to the point where you lose wearing this or other things around you.

Instead of just using the mantra, use emotions. Remember how it feels to have an emotion, use the concentrated state of mind that the meditation gives you to hold on to that emotion. Maybe design or create a mantra for the purpose of expressing the meaning of that emotion. if the emotion you wish to feel is love, maybe use a mantra made up out of the letters "el-oh-vee-ee- el-oh-vee-ee-el-oh-vee-ee-". make the experience even more powerful through the accurate and focused concentration on colors that have the same meaning as the mantra, such as rose quartz (pink).

There are many ways to do this and many attitudes that one can take to it, a slightly different attitude or state of mind when applied to visualization in meditation can have dramatically different results. One can do this to see how they feel when they are holding their attention on the object of meditation, or one can develop another state of mind, one that, for want of a better word, seems "open" or somehow receptive, seemingly changing the center of one's attention to receive something from the object of meditation and to see what appears in one's mind. You have to learn how to feel that openness. It can be described but it is another thing to have experienced it as an emotion or sensation in meditation. It seems at times as though the objects of contemplation have the capacity to communicate something to us, either symbolically through our visual imagination or somehow cognitively or emotionally. If one can learn that "open" state of mind, something strange can occur. You need to practice it to fully understand it.

Sometimes to assist in the visualization exercise, you may need to bring more energy into the brain in the form of oxygen. This requires breathing control. It is not always essential for all exercises that you do. We all have different bodies and brains so what is needed at one time for one person won't be needed either by the same person at another state on their journey or necessarily by anyone else at all. However, it is another one of those good habits to get into. Breathing in this manner is something that I have used for many different reasons in the past, including to help my body recover from having taken too much coffee when I was a student staying up late to finish an assignment!

It is cyclical breathing, in which you breathe in for the same period of time that you hold your breath once you have inhaled, and you exhale at the same duration, and then hold your breath with the lungs empty for the same duration prior to inhaling again.

Try to make sure that you don't do this in a manner that is uncomfortable. Don't strain yourself. Do it steadily. There are no hard and fast rules about this and you aren't going against the actual technique if you use a count of five or of two. For some reasons that I don't fully understand and haven't fully researched, the manner of breathing helps with the visual ability and does bring more oxygen into the bloodstream and therefore will help the brain to function. Try it and see. Maybe start your meditation and when you are ready to start the visualization, commence the breathing exercise and work on the visualization exercise. You may be surprised at how much easier the whole exercise gets.

It is easy if you read a New Age book to assume that the exercise in question that is being written about can be achieved as quickly as it takes to read the words on the page. This is a fallacy and it's worthwhile remembering that. Although I have given you a list of things to use for your visualization exercises, it is by no means a definitive list and if I was to provide some simplistic instructions, you might assume that just finishing off the tasks that I have listed would be all that is required to make you as great in an occultist as Merlin or as much of a miracle worker as Jesus Christ. It is actually much more complex than that and you will need to do some research, use your creativity and experiment.

And some of the older, more traditional occult texts and indeed in some more modern ones, there is the occasional mention of a search for spiritual truth. It's a subject that is full of issues in its own right. If I see a ghost, for instance, have I got objective proof of life after death or have I just had a strange experience that is culturally defined by certain apparently optical phenomena? It's impossible to say, so why not doubt the idea that approves life after death and just enjoy the experience?

Trying to investigate any form of spiritual reality from the comfort of your own mind has many issues. On the more positive side of things, if the world religions were the product of human thought, then maybe if you were to take something that is made of human thought (you!) and was to use meditation and inner Journeys to investigate its workings, I am sure that you would find some correlations between certain faiths and the things that arise in your own mind's eye. However, that is where the similarities do stop. The mind has a fantastical ability to play tricks on you. A slight change in the digestive system, maybe a touch of insomnia or a few bad experiences in life can set you into a state of misinterpretation or believing in something to a greater extent than you should have to. You may end up developing some beliefs that won't necessarily have the capacity to do you any good, such as thinking you are the reincarnation of a famous person, or maybe an alien from a distant galaxy. Some of these strange beliefs are not too pathogenic if they are mild or weak. However, some of these beliefs can get too much for the individual and they can start to do something silly or indeed out and out dangerous purely on the basis of what appears to be true based on these apparently real spiritual ideas.

I knew one lady who was an active meditator. At one stage in her life she started to have experiences that appeared to be angelic beings. She believed that they were real and didn't even try and doubt her experiences. Her lack of self doubt and self criticism led her to believe that she should trust these alleged spirits. This lack of doubt was very dangerous for her. As the years passed by, she trusted the spirits more and more. Eventually, these "spirits" were telling her that she was personally responsible for the evils in the world and that she would suffer in Hell for all eternity. One of them even told her to take more and more paracetamol. She was in serious danger of an overdose. She found it hard to take my advice (to go and see a psychiatrist) as the spirits were identifying themselves as great teachers such as Jesus Christ, the Archangel Michael, Buddha, Confucius and many others. These were holy people, so in her mind's eye she thought that they were to be highly respected and trusted. She had got herself into a vicious circle that was highly dangerous to her mental and physical health. One needs to learn the importance of doubt and to learn when you have had enough and need to stop for a while.

We also have to be careful about the way that literature and the media affect our perception of reality. I knew personally a young man who was fond of reading both the writings of well-known clairvoyants and science fiction books, but he had reached a stage of obsession with both and had come to the incorrect conclusion, as a result of his reading poor quality literature that made thoroughly unsubstantiated claims, that science-fiction was in fact the memories of past lives on other planets being remembered, and that all fiction stories were in fact scientific studies that we should regard as being factual. This most dangerous combination led him to think that if he was to, in meditation, visualize his whole body disintegrating, it would actually affect his physical body and he would be able to teleport to other regions in time and space. He attempted this as an experiment and didn't manage to get any result, funnily enough! I asked him whether he was surprised by this and he replied that he was, but was still highly convinced that his ceremonies had the power to unbalance the whole natural order of the universe. The poor man had driven himself clinically insane as a result of losing sight of reason.

It does concern me that these are individuals who are representative of a social, psychological and cultural demographic that is probably larger than we in the advanced and civilized West would like to think. Even more frightening, they seem to be just as numerous in our own educated nations as abroad. These individuals are primed and ready to propagate their beliefs and to think that they are doing so for the betterment of society. Some become completely diseased to the point of megalomania and believe that they should take over the world.

There needs to be more self-doubt in the New Age world, but we are often taught in schools, in our families when we were children and in the workplace that we should believe in ourselves, but many people stop there and think that believing in themselves is more important than thinking, or that self-belief means that we should believe everything that we think. The very idea that we should believe in ourselves exists to motivate lazy schoolchildren and to get apathetic salespeople to start making more money for the company through getting on the phone or getting out in the car and making sales. It is not an idea to take it to every area of life and should really be discarded at the school gate when the children leave education to enter into the real world. Too many people take the thinking that they were taught as a child into adult life.

But is there a way of investigating the seemingly spiritual without losing one's mind? If there is, it would have to be down to the way that we approach the subject and the exercises that we are going to do. Let's say that I wished to do a particular exercise that was well-known in occult circles, a pathworking exercise as it is sometimes called, a powerfully visualized journey performed in meditation in which it is believed by some that the occasional anomalous occurrence happens. Let's say for argument's sake, that I have already been practicing to agree with meditation and I have trained myself up to a sufficient level of proficiency and I wished to perform the exercise for a specific reason to contact an alleged spiritual entity.

I would start for the presupposition, that there is insufficient evidence to say that these things have any objective reality, but I accept that occasionally under some strange circumstances, some strange things happened. It is my desire to see whether I can trigger one of these strange occurrences. I take it as fact that even if I do have some strange experiences as a result of this exercise or sometime thereafter seemingly as a result of the exercise, that, although I can speculate for fun as to what the experience might mean, I can't prove, by any stretch of the imagination or by any methodology of reasoning, that the experience was indicative of any spiritual fact. The only real fact is that a strange experience may have happened and what it means I don't know and cannot know. At a stretch, I may wish to develop some weak theological beliefs as a result of the experience, but all that will do is to give me some DIY religion and not give me any facts of the way that the world works. I admit I may have touched upon some factor about the working of my mind, but what that is I cannot say as I don't actually know any environmental, physical and mental confounding variables will affect the result

301

dramatically. All I can do is perform the experimental experiential activity and see what happens. However, during the exercise, I will choose to enter into a state of suspension of disbelief through the use of theatricals that can come from any source that is comfortable to me and has some bearing on the operation at hand. These tools may be of a religious nature, or may come from any fictitious or real life source that seems appropriate, but, although to all intents and purposes, these tools will be sacred to the operation, figuratively speaking, after the activity is completed, I will have no compulsion to view them as anything other than normal ordinary everyday items. I certainly shall not be afraid of them and certainly shall not develop any superstitious beliefs about them. It is only during the operation at hand that they will have any significance. After the operation, I will return to my normal state of mind, being skeptical and secular.

So, let's say that the exercise in question is to contact the Spirit of Mercury, which in the Judeo-Christian occult tradition is the Archangel Raphael. I may do chanting beforehand with an altar setup that is simply two candles, one yellow and one blue, colors that are associated with Mercury in some writings, and in between the candles I may have the planetary symbol of Mercury drawn on a piece of paper. I will have already spent months saturating my mind with images of Mercury, watching films that are to do with the entity, contemplating religious art that might have an Angelic creature in it, looking as deeply as I can into what this entity might be. Maybe I will start the exercise sitting in a comfortable but upright position at the "altar" (probably just being my desk) staring with half-closed eyes at the Mercury symbol that is illuminated by the candlelight while chanting the syllables "rah-phay-yell-rah-phay-yell-rah-phay-yell-" over and over, slowly, reverently (if you can do it!) for about ten minutes to help still the mind and fill my mind with something that is by its nature raphael-ian. I will then close my eyes and create for myself a journey that is full of ideas that are mercurial.

Let's say that the "pathworking" (a name that is rather pretentious I know, but for the moment will suffice) has been well scripted by you, with a good beginning, middle and end. It has a good storyline and you have been, to a degree, rehearsing it as you have been writing it. Being skilled in meditation after a long period of self training, you are confident that the state of mind that you will go into will be sufficiently deep for you to make the visualization exercise a good suspension of reality in its own right.

Let's say the journey starts off with you being surrounded by a milky white mist that completely obscures vision. You then visualize the mist clearing and find yourself in a woodland, beside a rocky outcrop, maybe of the type that you might be familiar with. You try and visualize the scene as accurately as you can, knowing that you won't be able to get it perfect, but you try your best. Relaxed, focused attention.

Inside the rocky outcrop is a door, maybe old and made of gnarled wood with iron studs in it like you might find in an old church. You push the door open and step into a tunnel that is completely round, like a large drain pipe, but seemingly made by natural means. Its walls emanate a bluish yellow light and so you don't need any for illumination. Feel and visualize yourself walking through the tunnel, sense the damp and chilly nature of the tunnel, maybe even the moisture in the air. The tunnel leads to a chamber that seems to be like a scientist laboratory, but the scientific tools seem to be antiquated or maybe of a pre-Victorian nature, glass jars, brass clamps for the glassware, oil lamps instead of Bunsen burners. Everywhere there is a chemical aroma as if many years of alchemical experiments have happened in this room. At the far end, a man dressed in blue and yellow sits reading through some manuscripts. Ask him if there is anything he wishes to tell you. He may answer you or he may not. Thank him anyway and then leave his presence, going back through the tunnel, leaving through the door, allowing the mist to envelop you and then opening your eyes and, ideally, writing down as much of the experience as you remember. It can be fun, but it can also open your perception to the fact that maybe the exercise has more to it than meets your expectations. The things that you notice in the exercise, the things that you haven't scripted, those are the things to pay attention to.

When you were standing outside, were there any wild animals there? If so, what were they? What does that animal type mean? What color was the mist? Did the visualized landscape change to something that you didn't expect? What was the weather like? When you went through the tunnel, what did it look like and feel like?

There are many different dimensions to this particular exercise that can be interesting or useful in some manner or other. I once, early in my psychic career, did a reading for a man who was going abroad to a hot country and he asked me to read on the journey and what would happen. All I saw was rain and cold weather. He told me that I was wrong. But, within a few days, I had come down with one of the most appalling doses of influenza that I have ever had. Was my subconscious mind warning me about my own state of health before the illness had fully manifested itself? So, hypothetically, the weather that you see in your imaginary journeys are important to self understanding and self understanding of the mind-body connection that can occur when you do exercises like these. What about the journey into the tunnel, how could that be useful? After a particularly heavy few months of meditation, I opened a car boot and looked inside. For a brief moment, I hallucinated that the boot of the car was coated in slime. The hallucination then vanished as quickly as it had appeared, but shortly thereafter, I felt very nauseous. So, was there some kind of semantic meaning between the cavernous boot of the car and my stomach? And therefore, would there be some kind of connection between things that are seen in meditation and the body? Could you use this eventually, not for self diagnosis, but as a way of forewarning you of any minor health problems that you might have, but are unaware of? Quite possibly. However, this type of investigation has not been turned into a hard science, so please do not fall into the trap of trying to diagnose yourself with diseases. I also admit that at times it does seem like there is some kind of supernatural phenomena associated with some of the things that you might "see" in a pathworking, but that is even more hypothetical and even less empiricist than mind-body perception though exercises like this, so basically, don't worry about it.

When you actually got to the laboratory, did it look as you expected? If not, think about why not. Go through an in-depth period of introspection so as to ascertain why these things didn't appear as planned. Correlate the results of this visualization with your own personal history and life experience. What about the man who appeared at the end? Did he dress as anticipated, did he communicate with you, verbally or non-verbally, what was the meaning of what he communicated? Did he look like what you thought he might and if not, why not? Sometimes the characters that appear in the visualization do not at all correlate with your life experience at all and the messages that they seem to convey are unearthly and sometimes religious in nature. By all means take notes of them. After all, these experiences can be curious as they say something about us as human beings, but what they say at this stage in our limited understanding just down to speculation I did not fully crystallize into a hard science.

Humans in general have the capacity to jump to conclusions, something that we as a species really should have grown out of by now. We do this in accordance with the Outlook that we have developed often as a result of our upbringing and the sources of information that have influenced us. This is a problem that is at the core of the New Age movement, as well as many other movements that is present in our lives today. If a person was to have an anomalous experience in this pathworking exercise, they would attribute it to something that they believe in. Doubt or self-criticism rarely features in the assessment. But if you come to a conclusion, how do you know that you are right? How do you know that the assessment that you came up with his correct and indeed the sources of information that have led you to that conclusion are at all reliable? If you trace your thinking back far enough, you may well find that you're unsure and you are left in a state of ambiguity, of unknowing.

Unfortunately for us, that state of ambiguity is the right state to be in. There are always people who wish to take that ambiguity away and replace it with some kind of Illusion of knowledge.

Let's take another hypothetical example. An individual who does the above-mentioned pathworking exercise, but that person believes heavily in the spirit world. Something abnormal happens when they are going through the experience, the man in the laboratory speaks to the believer saying some words of wisdom. The believer would then assume that they have had some direct contact with the spirit world. Can this be true? Considering that we don't have empirical knowledge of the existence of the spirit world nor how it operates, that cannot be a wise thing to state as a claim. If a claim is unsubstantiated or unfalsifiable (testable by the standards of the natural physical sciences), then it will be considered in a dim light. As a truth claim, therefore, the idea that the enquirer really had contacted the spirit world and had participated in a conversation with Archangel Raphael himself would be daft. All one could say is that the experimenter has had a strange experience and can try and define that experience in some way or other, and it has some characteristics that modern folklore would call a communication with a form of spirit. That's all, just a strange experience. The experimenter might protest and say, "Well, what about all the people who say they have been to the spirit world and have found out?" Surely these apparently wise individuals would have to spend so much time in the spirit world in order to have that quantity of knowledge that they wouldn't have time for physical existence. There are people in my city who have lived and worked here all their lives and still

307

have very little knowledge of its history, geography or the administrative organizations that run the place, so how can we say that a person who has done some meditation has total knowledge of the alleged to spirit world? We can't. All we can say is that if they are being honest and accurate (and in the cases of many New Age authors, that is hard to believe), that all that has happened is that they had a strange experience and that's all. Surely these people are providing a disservice rather than a service to humanity? Also, if they are not trying to explain in great detail how they managed to generate the experience, and they are doing a secondary service to humanity, as if the experience is real (whatever the experience in question may be) it says something (as of yet, not understood) about what we as humans are, and are capable of. For this reason we have to have a great quantity of disbelief by the claims made by psychics, clairvoyants and occultists of all kinds.

Can we actually know for sure what any vision means? Not really. There are too many variables in the natural world for us to be able to make any real, hard and fast claims at all. It is easier in the examples of indigestion and influenza that I have mentioned above to be able to say that there was some kind of real and noticeable physical connection between what was seen in the "vision" and what was real in the physical world. How far can we take this? Not very far if we are to be accurate and honest. We could say that there is some kind of guidance or an indicator that has been put our way by the vision, but precisely what it means we cannot say. We have to be fortunate enough to be in a highly sound state of mind to be able to make sure that we don't lead ourselves astray and start to come to all manner of superstitious conclusions about what division might mean. We can try our best to objectively take notes, taking care to be as accurate as possible and to make sure that we don't delude ourselves to following our extrapolations too far, and then believing what we think might be correct. Generating a weak belief is one thing, generating a personal theology is another, stating that personal theology as if it were a fact is yet another and we must guard ourselves against it. We can only do that with the help of re-educating ourselves in reasoning.

If we were to use other New Age source books as a way of trying to find out about certain phenomena, we have to be even more careful. Humans are great at using words badly. We can make some errors in judgment just reading what others have written. Humans also cherry-pick certain ideas and use those ideas or words to justify any agenda. How often do we see this in religious groups when some passages of religious texts are used to justify slavery ownership, stoning adulterers to death or hatred of ethnic groups or groups of people defined by their sexual orientation? Apply your reflective reasoning to the New Age world knowing that the New Age world has a strong commercial aspect to it in which new ideological demographics are being created and recreated all the time. Do you think that some writings may be created either for the purpose of maintaining client bases, getting members of the crowd more impassioned about a subject so that they go out and evangelize for that movement or sector of the New Age business community? Could this happen at times through misrepresenting arguments for the purposes of undermining the authority of the opponent (committing a "strawman logical fallacy")? Naturally! But, also we find ourselves doing this and we can often find ourselves starting to believe that we have misrepresented, possibly to confirm a belief that we have had (which may be false). All of these contortions of thinking take us away from the facts. A strange experience has happened. What it means, we cannot be totally sure, but there is some strange excitement about these strange experiences, something that entices us to experience more of them.

Tarot and Divination

All card and tile games seem to have their ancestry in China. The Chinese used to play games using their money as playing pieces. These playing pieces eventually became our modern day cards, mah jong tiles and domino tiles. The Chinese money games started to move from the east to the west as a result of trade and conquest. The games that were played also evolved as cultures added their own special flavor, and likewise the imagery that appeared on the cards and tiles also changed with the times. The movement of card games picked up middle eastern ideas and imagery as the Mesopotamians created what could possibly be considered to be the first properly recognizable cards with suits in a design that looks a lot like what we have today. Middle eastern influences also make some people (myself included) think that there may be some kind of Jewish Kabalistic connection to the history of the cards. There is evidence of the ancient Greeks using a four suit system to the packs of cards and the fifth suit being the trumps. In the Ancient Greek times, the trumps were images of the Gods of Athens, pagan religion being, one might argue, the main form of popular culture of the time.

When card gaming entered into Europe, the decks developed Christian imagery, probably from the Triumph procession, a celebration of the victory of Christianity over Paganism and Christ's victory over death. Little is published these days about the Christian Triumph procession, but the characters in the Major Arcana of the Tarot, do still have some traditional religious overtones. The number of major arcana cards have changed a lot over the years and what the cards have been used for has also changed. Some nations banned the playing of games with tarot cards, not because the Tarot was evil or of the Devil, but because it was considered blasphemous to do gambling with cards that had Christian imagery on them.

Tarot as a game is still being played and, especially in these times, with mass internet communication, there is even a revival movement to bring tarot game playing into the mainstream. This can only be regarded as a good thing, as it will help to make Tarot more commonplace and will remove the fear that certain superstitious people have over the cards themselves.

But what of divination, fortune telling and other allegedly occult pursuits? Does tarot still have a role to play there? Definitely.

But what is the history of divination? Well, although there may be artifacts of archaeological importance that we can refer to, we still can't say how they may have been used at all. What we can say, knowing human nature the way that we do, is that humans will always try and make sense of patterns and if there is a device that creates patterns, humans may exploit that for some reason.

What we can say about divination is that there has been evidence of cards with images of nature that was accompanied by books that had the apparent meanings of the cards included with it that was discovered in Germany. The find was centuries old, probably medieval in origin. So the new-agey tarot packs and reading cards that we see in certain bookshops of certain types these days are in fact continuing an ancient form of popular culture. Divination cards are part of our European popular culture, have been for centuries, and are a small part of what defines us as Europeans.

The application of meanings to symbols is what we as humans do. Think about what you are doing at the moment, reading. You are just looking at a group of symbols that have been culturally used for the purposes of communication of a message in a certain way. That is all. Your culture defines the meanings of the symbols, and the way that you use them, and you go right ahead and read the message in front of your eyes. A balance sheet or a counter receipt uses different symbols and uses them in a different way. In the history of tarot, there are some tales of messengers falling mute and unable to pass on a message of political importance to a baron and then pulling out a pack of cards and using the characters therein to express a message. One could guess that the messenger might also have used a complex system of charades, probably made up on the spot. In the 19th century, in parties, people would treat tarot as a party game and deal out the major arcana cards and explain with their wit and charisma why they were dealt that card. So, with creative thought and intelligence, one can use images to express a message from one person to another as a form of prop or aide to storytelling. To use any group of images and symbols in a widely diverse number of ways, one must have the intelligence and flexibility to be able to see those symbols from different points of view depending on the usage in which you wish to put them. As such, one cannot just give the tarot, a set of rune stones or any combination of divinatory symbols with any singular meaning. Nor should we consider that there is only one approach to the cards or symbols. We have to do something that most humans find difficult, namely to think about what we are doing and to make some intelligent decisions as to what we are going to do and how to use the cards.

Within the past three hundred years with the development of spiritualist and occult movements, certain French occultists started getting their hands on tarot packs and doing what humans do, seeing patterns and using their creativity to fill the gaps. Elipias Levi (Alphonse Louis Constant) was one of the first people to draw a parallel between the suits, the pip cards, the major arcana and the tree of life from the Kaballa. This not only paved the way for tarot to become a form of religious instruction for pagan revivalist movements, but also changed the use of tarot from being more of a game to being better suited for divination (or the expression of ideas and messages). Crowley, a very misinterpreted occultist, gave the first beneficial instructions on how to perceive the tarot and the tree of life for contemplative purposes. Namely, to apply one's own life experiences to the various semantic meanings that are present in spheres and paths of the tree of life and therefore, by inference, the tarot.

In practice, there is no restriction on what can be used as a divination tool, how any given divination tool can be used or on the point of view that a tool of divination can be perceived, including atheistic points of view. However, one should use one's intelligence to ascertain which point of view one is going to use, to make sure that one can choose a point of view that makes sense, to be open when one is getting any messages, but to be intensely skeptical and analytical after the experience has happened without falling into the trap of developing beliefs. For instance, some divination exercises require no tools apart from meditation and visualization exercises, however, some people make the most obvious mistake of thinking that the experience has given them an answer, when in reality, what it has done is provided an experience which raises more questions. Divination is more about getting experiences that assist in the creative problem-solving process rather than getting answers which are cut in stone.

We have to think carefully about the context in which the symbols are being used and how we go about using them. The sounds you make when you are on the phone with someone, the phonetic syllables, are just symbols, but they can be culturally used to communicate a message. The more simple symbols of musical notes articulated by musical instruments or digital music software and played to you serve to tell a story and make an effect happen in you, a change in mood. But if you communicated to your friends over the phone by music, you would be considered to be insane. Also, have you noticed that the attitude that you take when receiving any communication dramatically affects your ability to understand the message? If you are up late surfing the net and reading blogs, if you are overtired or emotionally distraught, you will read the information and get a totally different message then when you are in a different mood, have slept well and are basically in a different state of mind. So be careful when you are trying to interpret any information at all. Example, if you are approaching this text from the point of view of someone who is interested in the supernaturalist ideas, you may be thinking that I am trying to explain the subject from a supernaturalist standpoint, which would be incorrect. If you are approaching this text with the presupposition that the author is a supernaturalist and therefore he must be daft, you will probably be laughing to yourself thinking, "How can anyone believe that rubbish?" when essentially I am not explaining the subject from that point of view, so you would also be wrong and reacting in a way that is very unintelligent to some rather objectively written text. Try and pay attention to the information that is being given and leave the presuppositions at the door! This is a very important attitude to have if you want to look into the world of divination, and even if you want to do any form of intelligent assessment of any ideas that are out there in the world.

My own personal opinion is that learning any form of divination is a lifelong task. I have about 20 years' worth of personal history with tarot and on reflection I seem to have gone through a series of stages for the purposes of developing the way of thinking that I believe a good diviner could use. I don't believe that there is a fixed structure that one needs to go through, and I certainly don't believe that there is anyone singular "actual technique" (and to be quite frank I tend to look down on people who think that way), but in retrospect, I can say that there are two types of stages that I have been through, firstly the academic or intellectual, and secondly the introspective and creative. But before any of those stages can occur, I had to get over any fear and dread that I had with the tarot or any form of apparent or alleged occult ideas. I then had to move away from literalist or dogmatic interpretations of anything. Which, if you are in the company of New Age people, can be hard. So, I do recommend that you either move away from New Age circles or don't tell them that you are interested in improving your skills. If word gets out, some twisted individual who is still getting over having been bullied in a church many decades back, or who has some other issues be they psychiatric or just neurotic, will probably make your life much less comfortable than it is. New Agers make claims, it would be more profitable for you to ignore the claims and just think about what you can work out from experience and intellectual assessment of experiences and not through looking for corroboration of any particular belief system.

The next stage is to go through a period of researching the different interpretations of the symbology of the tarot or of any other system of divination that you might be interested in. Don't rush. This is no race. Any source can help with this, but one with just one point of view would be useless. There is too much punditry in the New Age world anyway, too many people trying to sell their own cult or religion and trying to get you to become a follower. That is another reason why it is worthwhile being skeptical of people's claims to anything. Look into the history of magical symbols, the way that a shape is used, the difference between the vertical line and the horizontal line, the difference between a square and a circle and a triangle, what they all traditionally meant and what humans make of these shapes religiously and intellectually. Symbolism is there to communicate a message. Learn the language that the creators of any type of symbology are trying to create. Spend a bit of time on one set of symbols, then move to another. Build up an understanding or a relationship with each combination of symbols. Look at how different religions and cults use these things and interpret them. This can be a confusing exercise after a while, because you may be tempted to think that there is no singular meaning for any color, shape or symbol. Unfortunately, you might be right, but the intellectual stage seems to be essential to get a good and well-rounded understanding of what the cards could mean. After a time, a set of meanings that you are comfortable with will start to present itself to you, but that could take a long time indeed. There is no rush. One could argue again that this is a stage that carries on forever but needs to be focused on much more in the early days of learning the personal experiential experimental art form that is divination.

This intellectual stage is quite important, but it really isn't something that you should get into argument with other people about, as you will just end up getting into arguments about different dogmas about what various symbols mean and the importance to you of becoming a diviner will become downgraded to a lower level. Instead of trying to master the art form, you become obsessed with winning a debate, and debates don't assist anyone in getting closer to the truth, they usually just devolve into arguments about who is the best at misrepresenting the other person's position and therefore become completely useless when it comes to being a searcher for the truth. Keep your research to yourself.

Next, you need to get a handle on using intuition. Intuition is a word that is misused too much, especially around New Agers, so be careful of what people say about that. If you have done the intellectual stage of research into the symbology of the tarot or similar system, you will have already filled the mind with a mass of ideas. That is good, but now the consciousness must learn how to let some selective meanings come to the fore all by themselves and that is where one needs to start altering your own mind, training yourself to get to that stage whereby meanings flow, stories can start telling themselves and you can react spontaneously to a complex combination of symbols that are presented to your senses when in a divinatory setting and context.

Without not only giving yourself an excellent education in how to reason and also giving yourself an excellent personal history of a wide variety of meditation techniques, you cannot become a diviner. You need to have the education so that you can learn the most important intellectual skills in the world, to be self-critical and to see any issue from a wide variety of different points of view without having presuppositions or jumping to conclusions, and you need the experience in meditation to increase the creative, introspective and intuitive parts of your nervous system, thus to give you new skills of thinking. If you do not do these things, you will be the poorest diviner in the world.

Meditation is all important, but so too is the skills of thinking as if you were having to think on your feet and to force yourself to think faster and to break down the impressions that you will undoubtedly receive as a result of doing the divination exercise.

The best varieties of meditation include mantra, prayer and visualization, but it is also essential once you have been practicing a technique for a while to move on to a new way of doing these things so that you can get greater flexibility of psychological states.

One of the many things that can happen doing a divination exercise is some kind of mental phasing out, a moment when you start to get some vivid imagination, a kind of very mild hallucination not much stronger in quality than a daydream, but it seems to come to you very quickly and passes as quickly as it has come. It often seems like an irrelevant piece of visualization, but if you then discuss it with the enquirer, it can sometimes be connected directly to something that they have been experiencing or doing in the recent past. It is one of those strange experiences that we have no real explanation for, but is still some kind of spooky apparent corroboration of the skill of the diviner. For one to feel comfortable with these temporary slips of the mind, one needs to get used to changing the state of consciousness, the actual brain waves themselves. Practice with visualization will give you the ability to use your visual cortex much more and from that point, you will be able to start putting all the meanings that you have accumulated through the symbolical research that you have already done. Again, this is another lengthy process and one can't rush it, but one can start to notice subtle ways in which one is learning how to use this self-training. For instance, after a while, you may find yourself solving problems in your mind's eye without using words. This is a much faster method of data processing in the brain. It's very useful if you want to be able to think on your feet, so long as you have also, through your education and life experience, developed enough skills at verbally expressing yourself to articulate the ideas that are in your mind. Don't give up on the use of a vocabulary though, as we use language to help structure our thoughts.

Tarot spreads are a method of structuring the story that the reading is telling the tarot reader. No matter what spread you use to provide a perspective on any particular issue or question, it has to make some kind of sense. The positions that you use need to represent something that is part of the story. Unfortunately, many people lack the creativity to be able to develop their own tarot spreads. So, if you are going to be a good diviner, it would make some sense to study other spreads that people have used in the past. Much occult research has a component of researching traditions that others have used to attempt to bring about some kind of strange experience anyway. Although it might seem silly, start reading books on ordinary fortune telling, the kind of books that a serious researcher might not want to use, but play is important and can help to release some creativity. I am sure that if an individual had access all the time, at each and every waking moment to all the knowledge that he or she has managed to accumulate throughout all of his or her life, being a diviner, no matter what attitude one takes to the subject of divination would be a breeze, a walk in the park. However, as there are no super humans with memories, intellectual abilities and qualities of emotional control that are quite that powerful, we have to reply upon other ways of dredging up the knowledge that we have. The processes that l have already outlined start to pays dividends with the passage of time as more and more knowledge becomes accumulated throughout your life.

When we are using tarot symbolism and the symbolism of (nearly) any form of divination tool, we are using some kind of random arrangement of symbols to create a message. It is possible (and likely considering much of my experience as a diviner) that the same message can be obtained despite the fact that many different combinations of tarot cards actually turn out. The cards are (in varying degrees depending upon the tarot pack in question) remarkably complex in the possible meanings that they can portray, often seemingly self-contradictory if one was to just rely on some kind of book meaning of the cards. There is no singular meaning for any card, and just as one lady might get a positive message about her love life with the devil, hanged man, lighting struck tower and death card all in a row in that order, another lady might get another message that is completely different as a result of the same cards coming out. The word that is used to describe these exercises is often called "psychic" but so many people don't realize that the word "psychic" just refers to something of the mind and not some kind of paranormal power. I would say that it is, in this context, more like a psychological skill that seems to develop with the passage of time and part of whose nature and origin we cannot say anything about because we as humans have no real knowledge of these things. We can speculate until the cows come home about the astral energies and the like, but that has to remain just speculation of a religious nature and not a hard and fast scientific fact of the way that the world works. Why is it that in some divination sessions I can get images appearing to the visualization that seems to have some kind of direct connection to something that is of the enquirer and specific to them and no one else? That I can't say. I can hypothesize that all the years of accumulated self-training and brain training that comes from doing the mind altering exercises that are religious in nature have some brain altering effect, to bring the reasoning faculties of the brain and the visual imagination together to the point whereby on a subconscious level, one processes information very quickly and it then gets played back to one in one's own visual cortex creating the hallucination. Or maybe it is something to do with astral energies after all. Or maybe a green gnome on Proxima Centuri belched and that created some telepathic effect (sorry, couldn't resist, that stuff about the green gnome was a joke by the way, had to mention that just in case you were the type of reader who takes everything that is written on face value). The bottom line is that we just don't know. On top of that, I also don't know all of the ins and outs of the computer that I am using to write this essay, but the fact that I don't understand it, certainly isn't going to stop me from using it and seeing what I can do with it.

So, if we are going to use tarot spreads that we have discovered in a not-so-old and dusty volume that we have picked up in a second-hand book shop, why are we using it? Is it because we have heard that the author in question was a "great" reader, or occultist or magician? Hopefully not. If we are to read the tarot, we could be using it to see how our self-training and our ability to connect ideas has developed, to see whether we are capable of creating a pattern using the cards dealt out at random to answer something in a way that is allegorical (you certainly won't find the cure to your irritable bowel syndrome or any other disease in a reading, so don't go looking for a medical cure in any reading or from any reader!).

Use a tarot spread, one that you have learned or one that you have developed to paint a picture. A good playwright knows that he needs to have different characters in a story, different stage sets and different theatrical props to portray the story. Your spread has positions, each position acts like a character in the story, its position in retrospect to the other positions in the spread is somehow connected to the nature of their role in the story, the progression of the positions to cover future events are also part of the story and so on and so forth. The cards themselves are indications of the character, rank or nature of the thing that is in that position in the story. A mercurial card in a position that has a meaning relating to a character will have a different meaning to a mercurial card that is in a position that is in relation to a vocation or the feelings that a person has with another person. On top of that, what happens in the mind of the reader will have an effect that can completely go contrary to any meaning of what "mercurial" might mean and thus can lead you as a would be reader in a position of potential despairing about what readings are about anyway, that is if you can't get the intellectual complexity of what l am trying to convey to you.

I once described tarot reading as a personal art form in which the question from the enquirer interacts with the mind of the reader creating two parts of a conversation and the third part of the conversation was within the symbols in the cards. You can't get the full gist of a conversation by just looking at what one person says in the conversation, so why is it that people try and simplify what a tarot reading is though assuming that some simplistic and literalistic meanings of the cards are all that you need to know?

Unfortunately, there are always members of our species who desire to take away that ambiguity and replace it with superstition and simplistic literalism. Fiction authors make their living more through finding an emotional need and then satisfying it then by providing good entertainment, politicians and religious people (more so in the New Age than any other combination of denominations) make it their job to minister to their flocks emotional needs, atheist pundits build their careers through misrepresenting arguments to make their cheeky followers feel like they are fighting for a cause, and humans wander further and further away from the search for the truth. Please try and look beyond that!

When you are researching spreads or layouts, see it as an intellectual exercise and not one that is just based on acceptance. Think about the quality of story that you want the reading to express, the characters in the play if you will. When I was studying to be an accountant, I learned that there are different qualities of knowledge that are needed for different things and as such when you are creating a reading or choosing the divination style that suits you, think about the quality of assumed information that the reading is supposed to be giving you. If a spread doesn't help much, then think about how you can change it. If you go on well with a spread that is rather psychoanalytical, but you want to use it to answer relationship questions, think about how you could adjust it to fulfill the needs of two people and not just one. How would you adjust it to take into account a third party as in an adulterous affair? How would you adjust it to take into account issues relating to property and money in a divorce case? If you are the diviner, then create your own traditional spreads, but make sure that they make sense and can represent the forces that you are assuming exist in the setting of a divination reading.

When I designed the principal relationship tarot reading that I use in my work, I based it on some very simple ideas, one position (with two cards) signifying the enquirer, one position (again with two cards) signifying the person that the enquirer was wanting the reading upon, one position (with one card) for what I called the forces between them, the nature of the connection that they had. These five cards gave a snapshot of the here and now. I then extended the reading by a further three cards to signify the progression of their relationship over the coming time periods of short-term future, mid-term future and long-term future. Usually I kept these time frames specifically vague, but sometimes I would regard them as being up to three months, up to six months and up to nine months (or over six months) respectively. However, what precisely the time periods meant, I would leave up to the reading to explain to me intuitively. The process is simple, as simple as offering a good way of starting a rather intricate exercise of reason, introspection, collation of ideas and explanation. It always starts with asking the enquirer their first name and date of birth and then the relationship question. If they don't give me the first name of the person I want them to read upon, I asked them for their first name. It seems to give me some more of a feeling of familiarity with him (despite the fact that I have never met them, and they could even be on the other side of the world for all I knew). Then I ask for the question about the one that is enquired about and the rest of it is just up to the reading itself and for me to try and decode the meaning of what the reading seems like it is trying to explain to me and to give that in context with the question using all my skills of personality to bring about the right explanation for the enquirer. Sometimes the enquirer asks a question of what requires a different state of mind, so that is where my skills of meditation come into play and I try to change my center of attention, as it reaches forward or backward in time, or to a different location on the face of the planet to try and get answers. When I do this, is my soul really traveling in time and space to find an answer? I don't think we can say either way. But sometimes it definitely feels like it. However, it could equally be that the exercise in this context is more about opening up the mind to different possibilities and making sure that any hidden cognitive skills that I have can get activated and can become part of the problem solving process. Either way, I do tend to get many customers coming back to me time and time again telling me how accurate I was. So, I guess I must be doing something right.

In conclusion, I think you can see that although to create some kind of strange phenomena, something of a religious nature may need to be used (such as mind-altering meditation or the self-hypnosis exercise of prayer and ritual), but it is stupid in the extreme to assume that a religious explanation for the phenomena when it happens is justifiable. Members of New Age communities often state that their "Magick works," but are often most resistant when you suggest to them that they should prove their claim that their magick works through being quarantined, getting them infected by every deadly disease on the face of the planet and then attempting to cure themselves of the diseases before 9 a.m. the next morning.

Strange experiences do happen. My personal experience dictates this. Although I can develop weak beliefs about the way that the universe seems to operate, I can't state these as hard and fast facts of the natural world, but I can encourage people to experiment and explore. Magick, if it exists as a practice at all, is a personal experiential experimental art form and not a hard science. If New Agers wish to use the "art and science" definition by Aleister Crowley, they must be able to demonstrate pure and perfect scientific thought, which they do not do.

If, at any point in the future, psychic research (in this context I am referring to sci phenomena, things currently regarded as paranormal) is to become more scientific, it is essential that the religious component be removed from occultism for all time. Strong truth claims also need to be obliterated completely from occult and New Age culture and modern Pagan religions should be dissuaded from using magic as something to frighten people with in order for them obey or to convert them to the pagan faiths.

For Bulls coach, God is no game (excerpt)

By Phil Jackson

Excerpt from "For Bulls coach, God is no game,"
then-Chicago Bulls head coach Phil Jackson
interviewed on religion by sportswriter Michael
Hirsley of the *Chicago Tribune*, April 27 1990,
Section 2, Page 8. This is the seminal and ultimate
quote of the piece, spaced for effect.

"I've always liked the concept

of God being

beyond anything that the
human mind can conceive.

I think there is a
pantheistic-deistic-
American Indian
combination religion
out there for Americans.

That rings true to me."

Souls, Gods, and Afterlives in a World of Matter

By Douglas M. Stokes

Douglas M. Stokes received a BA (*magna cum laude*) from Harvard University and a PhD in experimental psychology from the University of Michigan. He was a frequent contributor to the academic literature on parapsychology and published three books on the subject: *The Nature of Mind* (1997), *The Conscious Mind and the Material World* (2007), and *Reimagining the Soul* (2014). He was published widely in parapsychological journals as well as in skeptical journals such as the *Skeptical Inquirer*.

Introduction

Modern scientists and philosophers appear to be finally abandoning the untenable position of radical, eliminative materialism like proverbial rats leaving a sinking ship. This trend is further exemplified in the recent anthologies *The Waning of Materialism* (edited by Koons and Bealer),[1] *After Physicalism* (edited by Göcke),[2] and *Beyond Physicalism* (edited by Kelly, Crabtree, and Marshall[3]).

There also appears to be a renewed interest in the soul "concept" in mainstream philosophy and science, as witnessed by the many recent books bearing the word "soul" as parts of their titles, such as Baker and Goetz's *The Soul Hypothesis*,[4] Goetz and Taliaferro's *A Brief History of the Soul*,[5] and Humphrey's, *Soul Dust: The Magic of*

Consciousness.[6] At the same time, the mountain of evidence amassed by neuroscientists over the past few decades demonstrates the fundamental and intricate dependence of memories and personality traits on the state of the physical brain. See the recent anthology *The Myth of an Afterlife*[7] for a detailed review of these findings. In view of this evidence, it seems unlikely that you would be able to survive death with some portion of your memories and other personality elements. intact, as in the depictions of the afterlife in many religious traditions as well as in parapsychological investigations of mediums, ostensible cases of reincarnation, electronic voice phenomena." etc.

Physicalism, the doctrine that the world consists of particles of matter-energy obeying the laws of physics (or some suitable modifications thereof) has become the ascendant metaphysical *weltanschauung* of modern Western science. Most scientists take it for granted that there is no room in this worldview for the notions of souls, gods or afterlives Rather the universe consists of material particles careening around in blind obedience to the laws of physics.

This article explores the nature of souls, afterlives, and possible gods that would be compatible with modern physicalistic science, within the context of philosophies such as pandeism.

Survival of Personality Elements.

I have reviewed the evidence for personal survival (i.e., the survival of death of personality elements such as memories, thoughts and emotions) in my book *Reimagining the Soul.*[8] This evidence includes apparent messages from the departed received through mediums, the recollection of past lives, out-of-body experiences, apparitions and ghosts, electronic voice phenomena and so forth. It should be noted that the survival of such personality elements would represent forms of information transfer that are inexplicable under modern theories of physics and are consequently rejected by modern science.

The evidence for the survival of personality traits is largely anecdotal in nature and in most cases is subject to alternative, more skeptical explanations that will be discussed in more detail below. For this reason, psi effects such as telepathy and precondition and other paranormal processes are largely excluded from this analysis, which is directed at conceptions of souls, afterlives, gods and deities. that are consistent with mainstream physicalistic science.

The Dependence of Mental States on Brain Activity

Neuroscientists have amassed a mountain of experimental evidence demonstrating the intimate dependence of mental states on brain activity. Much of this evidence is presented in the compendium *The Myth of an Afterlife*, edited by Martin and Augustine.[9] In view of this evidence, it is unlikely that personality traits or memories survive the death and dissolution of the brain.

Modern Physicalism

Consciousness Denial. For over a century, the mainstream philosophical and scientific position has been that the only true reality is that of the material world as described by modern scientific theories. This view of the world appears to allow no room for consciousness, souls, or spirits to influence the behavior of matter, including human bodies, which are merely collections of material particles whose behavior is almost completely, albeit probabilistically, governed by the laws of physics. In the words of the philosopher Gilbert Ryle, there is simply no place for a 'ghost in the machine.'[10] Some have suggested quantum indeterminism may provide such a window for the soul. but hardcore materialists have argued that quantum events are for all practical purposes completely determined by the formalism of quantum mechanics, leaving little room for any kind of free will based on quantum events. It should be noted that some parapsychologists have reported evidence that conscious observers may be able to influence the outcomes of quantum processes. However, these experiments are largely rejected by mainstream scientists, based on their inability to replicate the parapsychologists' claimed effects.[11]

Subscribers to the materialist view of the mind have gone so far as to deny the very existence of consciousness itself. In the first half of the twentieth century, the entire field of experimental psychology was held in thrall to the doctrine of behaviorism as articulated by John Watson and B. F. Skinner, which in its extreme forms denied the existence of mental events altogether.[12] I have heard it said that the fastest way to rise into academic prominence is to propose an absurd theory and defend it at all costs. As the theory comes under attack, one's fame and citation rates will skyrocket.

Skinner and Watson, incidentally, are by no means the last modern thinkers to deny the very existence of private conscious experience, or "qualia" in the terminology of philosophers. The prominent materialist philosopher Daniel Dennett has asserted that 'contrary to what seems obvious at first blush, there simply are no qualia at all.'[13] This point of view is called eliminative materialism. Some modern scientists and philosophers, such as Daniel Dennett,[14] Susan Blackmore,[15] Thomas Metzinger,[16] Paul Churchland,[17] his wife Patricia Churchland,[18] and Bruce Hood,[19] continue to deny the very existence of continuing selves, or "Cartesian theaters," as these self-proclaimed "skeptics" disparagingly call them. The self, these "skeptics" maintain, is a merely a convenient "story" we tell ourselves in an attempt to render our experiences coherent and consistent. As such, the self is an entirely fictional concept, and "we" are nothing more than the scattered contents (fleeting sensations, thoughts, and emotions) of "our" minds.

The philosopher Galen Strawson calls the period of the hegemony of this view (that consciousness does not even exist), which reigned over psychology and the philosophy of mind from the 20th century and continues until this very day, the "Great Silliness."[20]

To most people the existence of a continuing self is immediately given and cannot be doubted. Any theory that denies the existence of any centers of consciousness is quite simply wrong. Such selves are an integral part of our essential existence.

It should also be noted that Bernard J. Baars, a prominent theoretical neurobiologist, has provided considerable evidence for the existence of a "global workspace" in the mind in which contents of various subsystems are melded together.[21] This global workspace is very similar to the "Cartesian

Theater" disparaged by Blackmore, Dennett and their ilk.

If Blackmore and Dennett are correct, there is no need to worry about whether the self will survive death. Indeed, the "self" does not even survive from moment to moment and in fact does not even exist at all.

Modern Panpsychism. Perhaps contra Ryle, the ghost may in fact be the machine or part of the machine. There appears to be a growing acceptance of the doctrine of panpsychism among philosophers and scientists, which posits that all matter and energy possess consciousness or awareness. One recent example of such a convert is the prominent neuroscientist Christof Koch.[22] Koch is well known for the reductionist (materialist) theories of consciousness he developed in concert with the Nobelist Francis Crick, co-discoverer of the structure of DNA.[23]

The increasingly popular philosophical doctrine of panpsychism finesses the seemingly intractable philosophical problem of accounting for how consciousness could arise from insensate matter, It didn't. It was there all along. It was there at the Creation (i.e., Big Bang) and perhaps even before that (as part of whatever collective mind or agent set up the current laws of physics and then somehow caused an explosion to make them so).

Under the panpsychist view, each proton or electron in your body possesses some form of awareness. In fact, under the well-established theory of quantum mechanics, these particles are each entangled with a large number of particles spread out over a wide region of space, and their behavior is governed by a complex wave function that takes these entanglements into account. In other words, these particles respond to (and thus may be said in some sense to be aware of) other events occurring over a relatively wide region of spacetime. Many of these particles, such as protons, are essentially immortal.

Persistence of the Self. We experience ourselves as simple, indivisible centers of consciousness. Could you in fact be something like a proton? If so, it is likely that you entered your body well after your birth, as the material particles in our bodies are continually being recycled, and it is estimated that they are almost completely replaced after seven years or so. Some estimates suggest that the matter in one's brain is completely replaced in one month or so.[24] The fact that you remember events that occurred more than more than one month ago may be due to the fact that these memories are stored in patterns of brain activity and neural connections that serve as "notebook" reminders of events in the remote past. Thus, if you are, say, a proton or something like a proton, it is likely that you will exit from your body long before its death. In this case, the afterlife would be whatever system of material particles you become "stuck in" after you escape your present body, whether it be an animal, a plant, or part of a circling cloud in the atmosphere of Saturn's moon Titan.

If each of us does has a self that endures from moment to moment, from day to day, and year to year (however much it may be extinguished at death), then that self cannot be identical with any specified collection of material particles. Yet, you perceive that you are the same self you were several months ago. If this perception is correct, then you cannot be identical to any particular collection of material particles, including your present physical body. Indeed, you have already survived the death of many physical bodies within your present lifetime.

The Death of Determinism. The Newtonian clockwork universe that still underpins the world view of the majority of today's reductive materialists was actually overthrown a century ago with the development of quantum mechanics. In quantum mechanics, the future state of the universe is not completely determined by the present state. Rather, the present state may give rise to many possible futures with macroscopic differences among them, such as the fate of Schrodinger's hapless cat, whose life or death depends on a single quantum event. Under this widely-accepted and highly-verified model, a nonmaterial mind might conceivably be able to select which of these possible futures will actually occur. Thus, there may indeed be some room for a ghost in Ryle's machine.

However, as noted above, many mainstream physicists maintain that, at the level of brain processes, quantum-mechanical processes are essentially deterministic.

Gods, Afterlives and Souls. Various concepts of the afterlife will be examined. A mountain of evidence amassed by neuroscientists over the past few decades demonstrates the fundamental dependence of memories and personality traits on the state of the physical brain. As already noted, some modern panpsychists[25] assert that elements as small as a single neuron or a single elementary particle may house centers of consciousness that are entangled with (aware of) wide regions of brain activity as well as external events.

There may be a hierarchy of such centers of consciousness, each contained within the next (e.g., an electron, an atom, a molecule, an organelle, a cell, an organ, an organism, a country, and beyond). Such entities were called "holons" by Arthur Koestler.[26] Several scientists[27] (e,g., Hölldobler and Wilson), have proposed the existence of collective minds or consciousnesses, such as that of an ant colony or that of the Internet combined with all its users. Research with split-brain, cortically-blind and hypnotized subjects suggests that each human body may be associated with multiple centers of consciousness. Many of these centers likely fall under ,the delusion that they are the sole center of consciousness "in charge" of the body.

Evidence for the well-known "anthropic principle" in cosmology suggests that the laws of physics and the initial state of the universe appear to be fine-tuned to allow emergence of conscious observers. This suggests that the creating agents (if any) may even have played a role in designing the fundamental laws and initial conditions of the universe to enable the evolution of, or at least the possibility of, conscious beings. To avoid circularity, one might suppose that, at least initially, such creative agents inhabited a region or realm that lies outside our own spacetime continuum. If so, these creative agents might collectively be thought to be essentially playing the role of god or gods in a deistic universe (in which the gods do not intervene in the universe once it has been created, but allow the universe to unfold in accordance with the specified laws of physics and the initial conditions set by the creating entities). Under such a deistic conception of the creators, the gods or creators merely observe material universe as it unfolds without intervening in its outcomes. Under the theistic conception of god, the creators actively intervene in the universe, perhaps by altering or suspending the laws of physics locally in order to achieve a desired outcome

God may be akin to a introductory calculus student who types in a random set of equations (say those of general relativity) and initial conditions into a (hyperdimensional) graphing calculator to see what will happen. In this scenario, the role of God is played by the lowly student, and the laws of physics by the equations and initial conditions selected by the student godling, and the universe is comprised of the four-dimensional graph so generated. Please note this version of the universe corresponds to the timeless block universe of relativity theory, in which past present and future are equally present in a timeless array of events, analogous to the spacetime continuum of relativity. To accommodate quantum theory (which is incompatible with general relativity by the way) a stochastic (random) element could be introduced into the equations)

In the graphing calculator example above, the plight of a primitive soul might be modeled by a point-like center of consciousness (perhaps an proton moving along a branch of the graph, which would comprise the trajectory, or "worldline" of the point consciousness, for those of you somewhat conversant with relativity theory). Such a moving point-soul might be expected to experience a sense of "time flow" in which it successively experiences the events along the chosen branch of the graph, as opposed to the timeless, static array of events that comprises relativistic spacetime. Such a moving point-soul, might experience a succession of events on the selected curve, emerging from the future, briefly becoming the present, and then receding into the past.

From the perspective of an observer outside the universe (such as the creator/student contemplating the graph in our graphing calculator example), the universe might be experienced as a static, timeless array of events (i.e. the graph), in which there in no distinction between past, present and future. This would be analogous to the Minkowski spacetime of special relativity, which Lawrence LeShan[28] compared to sense of timelessness and one-ness that characterize mystical states under what Aldous Huxley[29] called the Perennial Philosophy.

Under the theistic conception of god, at any moment, the god/student may delete or alter the graph (i.e., universe) if it doesn't tickle his fancy or if the nasty behavior of some particular point-soul pisses him off in some way. (Think Noah's flood or the Boxing Day tsunami of 2004, which killed 230,000 people.)

This would be a far cry from the supposedly omniscient, omnipotent, and omnibenevolent theistic god of the Christian Old Testament, which Dan Barker[30] has called the most unpleasant character in all fiction. The existing data and the course of human history and suffering would seem to rule out the supposedly benevolent god of the Abrahamic tradition in favor of a god that takes sadistic delight in tearing off the wings of houseflies while they are still alive.

At each point along the world line, the point-soul may be aware of other events on nearby branches of the graph, analogous to our own sensory awareness of nearby events in our own spacetime. Such interactions would be governed by the laws of physics chosen by the creator/godling to govern this particular universe.

If the god-student can view the entire universe (i.e., graph) from all possible perspectives, including magnification and "microfication," then the god/godling could be said to be omniscient (or at least potentially omniscient) regarding the static spacetime of the graph-universe. A time variable might be introduced to enable the godling to experience a sense of "time flow," in which time is experienced as moving toward the future and away from the past, as described above. It should be noted that science currently has no explanation for the experience of time flow. An injected or immanent god might be able to experience time flow along all the spacetime geodesics in the universe, one at a time. In this case such a godling could be said to be potentially omniscient, although by restricting this awareness to events on his chosen/assigned spacetime geodesic, the godling would not be omniscient at any given time to all the events in his spacetime. In fact, a sense of time flow may be a perquisite for the acquisition of knowledge and even experience itself. If the universe were a static array of events one could easily expect the godling to grow very bored with the unchanging timeless array of events in which nothing ever happens and he might pass out or go to sleep, as Pope Benedict suggested God had done in his farewell address.

It is amusing to speculate that our godling, by squinting really hard, might be able to make out himself typing on his calculator, a form of what the Buddhists call interdependent arising and the physicists might call a closed causal loop or timeline. Who said causation must be a one-way street or an irreflexive relationship?

Thus, the creating mind or minds (if any) may be looking at various combinations of physical laws and initial conditions to see what universes are generated as some sort of virtual parlor game and then letting themselves get lost in the resulting Dream or Thought This may explain why the universe does not appear to be designed by an all-powerful, all-caring compassionate God (for which there appears to be little or no evidence, given the seeming lack of correlation between the favorableness of events and one's moral virtue). It may have been designed by mad scientists in the preuniverse for their own fun and entertainment. If they are looking at the universe from an external point of view (such as when our student contemplates the graph on his graphing calculator), the universe might be considered to be an some sort of artwork displayed in some sort of gallery showing the outcomes of various attempts to spawn a cosmos. This gallery would be similar to physicist Hugh Everett's multiverse[31] in which all possible outcomes of quantum processes are realized in a Hilbert space that contains all possible histories of the world that are allowable under the laws of quantum mechanics. Each time a quantum mechanical state vector collapses into a definite outcome through an act of observation (say into state A rather then state B), two alternative histories of the universe are created, one in which event A occurred, and one in which event B occurs. The two universes would then continue to evolve in accordance with laws of physics and then branch into alternative universes each time a quantum mechanical state vector is collapsed through an act of observation. This of course implies that there are an uncountable infinity of alternative universes. This seems like a profligate model, given that at the present time, we can only observe one of these literally countless alternative universes.

Thus, God may be akin to a deranged particle physicist who is not particularly concerned with the fate of whatever life forms may inhabit any of the universes he inadvertently creates in his basement tinkerings.

This may be similar to the Hindu doctrine of Atman-Brahman (person-God) identity and the view of process theologians that God is immanent in the universe and that human consciousnesses may be aspects of a greater divine mind, a doctrine that receives some support from the evidence for the anthropic principle as discussed above.

Pure Consciousness. The self that (seems to) persist over long time periods (from birth to death in the popular, most common view) is not the conglomeration of one's thoughts, feelings, memories, and sensations themselves, which is constantly changing, but rather the field of pure consciousness within which these qualia act out their drama. In other words, we are vessels of consciousness rather than the contents of those vessels, we are the movie screens rather than the movies.

The Evanescence of the Person. The reason that we think that we ride our present brains from birth to death is likely that we have fallen under the powerful illusion that we are the Person. Much like an oxygen atom temporarily trapped in one's body, we may have jumped on board well after birth and may depart well before death.

Our core selves, if conceived as centers of pure consciousness, appear intuitively to be unitary and not divisible into components. We might even enjoy the same ontological privileges accorded to fundamental physical particles, including conservation over time. Perhaps we are even identical with particles or fields already known to physics (much like a proton responding to a complex quantum-mechanical field connecting it to the rest of the universe may be said to be in some sense aware of that universe). On the other hand we may be fundamental entities yet to be identified by modern science. In either event, your association with any given brain or other physical system is likely to be more ephemeral than we think. The illusion that you have continuously inhabited one's current brain for decades likely arises from the memories stored in your connectome (patterns of neuron connections) combined with your cognitive construction of the social entity known here as the Person.

The illusion of being the Person, the conjunction of our physical bodies and personality traits such as memories and desires, likely arises in part from this false identification with the physical body and its needs, which may serve our biological imperatives but perhaps not our spiritual needs.

Our universe is one of conservation, of mass-energy, baryon number, and angular momentum to name but a few such conserved elements. It is a universe of rearrangement, not destruction. If, as centers of pure consciousness, we are granted at least some form of parity with such seemingly (to us) mindless and insignificant entities as quarks and electrons, then it is likely that we, like they, are recycled from system to system, continually falling into the murky depths of one system of primitive awareness after another, but perhaps from time to time becoming united in a "supersystem," compared to which our present human consciousness will appear like that of an amoeba.

If the materialists are correct in their view that we are nothing but matter and energy and if our intuition is correct that we are unitary, much more like a quark or an electron than like a temporary conglomeration of atoms, then the pro-survivalist may rejoice. The universe conserves mass-energy, recycling it from one part of the cosmic show to another. Uncountable beauties and terrors may await us as we are torn free of our human form and the illusion created by our stories of the self and our false identification with the Person.

Just as the collection of atoms and elementary particles making up one's physical body undergoes continual change and replacement, so do one's thoughts, emotions, memories and personality traits. One's essential self persists, despite these continual changes in the contents of your consciousness as well as in your brain (and, we might add, in your subconscious and unconscious minds as well). Thus, you cannot be your personality or its "contents," such as your thoughts, emotions, and memories, which come and go while you persist.

Consciousness and the Soul.

In view of the explosion of modern science's knowledge about the dependence of psychological states on brain activity, the most plausible candidates for souls that could survive the death of the physical body are centers of pure consciousness. Modern science is not even close to explaining the existence of such centers. This has led some materialist philosophers to deny the existence of consciousness altogether, as already noted, surely an absurd conclusion.

Consciousness may exist at many levels, from an electron, as is postulated by some modern-day panpsychists such as David Skrbina,[32] to a single neuron as proposed by Jonathan Edwards[33] to assemblies of neurons as proposed by Christof Koch and his collaborators,[34] to the entire Internet combined with its users, and all the way up to the Universe and beyond as suggested by Teilhard de Chardin.[35]

We will use the term "macrosouls" to denote spheres of consciousness associated with macroscopic objects such as a human brain, "microsouls" to denote spheres of consciousness (if any) associated with microscopic objects such as individual neurons or protons, and "megasouls" to denote spheres of consciousness (if any) associated with supraindividual objects such as ant colonies or the network consisting of the Internet conjoined with its human users, and "megasouls "to denoted spheres of consciousness associated with gods and Creative Intelligences, if such there be.

Such centers of consciousness might be recycled in much the same way as oxygen molecules and atoms are. Skrbina[36] suggests that such atomistic entities are associated with centers of consciousness. This would correspond to a form of reincarnation, likely without memory of the previous incarnation.

It is likely that such centers of consciousness would enter the body well after birth and will exit well before death. Thus, each incarnation may be a fleeting thing. So you might as well enjoy it while you can and make the most out of it (hopefully in a responsible way, as it might well turn out that you will be stuck in your brain for a quite a while). Also, follow the Golden Rule, as you may find yourself in another's brain in no time.

It is thus an intricate conceptual web that we will explore in these pages. We will begin by developing a taxonomy of souls.

Conceptions of the Soul

We now explore the possibility that souls are real, and if so, what their nature is. It will not trace in minute detail the considerable evolution in the soul concept over the centuries in the world's major (and minor) religions. However, religious conceptions will be discussed from time to time, where relevant.

In some cases, the word "soul" may be used in nonstandard ways. As we will see below, the word "soul" may mean quite different things, depending on one's religious or philosophical stance. We will use the term" thanatope," to denote that portion of one's self (if any) that survives the death of the physical body. We will consider seven types of thanatope:

Thanatope #1: The Person (the union of one's personality traits such as memories, emotions and skills and current physical body),

Thanatope #2: The soul embedded in a dream body or astral body inhabiting a dream world and bearing many of the personality elements of the deceased person,

Thanatope #3: One's personality or partial personality,

Thanatope #4: The soul as a center of pure consciousness,

Thanatope #5: The doctrine of no soul or self as promulgated by some Buddhists and some modern philosophers and scientists such as Daniel Dennett[37] Susan Blackmore[38] and Thomas Metzinger.[39]

Thanatope #6: The doctrine of multiple souls or selves, as found in ancient Egyptian mythology and Aristotelian philosophy and more recently proposed in the writings of modern neuroscientists such as Jonathan Edwards,[40] and

Thanatope #7: The doctrine that one's self is part of a collective mind or consciousness, as promulgated by such disparate thinkers as C. G. Jung[41] the Jesuit priest Pierre Teilhard de Chardin,[42] and the renowned entomologists Bert Hölldobler and E. O. Wilson, with respect to ant colonies.[43]

We will distinguish four types of afterlife:

Afterlife #1: Physical, quasiphysical, or cybernetic resurrection,

Afterlife #2: A collective dream or astral plane,

Afterlife #3: Absorption into a collective mind, and

Afterlife #4: Reincarnation.

Thanatope #1: The Person. We will define the Person to be the conjunction of one's physical body, its mental states, and its center(s) of awareness. This corresponds with the usual use of the term (with eliminative materialists of course denying that there are mental states or centers of awareness, but being happy to grant the existence of at least the physical body).

The Person by definition cannot survive the death of the physical body. This does not mean that there is no afterlife for the Person, as several religious sects postulate the resurrection of the physical body (and its associated mental contents) at some future time, such as on the Day of Judgment as prophesized in the Abrahamic religious traditions (Judaism, Christianity, and Islam). This resurrection may take place in a "Resurrection World" that is distinct from the present physical universe.

Several scientists, including Ray Kurzweil,[44] have argued that one could survive death through downloading all the elements of one's personality into a cybernetic replica or clone of one's physical body. This type of resurrection would take place in the present physical universe and might be consistent with physicalism. The resurrection of the Person is explored in much greater detail below.

Afterlife #2: A Collective Dream World. The afterlife available to **Thanatope #2** might be imagined to be a collectively-constructed dream (sometimes called the astral plane). This corresponds to **Afterlife #2** above.

Such dream-worlds include the realms of the gods in the mythological traditions (e.g., Olympus, Asgard, and the Dream Time of the Australian aborigines) and the various hells and heavens postulated in world's major religions, from the mythology of the ancient Greeks to the hells of popular Buddhism (even though more esoteric forms on Buddhism deny the existence of a continuing self or soul that might enter these hells, of which more later).

Survival of Centers of Pure Consciousness. The self that (seems to) persist over long time periods (from birth to death in the popular, most common view) is not the conglomeration of our thoughts, feelings, memories, and sensations themselves, which is constantly changing, but rather the field of pure consciousness in which these qualia act out their drama. In other words, we are vessels of consciousness rather than the contents of those vessels, the movie screens rather than the movies.

When Descartes famously remarked, "I think, therefore I am," his error did not lie in the second clause (the affirmation of the existence of a continuing and unified self). The experience of oneself as a continuing field of consciousness is immediately given. If one cannot even know that one is a field of consciousness that continues from moment to moment (at the very least over the course of the last five minutes or so), then one cannot know anything. To second Descartes' conclusion, the knowledge of one's own existence, at least from moment to moment, cannot be doubted.

Descartes' error in lies not in his conclusion (that he exists), but rather in his premise (I think). As a continuing field of pure consciousness, one does not think; rather, the brain prison in which one is somehow trapped does the bulk of one's thinking. As noted above, modern research in cognitive neuroscience has made it made abundantly clear that one's thoughts, one's feelings, and the other elements that make up one's personality are intimately dependent on brain activity. If that activity is radically altered or discontinued, they will not persist in any recognizable manner. However, one's true self, construed as a field of pure consciousness, might persist, either trapped in a vegetative brain or on to new adventures.

The evidence of a continuing self is not that it thinks, which it cannot do without massive assistance from a brain, but that it has feelings and experiences. Rather than thinking, this center of consciousness "has thoughts" in the same way that it has (i.e., experiences) emotions and sensations. A rectified version of Descartes' statement might be: "I'm queasy, therefore I am."

The Simplicity of the Soul. Many philosophers have proposed that the soul or self is an indivisible center of pure consciousness.

Aristotle, for instance, believed in a memory-less form of reincarnation in which nothing is retained of one's personal identity from life to life.[45]

The classical Greek philosopher Plato taught that soul is indestructible and imperishable, based on its indivisibility. Human bodies, on the other hand, are composite and continually changing, whereas the soul retains its identity. He taught that the souls were akin to the invisible Forms, such as mathematical truths, that are grasped by thought and not by the senses.[46]

Philosopher D. H. Lund notes that the manner in which a composite thing is destroyed (i.e., dissolution of its elements) is not possible for souls, which lack parts in his view. [47]

Similarly, Martin and Barresi[48] cite the 18th century Anglican clergyman Joseph Butler's observation that the conscious self is something indivisible and simple and thus cannot be identical to a material organism. Butler asserted that it is the simplicity of the soul, rather than its immateriality, that guarantees its survival of death.[49] Butler also thought that "gross organized bodies" are no part of our selves and that their destruction is not ours (Goetz and Taliaferro, 2011).[50] The contemporary philosopher and theologian Stewart Goetz[51] (2001) seconds Butler's view, observing that if you are not identical to your physical body, then it is possible that you survive the dissolution of the body. He conjectures that, if the soul is a simple and indivisible entity within the brain, it may be one of the simple "atoms" comprising the body. He notes that if you are a "simple self" that is located within the body and if the body is composed of such simple selves, then the possibility that you are one of these simple selves cannot be ruled out on an *a priori* basis. Thus, under this view, one might survive death even if the universe is the deterministic world of classical, Newtonian physics.

Martin and Barresi[52] observe that the 19th century philosopher Thomas Hobbs viewed souls as material entities and that this view avoids (or at least diminishes) the enigma of how minds and brains interact. To this, one might add that the fact that we seem to be somehow slapped onto our physical brains like so many pieces of chewing gum further argues for the physicality of a least some aspect of the soul (unless of course the universe is a very complex dream, hallucination, or thought, in which case nothing would be physical).

If the soul is unitary and indivisible, it could not be a compound entity such as a neuron, or even an atom for that matter. It would have to be something more akin to a proton than a protozoan.

Martin and Berressi[53] favorably cite the philosopher Edmund Husserl's view that the self is a transcendent ego or center of pure consciousness, for which everything that exists is an object.[54] Husserl asserts that consciousness cannot be investigated through observation, as can the physical world, but only through phenomenological investigation. Consciousness exists absolutely and is indestructible. If the world were destroyed, Husserl maintained, consciousness would remain, as it is the absolute foundation of the material world. Martin and Berressi note that Husserl abandoned these views later in his career.

Philosopher and theologian Keith Ward seconds the early Husserl in writing that "consciousness is the condition of any and all possibilities existing...and not merely a very complex thing that happens to exist."[55]

The Medieval Christian philosopher St. Thomas Aquinas viewed the soul as only one part of him, putting it on an equal status with his foot.[56] Thus, Aquinas asserted that the soul is not the person, but only part of the person. Consequently, he was more than just his soul.

The 17th century philosopher John Locke contended that one's identity is determined by the indivisible center of consciousness that is associated with one's physical body. The self remains the same even if parts of the body, such as one's foot and ear, are removed. Locke noted that this center of consciousness may become incorporated in other bodies after death, but without any memories of those previous lives.[57] Thus, this would not be a form of personal survival.

Goetz and Taliferro[58] note that Locke's writings suggest that he also believed that different souls (centers of consciousness) could be associated with the same body during one's present lifetime.

Thomas Reid, (1872) likewise an 19th century theologian, proposed that the soul is indivisible and is distinct from the fleeting contents of its experiences, such as thoughts, feeling and emotions.[59] Reid asserted that memories provide direct support for the existence of such a continuing self or field of consciousness. However, memories may be illusory.

The noted mathematician and philosopher Gottfried Wilhelm Leibniz proposed that the universe consists of centers of pure consciousness called monads. These monads form a hierarchy, in which the supreme monad is God. Leibniz called monads souls and proposed that each human being was ruled over by a "supersoul."[60]

Thanatope #5 Nothing. The existence of a center of pure consciousness that seems to persist while different sensations, thoughts, memories and feelings flow through it (or by it) and while the composition and configuration of one's physical brain and body continually changes seems patently obvious, at least to most conscious beings such as ourselves.

Pure Nothingness. If at this point you are frightened at the prospect that death consists of experiencing your own nonexistence for eternity, put your heart at ease. You can't experience anything it if you don't exist. Non-existence can no more be experienced than a one-armed girl can grasp her own fist. Also, in a state of pure nothingness, you will no longer have any problems to trouble you. If that is not a state of pure bliss, I don't what is. Unfortunately, pure nothingness may not have staying power. In his recent book *A Universe from Nothing,* Lawrence Krauss suggests that the universe may be the result of a fluctuation in the false quantum vacuum that preceded our universe.[61] Of course, this is not literally creation *ex nihilo,* as the false quantum vacuum and the laws of physics themselves had to exist before our universe tunneled itself into existence.

The Western philosopher Arthur Schopenhauer maintained that the entire universe is a manifestation of striving of one great cosmic will and that our individual wills are but splinters of this great cosmic will, as are inanimate material objects. He endorsed the Buddhist practice of attempting to extinguish craving to escape from this world of suffering, but did not follow this practice himself, preferring to engage immoderately in the material pleasures this world offers.[62]

The Buddhist Doctrine of No Self. One of the tenets of Buddhism is that there is no lasting self or soul. However, reincarnation is a Buddhist doctrine. What then is it that reincarnates, if there is no self? Can we not equate the Buddhist thanatope with whatever it is that reincarnates, which is presumably a complex of thoughts, desires, and cravings? If so, (at least some) Buddhists seem to be adhering to the view that the thanatope is some partial remnant of the personality. This conception has already been found wanting above. Also, the simultaneous postulation of an afterlife and denial of a continuing self seems to be contradictory. Thus, this appears to be an incoherent philosophical position. It is no more coherent when uttered by an obedient army of monks with shaven heads and orange robes than it is when uttered by philosophers and scientists such as Blackmore, Dennett, Metzinger, and the Churchlands. The Buddhist doctrine of "no self" is nonsensical. The same is true of any doctrine that speaks of experience without an experiencer. Such doctrines are inconsistent with our direct and core introspective experience. It would be easier to entertain the possibility that the material world is an illusion.

Many (although, as we have just seen, not all) branches of Buddhism and Hinduism teach that one's true self is pure consciousness, not the contents or objects of consciousness. Thus, rather than clinging to the hope that one's personality will survive relatively intact in some sort of afterlife, many of the Eastern philosophies teach that our personalities are transitory and not our true selves. One's true self in this view is the pure consciousness (Atman) that in Hindu philosophy is taken to be identical with all consciousness, including that of the World Soul (Brahman). Under the Vedantic worldview, there is only one pure consciousness, and each of us is the Universe looking at itself from a different perspective. Thus, according to this view, when persons temporarily abandon their individual identities and perceive themselves as merging with the Cosmos or as being in perfect union with God, as in the mystical experiences described by William James[63] and others proposing similar pantheistic and pandeistic hypotheses, they are seeing directly into their true selves, as all centers of consciousness are manifestations of the one Consciousness that underlies this and all other worlds. In this view, we are fragmented splinters of the World Soul, our selves at once separate from, and yet identical to, one another.

This is the "perennial philosophy" that stands at the esoteric peaks of all religious traditions, as described by Aldous Huxley[64] (and others). At the popular level, the various religions appear to be in irresolvable conflict, as their gods and godlings wear different faces and go by different names. At a deeper and more advanced level, one expressly proposed in pandeism, they may be the same.

It should be conceded that survival in the form of pure consciousness with little continuity of memories, emotions, and predispositions and other assorted baggage from one's previous biological life may not be what most persons would consider survival in the true sense (i.e., survival with one's memories and personality completely intact). It would, however, be survival of one's essential self, the central core of one's existence, freed of this lifetime's burdens.

We are not quite yet done with those who deny the very existence of a center of pure consciousness that continues from one moment to another. The philosopher Galen Strawson[65] for instance maintains that little transient selves are continually winking in and out of existence within one person's stream of consciousness, with none of them lasting more than an hour or so. He also asserts that, each morning one wakes with a new Cartesian "I." Thus, he does not deny that centers of consciousness exist, but maintains that they may be only transiently associated with a particular body. However, another way to parse this insight might be to maintain that the body is transient, especially in the long run, but that different spheres of consciousness may be continually attaching and detaching themselves from the brain, much like oxygen molecules. This view treats souls as quasi-material objects, but as they are after all, at least temporarily, trapped in brains, so this may be reasonable. This possibility will be discussed in more detail below Thus, there is no need to kill off Strawson's transient selves at the ends of their short lives. Perhaps they are only liberated.

The 18th century philosopher David Hume[66] noted that one can never perceive oneself by reflection, all that one can experience is some combination of perceptions or another. Holt reports that this view of the soul left Hume with profound existential depression, which he partially combatted by playing backgammon.[67]

Parfit's Part-by-Part Replacement. The philosopher Derek Parfit[68] has noted that if one were to slowly replace each neuron in someone's brain one at time over a long period, we would still regard her to be the same person she was before the replacement. Parfit compares our concept of a person to that of a social club, which remains the same club even if all the original members have defected. This is similar to Hume's comparison of the self to that of a country.

Suppose that one were to replace each neuron with an electronic component that functions exactly as the replaced neuron. Further suppose that this replacement is done gradually over time. At the end of this process, the person would have an entirely cybernetic brain. If this brain functioned in the same way as the original brain, we might well regard this cyborg to be the same person as she was before this transformation. However, it is an open question as to whether such a transformation is even possible. There may be fundamental principles at work rendering preventing such a transformation. Artificial intelligence is a long way from producing a computer that can successfully mimic a human being.

Whitehead's Process Theology. Another philosopher who denied the concept of the self is Alfred North Whitehead.[69] In his "process theology," Whitehead proposed that the universe consists entirely of "occasions." These are atomic (indecomposable) events that have both a mental and physical aspect. Each occasion arises from the previous occasions by "prehending" (i.e., sensing) them and then fades from existence as it is prehended by the succeeding wave of occasions. Thus, the universe contains no substances such as a soul or an atomic nucleus, but only processes and events.

The quantum physicist Henry Stapp[70] sees Whitehead as expanding on William James' view that "thought is itself the thinker, and psychology need not look beyond it"[71] Stapp notes that in Whitehead's process philosophy, each occasion occupies a restricted, microscopic region. As more and more occasions emerge from the previous occasions, the future spacetime regions are continually being filled in (by the collapse of quantum-mechanical state vectors in Stapp's view). Thus, both Whitehead and Stapp propose models that are based in the concept of the "moving" present in which future events (occasions) become fixed events, which then recede into the past.

Stapp notes that many of the "occasions" proposed by Whitehead may not have the "full richness of a fully developed 'high grade' human experience"[72] He suggests that the richness of an experience depends on the "complexity of the physical system upon which von Neumann's Process 1 (the observation and collapse of the state vector) acts." In Stapp's view, each Whiteheadian occasion is conscious to some degree, placing Stapp in the panpsychist camp (the view that all physical entities have some form of experience, which is discussed in detail later in this article).

The prominent philosopher Baruch Spinoza set forth a monistic philosophy (in which only one fundamental type of entity is assumed to exist, rather than two, such as mind and matter). Spinoza viewed sensations and consciousness simply as matter perceived from within.

The philosopher Whatley Carington[73] proposed a form of "neutral monism" in which the basic components of the universe are "cognita." Cognita are similar to what are now termed "qualia" in modern debates about the mind-body problem (i.e., thoughts, sensation, emotions, etc.). Cognita relate to each other by mental processes such as, in Carington's day, the psychological laws of association. Carington asserted that an individual mind is nothing more that a cluster of highly associated cognita.[74]

Klein and the Subjective Self. In *Current Directions in Psychological Science*, one of psychology's flagship journals, Stanley Klein argues that it is now the time to bring the study of the subjective self into the main arena of scientific of psychological science He notes that one's subjective self is not an object that can be treated as "other" and thus located, grasped and studied scientifically. The self is thus a seemingly poor candidate for scientific study. In Klein's view, the self is not an object, but an awareness, a consciousness, and as such is not knowable to anyone but the self. Thus, Klein notes, according to the orthodox view of science, the self would have to forfeit its subjectivity in order to become an object for scientific study. He goes on to say:

> What I am suggesting, therefore, is that although the scope of scientific analysis is well-suited to the study of behavioral and neural properties identified as components of self-knowledge, the ontological self, as a singular, conscious, knowing subjectivity, does not readily fall into the same scientific framework. To put this very complex matter in the form of a simple question: "How does a subjectivity, a unified, individual point of view, treat itself as an object of subjectivity while retaining its subjective nature?" Short of falling into the trap of a conceptual regress (e.g., the homunculus or Cartesian theater; cf. Dennett, 1991), the answer appears to fall outside the scope of current scientific inquiry."

Klein argues that "we need a new, more inclusive metaphysics in which "reality is not reduced to *only* that which can be manipulated by science." He goes on to cite the philosopher William Earle's observation that "we have no way of surveying the whole of reality... and we should not attempt to close our ignorance through impatience with the infinity of the absolute itself."[75] Klein recommends that in the future philosophy should pay more attention to psychology.

We now ascend the ontological hierarchy from realm of souls to that of the god(s) themselves.

The Realm(s) of the God(s)

The Ungodliness of God. Many people believe in the existence of a God or gods, although this belief has declined substantially in Europe in recent years. One of the first duties of any deity is, of course, to create the universe. The Abrahamic (Judeo-Christian-Islamic) God accomplished this in a mere six days, essentially by acts of fiat. In polytheistic mythologies, this creation is often accomplished by splendid acts of fornication, cannibalism and murder among the deities. Such gods seem no more refined than humans when it comes to spiritually, perfection, self-mastery, and tranquility.

If you consider such gods to be an archaic notion, consider the fact that before the Large Hadron Collider (LHC) recently built in Switzerland was turned on, there were concerns expressed that the collisions of particles in this detector might result in doomsday scenarios. These apocalypses included the creation of black holes or even white holes giving rise to daughter universes through mini-Big Bangs (and after cosmic inflation perhaps not-so-mini-Big Bangs). Lueptow[76] cites several prominent physicists who had expressed concerns that the LHC would produce mini-black-holes, and he notes that experts were split on this issue. He cites calculations by Otto Rossler of the Max Planck Institute of the University of Tubingen that "the chances are good" that such a mini-black-hole would be capable of expanding through inflation and devouring the Earth in a matter of 50 months.

Yet, we turned on the LHC anyway. For those seeking further comfort in the wisdom of the previous generations of scientists, the Manhattan Project physicists who exploded the first atomic bomb did so over the objections of the noted physicist Edward Teller, who calculated that its explosion would set the Earth's atmosphere on fire. They exploded it anyway.[77]

If any universes newly created in the LHC suddenly inflated into sizable "daughter universes," as it is thought our own universe did, the denizens of such universes might entertain the notion that their universe was created by a troupe of mythological gods resembling themselves. They would thus entirely missing the truth of their genesis, namely that their universe was created by hundreds of grant-seizing physics-nerd aliens in white shirts with hyperdimensional pocket protectors, who were not even aware of the universe they created largely through miscalculation and by accident. Thus, the lives of their real creators might be a sorry soap opera indeed when compared to the magnificent pornographic antics of a typical horde of mythological creator gods.

Is the universe in fact nothing more than the result of an experiment conducted by one or more mad juvenile alien scientists in a cellar workshop in some other universe or pre-universe? To cite the noted astronomer, physicists, and mathematician Sir James Jeans once again: "The stream of knowledge is heading towards a non-mechanical reality; the Universe begins to look more like a great thought than like a great machine. Mind no longer appears to be an accidental intruder into the realm of matter...we ought rather hail it as the creator and governor of the realm of matter."[78]

Perhaps as Pope Benedict XVI optimistically concluded in his farewell address, God is merely asleep. Were the god(s) in fact physicists of some sort, setting up complex equations to govern the structure and behavior of a (possibly simulated or virtual) universe? Does this account for what Eugene Wigner called "the unreasonable effectiveness of mathematics in the natural sciences" or the physicist James Jeans' observation that "from the intrinsic evidence of his creation, the Great Architect of the Universe now begins to appear as a pure mathematician."[79] Swedish philosopher Nick Bostrum similarly suggests that the universe may be in fact a computer simulation.[80]

The physicist Steven Hawking asks, if the world is nothing more than an elaborate system of equations and mathematical truths, why does it go to the "bother of actually existing?"[81] Cosmologist Max Tegmark[82] has hypothesized that all mathematically possible universes exist. Similarly, Robert Nozick a Harvard philosopher, suggested that everything one can imagine exists.[83] This would explain the evidence for the anthropic principle. Such observers would of necessity inhabit one of the mathematical universes in which their existence is possible, and all universes occur.

Another great physicist, Arthur Eddington called the fabric of the cosmos "mind-stuff."[84] More recently, another prominent physicist, Henry Stapp has observed that under the *Weltanschauung* of quantum mechanics, the world has "an essentially 'idea-like' structure."[85] In an essay in *Nature*, the flagship journal of materialist science, Richard Conn Henry proclaimed that:

One benefit of switching humanity to a correct perception of the world is the resulting joy of discovering the mental nature of the Universe. We have no idea what this mental nature implies, but - the great thing is - it is true. Beyond the acquisition of this perception, physics can no longer help. You may descend into solipsism, expand to deism, or something else if you can justify it - just don't ask physics for help...

The Universe is immaterial - mental and spiritual. Live and enjoy."[86]

One argument for the fundamental role of mind in the creation of the universe is that the laws of nature and the initial conditions and laws of the universe seem to be delicately contrived to give rise to complexity and to the emergence of conscious observers. This is sometimes chauvinistically called the anthropic principle (as if humans were the only centers of consciousness in the universe).

Perhaps the universe was created by a conscious Being or beings to serve as some sort of cosmic amusement park. Many other physicists, including John Wheeler,[87] have suggested that the universe itself, conceived as a quantum process, could not have come into existence without some conscious observer to collapse state vectors and thus to give rise to a definite history of the universe. Wheeler termed this view the "participatory universe." Wheeler noted that this may explain the evidence for the anthropic principle. Potential universes that do not support the presence of conscious observers could not become actualized in Wheeler's view, as there would be no conscious observers to collapse their quantum-mechanical state vectors in the proper "direction" to create such a universe.

The physicist Evan Harris Walker[88] proposed the existence of protoconsciousnesses dwelling in empty space which govern the collapse of quantum state vectors at locations remote from any human (or other biological) observers.

The Mind-Dependent Universe. The base reality of the world appears to be one of quantum probability waves inhabiting an abstract, multidimensional mathematical space rather than the solid, marble-like electron and protons zipping around in the four-dimensional spacetime continuum that we imagine to be the firm underpinnings of our material existence. The mathematical complexity and beauty of the laws of the quantum mechanics are remarkable. It does indeed seem as though the Creator is, as both Jeans and Einstein thought, a great mathematician.

Of course it could well be that the creation of the universe was a group effort, a kind of Manhattan Project involving trillions of microsouls embedded in an unimaginably complex "computer" made out of whatever passes for matter (if anything) in the "preuniverse." Given that we are embedded in organisms only a few genes removed from those a chimpanzee (and possessing fewer genes than many seemingly simple plants such as rice), it may be no wonder that our brains are unable to unravel the real mysteries of the cosmos, including the origin and role of consciousness. Perhaps Colin McGinn is correct in his assessment that our present brains, with their mere 100 billion cells apiece, will never be able to penetrate these mysteries.[89] There may, however, be nothing preventing us from one day in the distant future building a device or being that is capable of hosting a staggeringly large number of microsouls.

Such a cybernetic superorganism might not only be capable of grasping such mysteries, but may have the intellectual wherewithal to create new Big Bangs, giving rise to new universes (perhaps even with "improved" or at least more entertaining laws of physics). Such a superorganism might be considered to be a god under the definition of "deity" as the creating force or intelligence. However, whatever "gods" may have lurked in the preuniverse were perhaps just as puzzled by the mystery of their own existence as we are by ours. This is why recourse to any explanation of Creation in terms of a Creating Intelligence (CI) leads to an infinite regress, as one then is confronted with the task of explaining the CI's existence. However, such infinite regresses do not bother everyone. In his philosophical lore, Bertrand Russell was once told by an old woman that the world is flat and supported by an elephant standing upon a turtle. When Russell asked her what supported the turtle, she proclaimed, "It's turtles all the way down!"[90]

But if the universe is a thought as Jeans, Eddington and Stapp contend, whose thought is it anyway? Was the universe created as a vast cosmic "art gallery" for the entertainment of microsouls (perhaps even those embedded in the CI)? Why go to trouble of designing such an elaborate version of "Disney World for microsouls," unless One intended to enjoy it Oneself, if only vicariously? Are our individual consciousnesses just aspects (or perhaps former components) of the CI, embedded in the myriad creatures the CI has managed to generate from its mathematical invention.

A Plentitude of Worlds. There are ways of accounting for the evidence for the anthropic principle without assuming that the universe was designed by a CI. Barrow and Tipler[91] note that if one accepts Tryon's[92] view that the creation of the universe was a quantum fluctuation then Hugh Everett's Many Worlds interpretation of quantum mechanics[93] would imply that all possible universes must be created.

Mind as Immanent. Mind, viewed as the creator of the physical world, is literally deified. If the CI (if any) that created the physical world is somehow to be identified with the souls that now inhabit it, then that intelligence is unlike the post–Newtonian Christian God, who stands remote from his creation once it is complete (at least under the deist interpretation). Such a CI more closely resembles the Vedic view of the Universal Self that divides into the minds of the myriad creatures of the world, which derives from the *Brihadaranyaka Upanishad*. The philosopher Alan Watts was fond of comparing this Indian view of creation to God playing hide-and-seek with himself in the physical world.[94]

Consciousness and Matter

We now turn from an examination of the relation between gods and matter to that between consciousness and matter.

Descartes extended his mechanistic philosophy to encompass living creatures as well as inanimate matter. He viewed animals as mere machines. He did not, however, question the existence of minds in humans; indeed, he thought one's primary and most direct knowledge was of one's own mind. He viewed mind as a totally different kind of entity from matter. In Descartes' view, one's mind (or ego) was indivisible and hence lacked a basic character of matter—that of extension in space. Thus, the mind inhabited a different plane of existence from the physical world and could not be said to have a spatial location. Descartes proposed that humans are comprised of immaterial minds existing outside of physical space and their associated physical bodies. Descartes' soul included the rational mind (endowed the power of reasoning), but excluded emotions and memories. He contended that the rational soul is often unable to assert power over the passions, which results in human behavior being almost (but not quite) deterministic. Descartes viewed the rational soul as indivisible and eternal, whereas material things are composite and cease to exist when their components undergo dissolution.

He proposed that memory traces were just modifications of the pores through which the "animal spirits" were thought to flow, based on previous activity. This is amazingly close to the modern view that memory traces are stored in modifications of synapses (starring in the role of Descartes' pores).

The Mind-Body Problem

Materialism. The first "solution" to the "mind-body problem" is radical materialism, which postulates that only matter exists. Some radical materialists, including the founders of the behaviorist movement in psychology, B. F. Skinner[95] and John B. Watson[96] have even taken the position that consciousness and its assorted contents such as memories, thoughts or feelings do not exist. This position is self-refuting. If the writings of materialists do not express thoughts, then they are caused by meaningless keyboard pushes and thus cannot be taken seriously. Skinner himself maintained that his manuscripts were the result of conditioned patterns of keyboard pecks, for which he had been reinforced, through royalties and promotions, in the past. His plight was thus much like that of a hapless pigeon in one of his own experiments. (His own children's plight was more literally like that of Skinner's pigeons, right down to the Plexiglas box.)

It should be noted that Skinner did eventually retreat from this early radical version of his theory.

Closely related to radical materialism are neural-identity theory, central state materialism and double-aspect theory (often attributed to Spinoza), which assert that there is only one reality (the material world) and that conscious experiences are simply material processes experienced from within.

Most adherents to the above philosophical positions are physicalistic reductionists in that they believe that the behavior of material particles, including those that underlie consciousness, are completely determined by the known laws of physics. As the philosopher Thomas Nagel observes, "[I]t can seem that the only way to accept the argument against reduction is by adding peculiar extra ingredients like qualia, meanings, intentions, values, reasons, beliefs and desires to the otherwise magnificently unified mathematical order of the physical universe."[97]

Epiphenomenalism. A closely related view is that of epiphenomenalism, espoused by "Darwin's Bulldog," Thomas Henry Huxley.[98] Epiphenomenalists graciously grant matter the capacity to produce mental events such as thoughts and feelings that are not identical with the material processes in the brain that give rise to them.

However, they deny that such mental events can influence anything in the physical world, including brain processes.

Like eliminative materialism, epiphenomenalism is hoist by its own petard. The writings of epiphenomenalists are attempts to explain mental events. They are thus presumably caused, at least in part, by the very mental events that they claim have no causal powers. According to the doctrine of epiphenomenalism, the writings of epiphenomenalists are not caused, even in part, by mental events. Thus, their scribblings must be devoid of any evidence of mentation, a striking confirmation of the theory of epiphenomenalism!

The theory of epiphenomenalism cannot be true, because (in an archetypically and delightfully Gödelian fashion) it denies the existence of any theory, truth, or belief that can be verbally expressed.

Emergentism. Closely related to epiphenomenalism is emergentism, in which novel and unexpected phenomena, such as wetness, arise from the behavior and properties of more basic entities, such as hydrogen and oxygen atoms. One proponent of emergentism is the philosopher William Hasker, who asserts that the conscious self is an "emergent individual" and not just an emergent property of the brain.[99] Hasker considers the question of whether such "emergent individuals" could survive the deaths of their physical bodies to be an open question, comparing such postmortem traces to electrical and magnetic fields. In his later publications Hasker[100] asserts that only if the brain functions as a whole could there be unity of the visual field. As such neural unity has not been demonstrated, he maintains that the conscious visual field is not part of the brain, but of the soul.

Idealism. The philosophical theory of idealism is the polar opposite of that of eliminative materialism. It denies the existence of physical events and proposes that the universe is entirely mental, a great dream or thought. As the pandeistic idealist astrophysicist Bernard Haisch puts it,[101] it is not matter than creates an illusion of consciousness, but consciousness that creates the illusion of matter. The various agencies presumed by idealists to be responsible for producing the illusion of the physical world have included (a) God (in the view of the prototypical idealist, the eighteenth century philosopher Bishop George Berkeley), (b) a collective mind or collective unconscious, and (c) the illusion-producing state of craving and ignorance (according to certain schools of Buddhism).

Perhaps the universe is your own dream (especially if you are a piece of God, as the Hindus, not to mention some modern pantheists, panentheists, pandeists and panendeists believe). (of which more later). If the Universe is a dream, it is a whopper, produced by arcane mathematical laws of physics that few of us understand with our present cognitive apparatus. The universe certainly looks and feels real.

The reply of most modern scientists and philosophers of science to idealism is that scientific theories that postulate the existence of an objective physical world have produced more exact predictions about possible human observations than have idealistic theories and therefore should be preferred over the latter for that reason. (Such theories are even covertly preferred by most solipsists, who seem strangely reluctant to step in front of illusory oncoming trains.) The noted poet and essayist Samuel Johnson said of idealism, "I refute it thus," kicking a large rock and triggering one of the more painful sensations that can emerge from Pauli's exclusion principle in physics. However, despite Johnson's podiatrically self-sacrificing efforts in support of the anti-idealist cause, his pain remains just that, a sensation.

The physicist Amit Goswami[102] has contended that an idealist conception of the world is required in order to render modern theories of physics, in particular quantum mechanics, coherent. Physicist Richard Conn Henry contends that the only reality we can know for certain is mind. He endorses Eddington's view that the universe is entirely mental, as expressed in his 1926-1927 Gifford lectures[103] Henry contends that life after death is less improbable than the surprising fact of one's own existence. The philosopher Stephen Priest[104] asserts that mind rather than matter is fundamental and that theology rather than science is the fundamental vehicle of knowledge. Priest notes that we lose our souls when we picture ourselves from a third-person perspective and get sucked into the illusion that we are physical bodies rather than unchanging souls.

Solipsism. The ultimate form of idealism (and skepticism for that matter) is solipsism, the doctrine that only one's self exists and the world is just a very complex hallucination. Solipsism is irrefutable, but is unlikely to provide the basis of a generative research program. It is also costly in that one must give up the existence of the material world, as well as that of other minds. As noted above, the universe appears to be based on a very complex set of mathematical laws that would be a challenge for one mind (at least with a typical human processing capability) to design. If I am just dreaming this universe, my subconscious mind is a great deal more powerful than it seems to be as I go about my daily routine, which doesn't usually involve computing the second-by-second results of string theory, so far as I know. The remoteness and power of these unconscious regions of the mind might be more readily equated with the mind of God or with the manifestations of a virtual (i.e., idealistic) physical world. In any event, such a virtual and oftentimes surprising material world would seem to be, at least in part, dependent on something outside oneself. And this is what solipsism is designed to avoid.

Variants of Physicalism. If one were to charitably concede to the physicalists that the material world exists and in view of the undeniable reality of mental events (despite their denial by eliminative materialists), one is faced with two options. The first option is that mental events occur outside of the physical realm and there is a two-way interaction between brain events and mental events. The second option is to place mind within matter itself, as in panpsychism, pantheism, pandeism, panentheism, and panendeism. At this point, the reader's head may be spinning, trying to tease apart the philosophies of materialism, dual-aspect theory, neutral monism, panpsychism, pantheism, idealism, physicalism, panentheism and panendeism. (Deism is the doctrine that God created the universe, but does not act upon it after the universe's creation, letting the laws of nature enfold in an unmolested manner. Thus, the God of deism is not an interventionist God. A theistic deity continues to act upon the universe after it is created. Pantheism and pandeism, respectively, are the doctrines that a theistic (respectively, deistic)

God is coextensive with the universe and pervades all things, so that all is within God, and God is within every thing. Under the panentheistic and panendeistic views, God extends beyond the universe. These doctrines all appear to make the same predictions, so long as observable matter conforms to the laws of physics, as it appears to do. There seems to be no way of empirically or even conceptually teasing them apart, at least not if the Deity continues Her nap. Thus, these grand theories of the mind-body problem may all be operationally equivalent to one another. Paranormal phenomena such as psi and personal survival would throw a monkey wrench into the whole physicalist program insofar as they would violate the laws of physics or would at least be inexplicable by current laws of physics.

There have been many who have had difficulty conceptualizing how mind could interact with matter in view of the fundamental differences between them. (Descartes and many subsequent philosophers have regarded mind as immaterial and lacking any spatial extension). However, each of us seems to be somehow "stuck" in a human brain occupying a particular region in space, however temporarily. Thus, it would seem that the self, construed as a field of consciousness, does have some spatial properties, if only the property that it is, at least temporarily, stuck in a human brain occupying a particular region in space. (Under the panpsychistic hypothesis, the mind is conceived as a part of the brain, eliminating the need for such metaphysical Velcro.)

From this it does not follow that the self in its entirety is confined to a spatial location in the human brain or a circumscribed region of space. Even elementary particles of matter such as electrons and protons typically do not have any particular spacetime locations until they are forced to adopt one through an act of observation. Thus, even physical matter lacks the material properties ascribed to it by eliminative materialists.

We are a long way from having measured with precision every minute energy transaction in human brains. In the process of doing so, it is conceivable that some unexpected energy transactions will be observed. If science should progress to the point where the action of spheres of consciousness on energy transactions within the brain can somehow be mathematically (or otherwise) described, this might be a victory for the contention that immaterial minds can exert physical force. If such spheres of consciousness are identified with known material particles, fields and/or systems, the physicalists could claim victory. If not, the dualists could declare victory.

Pashler[105] has observed that consciousness may act as an information-processing bottleneck. The channel capacity of human centers of consciousness is stunning low. In a very famous article the cognitive psychologist George Miller,[106] presented evidence that only around seven items of information can be held in human centers of consciousness at one time. This is a surprisingly low number, when one considers that the brain contains somewhere between 10 billion and 100 billion neurons and around 100 trillion synapses. If we had a computer with that sort of capacity, we could easily program it to remember more than seven "chunks" of information at a time. Similarly, Leonard Mlodinow[107] notes that the human sensory system sends the brain about 11 million bits of information per second, whereas our conscious minds can process no more than 50 bits. Max

Tegmark[108] notes that, of the approximately 10 million bits of information that enter a human brain each second, we are aware of only 10 to 50 bits. Thus, the information-processing capacity of centers of consciousness is astonishingly low. Hence, such centers might be easy to fit into, say, a dragonfly.

Henry Stapp[109] asserts that only streams of consciousness exist and that there is no thinker, only thoughts. He cites William James[110] and Alfred North Whitehead[111] in this regard. Thus, Stapp falls into the "no soul" camp. In a dialogue toward the end of Stapp's book, quantum physicist Basil Hiley notes that some of the arguments of "New Age" philosophers appear to be circular, in that they assert that there can be no stability of matter without consciousness and no stability of consciousness without stability of matter. One way out of this difficulty, Hiley notes, is to postulate some form of universal consciousness such as that proposed in certain versions of Hinduism.[112]

Panpsychism. There are philosophical positions that avoid the scientific absurdities of consciousness-denying eliminative materialism, the cavalier dismissal of the material world by idealistic philosophers, and the dualist's difficulties in explaining the interactions between an immaterial mind and a material brain. Such doctrines include neural-identity theory, central state materialism, and double-aspect theory, as discussed above, and panpsychism. As already noted, the first three theories contend that mental events are simply brain processes experienced from within.

Panpsychism offers an easy way out (and perhaps the only viable way out) of the scientific conundrum of consciousness for those gracious enough to concede the existence of matter. Science cannot currently explain how brain activity gives rise to conscious experience (as opposed to identifying brain processes that are correlated with wakefulness or with *reports* of conscious experience). Many thinkers such as Colin McGinn[113] suggest than a full understanding of consciousness will never be achieved due to fundamental limitations on the cognitive powers of human brains, which evolved to invent more effective ways to brutalize a fleeing warthog rather than to probe the fundamental mysteries of the universe (although our probing has been rather astonishingly successful in the past few centuries).

Science also has no explanation for how consciousness (as opposed to cognitive powers) arose from insentient matter in the course of the development of the universe and our planet. The emergence of consciousness is perhaps the most vexing, fundamental, and seemingly unsolvable problem confronting modern science and philosophy.

To paraphrase Bertrand Russell's harasser, it is angels (not turtles) all the way down. Even an electron must somehow "sense" an electromagnetic field in order to respond to it. A white blood cell must "recognize" a pathogen in order to engulf it. A single neuron needs to sense the flow in order to go with it.

An electron may appear to lead a very boring life. However, quantum physics has taught us that even a single electron is generally entangled with a large number of other particles and thus must somehow sense their global state. Its experience might be very complex and beautiful as well as more tranquil than our own harried existence. It may just need to watch something like a complex light show, chipping in its own two cents worth every now and again, as it skis the mogul hills of spacetime.

Our bodies are composed of a vast number of cells and bacteria, with only a fraction of them (10%) from our own species. In fact, our bodies seem more akin to a ferocious battleground for microorganisms, which are replaced from minute to minute, than to a unified entity. If one is to grant consciousness to animals "all the way down," could not our white blood cells possess a (possibly dim) consciousness capable of recognizing their foes and engulfing them?

The Ruminations of Rocks. As discussed above, panpsychism extends the reach of consciousness to all things, including not only animals and plants, but even inorganic matter such as rocks.

And what of the highly-touted thermostat? Can it be said to be aware of the rise in heat? Might rocks as they weather and absorb radiation experience consciousness on an extremely slow time span? Perhaps the experience of a mineral might be something like the light show at the end of Kubrick's *2001: A Space Odyssey*. If so, it might be far more peaceful to be a rock rather than to be subject to the harried life we humans endure. Thus, the very dust from which we were born and into which we will die may well still carry still the stuff of mind.

Mysterianism. Then there is strangely appealing doctrine of "mysterianism," whose most notable proponent is Colin McGinn McGinn begins his book *The Mysterious Flame*[114] with a short story in which future silicon-based artificial intelligences stumble across the Earth and are astounded to find lumps of meat that can think (our brains). McGinn contends that the globs of 100 billion pulsating, amoeba-like neurons that comprise the biological wetware of our brains have evolved to discover how to better secure a stone axe head to a stick in order to beat our neighbor's brain into insensibility rather than to enable us to understand the realms to which our neighbor's consciousness has fled after we have completed our handiwork. In McGinn's view, the role of consciousness and the nature of the soul will forever remain beyond the grasp of our primitive primate brains. He even suggests that conscious minds may be remnants of a nonspatial world that preceded the Big Bang, and he hypothesizes that we may not be mentally equipped to solve the problem of how minds and brains interact.

Perhaps McGinn is right. Perhaps that is why consciousness is often referred to as the "hard problem" of the philosophy of mind. But, unlike our ape brethren, we have been to the moon and plumbed the creation of the universe down to the first femtosecond. It is premature to give up trying to understand the nature of our conscious minds. Such understanding may require us to relinquish core beliefs about the nature of our selves and the quasi-permanence of our association with any particular body.

Many of the most prominent practitioners of human thought have embraced some form of panpsychism, including Leibniz, Spinoza, and Alfred North Whitehead. Under the panpsychistic view, consciousness pervades all things, and the universe consists of a plenitude of spheres of pure consciousness, or "monads" in Leibniz' terminology.

Griffin's Panexperientialism. A prominent proponent of panpsychism is the philosopher David Ray Griffin[115] Griffin prefers to call his doctrine "panexperientialism" rather than "panpsychism," as he does not contend that rocks and other inanimate collections of material particles possess a highly unified and structured consciousness, but rather ascribes only vague "feeling-responses" to them. In Griffin's view, more highly complex and structured forms of consciousness are restricted to "compound individuals." Such compound individuals are composed of, or arise from, a hierarchical collection of more primitive selves or "individuals." For instance, a neuron would be a compound individual in relation to its individual constituents such as molecules and mitochondria. A suborgan such as the hippocampus of the brain that is composed of neurons would be a compound individual somewhat further up the hierarchy. All such "individuals" would have both mental and physical aspects under the panexperientialist view, although only hierarchically-ordered structures would be assumed to have a highly organized and structured consciousness. Griffin's theory raises the possibility that human societies may achieve a global consciousness that is beyond our ken, with each of us playing the role of a neuron in some sort of global "hypermind," much as each of our neurons is essentially a specialized cousin of unicellular organisms such as amoeba.

Hive Minds. What if our neurons could move? Might their collective then be considered an even more complex brain?

As noted above, Hölldobler and Wilson[116] propose that communities of insects comprise "superorganisms" and that evolutionary selection acts on the colony as a unit, rather than on the on the individual insects. Wilson has in fact written a novel featuring ant colonies as protagonists.[117] Can the whole of humanity be considered as a single super-brain, perhaps associated with global spheres of consciousness? Goldberg[118] has even suggested that in the future the Internet may develop into an "advanced intrinsic consciousness" (p. 54).

Cellular biologist Jonathan C. W. Edwards[119] and Willard Miranker,[120] a computer scientist specializing in neural networks, have proposed that that each single neuron in the brain is associated with its own center of consciousness. Due to the complexity of the input to each neuron, each such center of consciousness would likely identify with the body as a whole and would thus fall under the delusion that it is the single conscious self "in charge" of the whole body. Indeed, each neuron may have its own perspective on a wide area of brain activity, much as each part of a holographic picture holds the image of the whole scene rather than a single point or aspect of the scene. Regarding science's disregard of the observer, Edwards notes that:

Physicist[s] seem to assume that the thing with a point of view, the observer, is some big lump of stuff [the brain] that does not have to fit into theories about things that are observed.[121]

Semir Zeki,[122] a neuroscientist, has likewise proposed the existence of an array of micro-consciousnesses at each "node of neural activity." Neurobiologist Dennis Bray[123] compares neurons to amoebas having a complex array of inputs and thus possibly comprising centers of consciousness. He notes that neurons can grow, shrink, and move, and he observes that each neuron has a very complex input and can learn from experiences. Philosopher and theologian Phillip Clayton[124] offers living cells and electrons as possible centers of consciousness. Stewart C. Goetz, [125] also a philosopher, suggests that the soul may be one of the "simple atoms" in the brain.

Attributing consciousness to elementary particles would seem to ignore the usual roles attributed to consciousness by cognitive neuroscientists, which include attention and the binding of diverse neural activity into the unified perception of an object (as well as other functions, such as learning novel tasks and decision-making). In a review of studies relating to attention, Yantis[126] notes that process of directing attention remains unexplained by current findings in neuroscience. It does seem as though the center of consciousness that is the "master of one's brain" is somehow able to direct such behavior as the writing of this article. However, perhaps that center is just "lucky" enough to be in the right place and the right time to direct the writing of this article. (It might, for instance, be conceived as affixed to Broca's language area in the left hemisphere of the brain, as it does seem to choose the words one will use. Other macrosouls might for instance have the jobs of moving one's limbs. Sometimes when one stops to think about it, it is amazing that one's arm executes an intricate sequence of movements without any conscious "micro-management").

Skrbina on Panpsychism. The philosopher David Skrbina[127] has provided a comprehensive defense of the doctrine of panpsychism. He argues for instance that an electron must somehow sense the presence of a proton in order to respond to its attractive force. (An electron may even enjoy a certain degree of freedom of action due to quantum indeterminacy and may be able to sense a quantum field that is highly complex and global in nature.) Even a proton must somehow "sense" an electromagnetic field in order to respond to it. A white blood cell must "recognize" a pathogen in order to engulf it. A single neuron needs to feel the flow in order to go with it.

Bryan[128] has observed that both electrons and human centers of consciousness are indivisible, and he too has conjectured that individual electrons may be conscious, as has the neuroanatomist Robert Kuhn.[129]

As does Griffin, Skrbina associates more complex forms of consciousness with aggregates of matter, such as single neurons, or large assemblies of neurons such as hippocampi and cerebral hemispheres. However, it should again be noted that such aggregates of matter, much like one's personality and physical body, do not persist over time and thus cannot form the basis of a continuing self. Also, fields of consciousness appear to be unitary and indivisible, much more like a quark than like a molecule or a neuron.)

Skrbina points out that the panpsychist position solves the problem of "emergence," or how organisms acquired consciousness in the course of evolution (i.e., how insensate matter gave rise to consciousness). He observes that there is no definitive line of demarcation that can be drawn between conscious and nonconscious organisms, in either the present world or in the course of evolution. If all matter is imbued with consciousness or if fields of consciousness are fundamental constituents of the universe that have existed throughout its history, then the problem of the evolution of consciousness (and of how a three-pound "hunk of meat" like the human brain could generate conscious experiences in the first place) does not arise.

It should, however, be noted that panpsychism still faces the difficulty of accounting for the emergence of a unified mind or global consciousness out of a myriad of psychic elements, as was pointed out long ago by William James and, more recently, by William Seager[130] and Thomas Nagel.[131]

Consciousness Expanders and Consciousness Contractors. However, many other philosophers and scientists, following Descartes, deny the existence of consciousness in animals other than humans, or at least in most animals other than humans. The philosopher Thomas Nagel[132] famously posed the question "What is it like to be a bat?" The philosophical community generally translates Nagel's straightforward query into the indecipherable and muddled question "Is there something that it is like to be a bat?" Philosophers in turn seem to treat this last question as equivalent to the more straightforward question "Are bats conscious?"

Nicholas Humphrey. Psychologist Nicholas Humphrey notes that the hypothesis of personal survival of death requires the acceptance of a dualistic worldview in which the mind can function independently of the physical body.[133] He somewhat surprisingly states that dreams suggest that the mind can function independently from the body, although one would have thought that it has been amply demonstrated that dreams are closely tied to brain states. He even goes so far as to endorse the 19th century social anthropologist Edward Tylor's suggestion that "dreams seem to provide as good evidence as anyone could ask for that the soul can say good-bye to the body and continue its individual life."[134]

One might add here that you to have "emerged from nothing" at least once, namely when you were born. And as the legendary writer and satirist

Voltaire once wrote, it is no more surprising to be born twice (and one might add a billion times) than it is to be born once. However, to be reborn with memories of one's past life intact would indeed be quite surprising, based on our current experience (but see below).

Christof Koch. In his 2012 book, *Consciousness: Confessions of a Romantic Reductionist* neuroscientist, Christof Koch[135] embraces a form of panpsychism. While he describes himself as a "romantic reductionist" in the book's title, he differs from the typical reductionist who would deny any causal role to the mind and would regard conscious experience as either identical to, or an epiphenomenon of, brain activity. Instead, Koch sees consciousness as a fundamental property of the universe.

Koch asserts that, while human consciousness is an individual unity, there are numerous relatively complex lower level "modules" in the brain. He describes such modules as "zombie agents," as he views them as highly integrated as the core self. He counts among such zombie agents the cerebellum, on the basis that it is less interconnected and unified than the cerebrum. He notes that much of human behavior is caused by such unconscious "zombie agents" in the brain.

One would think that if Koch is going to grant a proton consciousness, the same courtesy should be extended to clumps of neurons in one's motor cortex, as they are surely more than their parts. Perhaps Morton Prince's term "co-conscious"[136] rather than the word "unconscious" should be applied here.

Koch contends that all complex material activity, including that of "every living cell on the planet" is associated with some form of consciousness. He endorses panpsychism, as well as Julian Huxley's observation that "Evolution is nothing but matter become conscious of itself."[137] In his recent book *PHI: A Voyage from the Brain to the Soul* neuroscientist Guilio Tononi,[138] whom Koch favorably cites, also endorses being. panpsychism and postulates that there are many centers of consciousness within each human being. When it comes to the soul, Koch likens it to a "crystal" that is constantly changing with the mind's experiences, feelings and thoughts and that returns to the "unformed void" after the person dies.

Finally, Koch endorses the view of the Jesuit priest and paleontologist Pierre Teilhard de Chardin that evolution is the means whereby nature becomes aware of itself and the universe is in the process of evolving into a global mind (Koch uses the Internet as an example).

Microsouls. According to Koch, a single proton would be a center of consciousness. However, as a unified center of consciousness, one might be more akin to an electron than a proton, as Koch notes that protons may be subdivided (into quarks and gluons, for instance). Such elementary particles are more akin to centers of pure consciousness than are clumps of neural ganglia, which are highly compound entities. Under this view one's memories, thoughts and emotions would not survive the death of the brain that generates them (nor is it clear what purpose would be served by their so doing, if one cannot act upon them).

If we are microscopic centers of consciousness, or microsouls, there may be billions of us inhabiting a single human body. In that case, it is likely that, like protons, we are more or less continually being recycled. The idea that we enter a human body as an embryo and remain stuck in it until it dies is likely is the result of the delusion that we are the Person, the (changing) collection of atoms and associated mental experiences that are our bodies and our minds. Instead of being imprisoned for long periods of time in our present bodies, we may be constantly recycled. Under this view, you might wake up in the morning as a dragonfly surfing the ultraviolet sunlight, with no memory of your temporary human incarnation.

In view of the complexity of the quantum mechanical wave function governing the behavior of individual physical particles, it might not be too big of a stretch to hypothesize that a single proton might possess consciousness in the form of "knowledge" of a complex array of inputs. Protons, despite their compound nature (they're made up of quarks and gluons), are essentially immortal. Their average lifetime is at least 10^{34} years, which is 17 orders of magnitude greater than the current age of the universe.

Elementary particles such as electrons and quarks sometimes become embedded in physical brains; these particles persist and remain stuck over "long" time intervals such as minutes and hours. If an electron can "incarnate" in a body for a period of time, then be expelled, and then be "reincarnated" in another body or physical system, then so might we. We may ourselves be material or quasi-material entities that can become stuck in individual brains on a temporary basis. We may be a particle or field already known to physical science, although it is more likely we are an entity yet to be discovered and explained.

We directly experience ourselves as single unified fields of consciousness that persist through changes in our brain states and bodily composition over periods of at least hours. We think we persist as the same selves over the lifetimes of our bodies. In this we may be wrong. If memories are, as an overwhelming body of scientific evidence indicates, stored as patterns of synaptic connections among neurons in our brain, how do you know that you are the same field of consciousness that inhabited your body when you fell asleep? If you can become attached to your brain shortly after conception (or in the view of some people at birth) and become detached from it at the moment of death, it stands to reason that you can also become attached to it long after birth and leave it well before death. Our association with our bodies may be only temporary. We may be breathed out and breathed in like so many oxygen atoms. Many philosophers (such as Descartes) have thought that minds or souls are not extended in space and time and are thus immaterial. However, we find ourselves stuck in physical bodies occupying particular locations in space and (even more mysteriously) located at a particular moments in time. This suggests that we too must (at least in part) be residents of spacetime ourselves, if only temporarily.

As noted above, if we are continually being recycled, then when we wake in the morning, we may not be in the same bodies (or objects or plasma fields) that we were in the day before. If our memories, thoughts and emotions are largely a function of our brain states, we would not remember our existence as, say, a crow the day before. Our previous "memory pad," namely the crow's brain, is lost to us. We cannot find those corvid memories in the same way that we cannot access a phone number written on a misplaced piece of paper. The telephone number and the pad on which it was written are not parts of our essential selves. Neither are we the memories stored in the brain of the crow that now perches outside our window or the memories and personality traits stored in the new human brain into which we have just awakened. What we will remember are the memories stored in that new human brain (sometimes after a period of momentary confusion upon awakening). We will feel the emotions caused by the intense firing of our midbrain neurons and the hormones and neurotransmitters rampaging through our cerebral cortex. Accessing the brain's memories of our sixth birthday party, we will immediately come to the conclusion that we have inhabited this brain and body for decades. The brain has evolved to serve the body and we are now made to serve that purpose as well, overwhelmed by the delusion that we are the Person, that is to say, the body and the memories, thoughts and emotions that result from the neural activity of that body's brain. We think we are in sole command of the body, whereas in fact our nerves, the neurochemical soup in which they bathe, as well as numerous other centers of pure consciousness also mired in the same brain, may have as much or more to say about the fate of the body than we do. In short, we fall under the illusion that we are the Person, the physical body that continues from birth to death, and the stream of memories, thoughts and emotions that courses through it, rather than the centers of pure consciousness that we are.

Once we have shed our present body along with the cognitive "self-cocoons" we have wrapped around us to keep us firmly identified with our present personalities, who knows what wonders may await us?

Afterlife #1: Physical and Quasi-Physical Resurrection. What most people mean by the survival of death is the continuation of the personality, including one's thoughts, feelings, emotions, and beliefs, after death. This is sometimes called personal survival to distinguish it from survival of consciousness without memory. In the most extreme view of personal survival, what survives death is the Person (i.e., one's physical body combined with one's personality, feelings, and memories.

The resurrection of the physical body complete with personality on the Day of Judgment is one of the central doctrines of the Abrahamic religious tradition (which includes Judaism, Christianity, and Islam). Many modern adherents to this tradition may not subscribe to this belief (or even know about it), but instead believe in a different, less physicalistic view of the afterlife. Some nonbelievers eagerly await their cybernetic resurrection in a robot, cyborg or memory-implanted clone of one's present body.

Supernatural Resurrection. The atoms in one's current body have resided in the bodies of countless other persons, which raises some difficulties from a literal interpretation of the Judgment Day prophesy that one's physical body will be resurrected. For instance, will you have to engage in some sort of spiritual melee with other ghosts on Judgment Day over who gets which atoms?

This problem can of course be avoided by denying that the resurrection body is molecularly identical to the premortem body or by asserting that the Resurrection World lies in a different space-time continuum than the one we presently inhabit.

Another good reason for disbelieving in the doctrine of bodily resurrection through the intervention of a deity is that there is no rational basis for believing in it, unless one is prepared to accept particular religious doctrines (out of a wide array of contradictory religious doctrines) as fact in the absence of any compelling supporting evidence.

Some of these difficulties with resurrection may be overcome by assuming that one's resurrection body is some sort of a glorified, super-healthy (indeed immortal) replication of the physical body one had on Earth or that the resurrection world lies outside of the spacetime continuum we inhabit during our present lives. The literal resurrection of one's physical body on the planet Earth does not conform to the conceptions of the afterlife and heaven held by most lay members of the Abrahamic religions today, who picture heaven as a dreamlike, albeit suprapersonal. realm.

The Lingering Death of the Quantum Observer. If not literally in the heavens (i.e., sky), perhaps heaven is a realm outside of our current physical universe, such as a dream world or one of the uncountable infinity of parallel universes postulated to exist in Hugh Everett's remarkably unparsimonious "Many Worlds" interpretation of quantum mechanics (in which all possible futures occur). Let us hope that it is not the latter, because then we might all be live Schrödinger cats, who (though an incredible streak of luck, or perhaps misfortune) never manage to die, perhaps because one's consciousness cannot observe its own death, as suggested by Anthony Peake[139] and Max Tegmark[140] We would thus become aged Methuselahs, forever breathing what we desperately hope are our last breaths. However, we would have to put up with this ghastly condition for only 30 more years until we reach the Singularity predicted by futurist Ray Kurzweil,[141] when nanotechnologies can repair and rejuvenate our aged and broken bodies and advanced cybernetics will allow our personalities to be uploaded into supercomputers. It should be noted that Kurzweil himself reportedly swallows 150 vitamin pills per day in an effort to prolong his life and make it to 2045, when the prophesized Singularity kicks in.

Artificial Resurrection. Several scientists, including Hans Moravec,[142] Grant Fjermedal.[143] Frank Tipler[144] and Raymond Kurzweil[145] among others, have suggested that one's thoughts, memories and personality could all be "downloaded" into a computer or robot, allowing one's essential self to survive after death in a cybernetic world or as a cybernetic simulacrum operating in the physical world. One's new brain might be entirely or in part biologically-based, and might be housed within an android facsimile of your body (possibly even within a biological clone of your own physical body).

Along similar lines, it could be argued that, if you are not the particular collection of physical particles that make up your present physical body, perhaps you are the particular *pattern* of molecules that make up your present body (including your brain configuration and thus personality). You would then remain the same person even if the physical particles that make up your body changed, so long as the general pattern remained the same. This is the basis of the famous beaming technique in the *Star Trek* television and movie series. In *Star Trek*, one can "beam" to a new location by undergoing a process in which one's physical body is atomized, information about the pattern of the physical particles that make up one's body is sent to a distant location, and a new body is reassembled (presumably out of new atoms) at the second location. Peter Oppenheimer[146] and Derek Parfit[147] have independently concluded that this beaming process would result in the death of everyone who used it as a form of transportation, followed by the construction of a replica of the person at the destination site. This replica may not be the original person any more than identical twins are the same person as one another.

Assume that more than one copy of the person is assembled at the destination site. Surely it would be difficult to believe that one's self could simultaneously inhabit all the replicas of one's physical body that are constructed at the destination site, insofar as a unified conscious self cannot have several separate and independent streams of consciousness occurring at the same time. The same objection applies to the "downloading" of one's personality into a computer.

Also, it might be possible that such a simulacrum of one's personality could be created before one's physical death. In such a case would your conscious self be located within the simulacrum or would you still reside inside your current brain? One suspects that the intuitive answer for most people is that one would still reside in one's original brain. We sense that we are somehow physically attached to our brains and that such brains are, alas, not so easily escaped. Thus, it is possible that the Person (your physical body and personality) might be resurrected and be recognized as you and accepted as such by your friends and acquaintances. However your essence, the center of consciousness that mysteriously inhabits your present brain, may be long gone and occupied in new adventures, while your simulacrum continues to fulfill your present role to the satisfaction of your friends, neighbors, and enemies, and spouse.

Personal Survival. If the afterlife is not a dream-world, might your personality (comprising your memories, sensations, thoughts, emotions and desires), or some fragments thereof, soldier on past your death? Evidence that such might be the case is provided by messages purportedly received from the dead and passed along to the living via mediums or psychics. However, much of this evidence may be explained on the basis of fraud, subconscious inference, sloppy scientific methodology, and the propensity for humans to see patterns where none exist. Suffice it to say that this evidence for the survival of personality elements is very weak and flies in the face of an overwhelming body of evidence that mental activity is intricately dependent on brain activity, as reviewed in detail in Martin and Augustine.[148] Surely it is absurd to postulate that personality fragments such as one's memories, emotions and thoughts can survive the dissolution of one's entire brain at this point in our knowledge of neurophysiology.

Afterlife #3: The Collective Mind. If you do not survive the death of your physical body cloaked in some sort of dream-body or "astral" body, perhaps you might live on in the form of your personality (comprising your memories, sensations, thoughts, emotions and desires). Possibly only a fragment of your personality is preserved after death. Perhaps several fragments, or "sub-souls" survive, as thought by the ancient Egyptians. Such clusters of disembodied personality traits are frequently postulated to reside in some sort of "collective mind."

If our dream bodies are mere hallucinations, might we be the dreamer rather than the dreamt?

Can facets of our personality such as our thoughts and memories survive in the absence of a body of any sort? Such incorporeal survival is not usually contemplated by believers in survival, as it is further removed from our premortem existence and such an afterworld may seem a dark and depressing place. But postmortem realms in which the departed are housed in some sort of astral bodies may only reflect the limits of our imagination as well as wishful thinking (i.e., not giving up anything from this life other than physical and spiritual ailments, certainly not one's clothes). However, it may be that if portions of the personality survive death, they may generate an hallucination of a physical body (and if this hallucination is continuous, it would be difficult if not impossible, to distinguish between this form of survival and survival in the "astral plane" as discussed above).

Survival of Personality Fragments. Many people identify their essential selves or souls with their personalities, including their thoughts, memories, emotions and strivings. Some theorists have proposed that at least some of these personality elements may survive death, persisting in a collective mind, such as those proposed by the early psychical researcher F. W. H. Myers, the psychiatrist C. G. Jung, the physicist and mathematician G. N. M. Tyrrell, and the prominent American psychologist Gardner Murphy.

Myers[149] postulated what he called the "subliminal mind," which was responsible for telepathy as well as ostensible messages from the dead.

Tyrrell proposed that people share regions of their minds at a deep unconscious level. He asserted that, at the unconscious level, the "midlevel centers [of the personality] possess in some degree both the qualities of selfhood and of otherness from self."[150] Tyrrell proposed that it is in these regions that our dreams and hallucinations are constructed. He asserted that, as this deep region of the unconscious has no organization in space or time, it enables telepathic exchanges to take place.

Afterlife #4: Reincarnation. The evidence for reincarnation comprises the strongest form of parapsychological evidence for the survival of death of at least some elements of the personality (and in some cases even of bodily appearance). Also, reincarnation provides the easiest afterlife to imagine, as no imagination is necessary. You are already there!

Reincarnation is an appealing doctrine because of its simplicity. The recycling of souls from one body to the next bears a resemblance to the great cycles of nature, including the seasons, the rising and setting of the sun, the water cycle, the oxygen cycle, and the recycling of atoms and molecules between living creatures and the worlds they inhabit. Another advantage of the reincarnation process is that it renders our present incarnated state less puzzling. Under the official Judeo-Christian-Islamic (Abrahamic) view, one lives but one human lifetime, which is but a flicker of an eyelash when compared to the 13.8 billion years or so that have elapsed since the Big Bang as well as the eons that lie ahead before the universe's predicted quiet end in a "heat death." Because our lives are such infinitesimal spans when compared to the age of the universe, each conscious person must marvel at the fact that this present moment in time just happens to be one of the moments when he or she (construed as the conjunction of a physical body and personality, as in the Western religious tradition) exists. If a moment were to be chosen at random from the history of the universe, the probability that any person would exist at that time would be essentially zero. The fact that the moment that has somehow mysteriously been selected to be "now" is a moment within the reader's lifetime would seem to be a miracle if the Abrahamic single life hypothesis is true. The fact that "now" happens to be a moment within your lifetime would become much less surprising under the hypothesis of reincarnation, as the "now" would only have to correspond to any moment in a potentially endless succession of lives rather than a single human life. If one were to allow the possibility of incarnation in nonhuman life forms, on one of the now countless exoplanets orbiting foreign stars, or perhaps even in other universes, it becomes more and more probable that you (construed as a center of pure consciousness) would exist now. The philosopher Friedrich Nietzsche endorsed a variation, the notion of the "eternal return," that one simply lives the same life over and over again.

Philosophical Objections to Reincarnation. Several objections have been raised to the idea of reincarnation. One, which was raised by the third century Christian philosopher Tertullian[151] and has more recently been dusted off and resurrected (or perhaps reincarnated) by the philosopher Paul Edwards[152] is based on population explosion. There are many more human beings alive today than have lived at any time in the past. Thus, it is claimed, there would not be enough souls to animate each new human body, as the number of bodies must surely outrun the number of reincarnating souls. However, this objection is mired in anthropocentrism.

Animals, of both the terrestrial and extraterrestrial varieties, could provide one obvious reservoir of souls, as would plants and elementary particles under philosophy of panpsychism.

It is also conceivable that souls might spend considerable amounts of time not housed in biological bodies, or indeed in any body whatsoever. The physicist Evan Harris Walker[153] postulated the existence of "proto-consciousnesses" responsible for the collapse of quantum mechanical state vectors governing events that are remote in space and time from human (or other biological) observers. Hill[154] has observed that, if the universe has been designed, it appears to be devised for creatures or consciousnesses that inhabit the vast, seemingly inhabitable regions of outer space. The design of such a vast cosmos for the mere purpose of creating a few randomly evolved, ephemeral sacks of protoplasm (such as ourselves) which crawl about on a minor planet of a second rate star would be most uneconomical indeed. Perhaps centers of consciousness are as common as electrons or quarks.

Objections Based on Memory. A second objection to reincarnation is that we have no memory of our previous lives. Actually, that may not always be the case. Much of the parapsychological evidence for reincarnation, to be discussed below, consists of instances in which persons have in fact claimed to remember details of their previous lives. Reincarnation could of course occur without any transfer of memory from one incarnation to another.

A considerable body of evidence now exists that memories are either physically stored in the brain or at least intimately dependent on certain brain structures. See the anthology *The Myth of an*

Afterlife by Martin and Augustine[155] for a recent comprehensive review of these findings. It would be difficult therefore to imagine that memories could in general survive the dissolution of the physical brain at death.

In fact, we do not remember the events of many previous days of our present lives, although we lived through them. Our system of memories changes over time, with some memories decaying and new ones being formed. Our essential selves, on the other hand, seem to remain unchanged over time. We are thus not identical with any particular set of memories. Thus, it would be easily conceivable that one's self could be reincarnated in a new body, while retaining no memory of one's previous life. Several writers, including Ken Wilber[156] and Stokes[157] have suggested that reincarnation might occur in just such a memory-less manner.

The Buddhist Doctrine of "No Mind." Reincarnation is a Buddhist doctrine. What then is it that reincarnates, if there is no self? According to many Buddhists what reincarnates is a complex of thoughts, desires, and cravings. These Buddhists seem to be adhering to the view that some partial remnant of the personality reincarnates. This conception has already been found wanting above. Not only that, but the Buddhist doctrine of No Mind appears to postulate the existence of experiences in the absence of any experiencer. Also, the simultaneous postulation of an afterlife and denial of a continuing self seems to be contradictory. Thus, this appears to be an incoherent philosophical position. It is no more coherent when uttered by an obedient army of monks with shaven heads and orange robes than it is when uttered by misguided philosophers and scientists such as Dennett, Blackmore, Metzinger and the Churchlands, who deny the very existence of continuing selves.

The Buddhist notion of "no self" as formulated above appears to be nonsensical. The same is true of any doctrine that speaks of experience without an experiencer. Such doctrines are inconsistent with our direct and core introspective experiences. It would be easier to entertain the possibility that the material world is an illusion.

In Buddhism, the goal of spiritual development is to reduce one's own suffering (and that of others) through the extinction of the cravings and desires that give rise to suffering (to the extent that they are invariably unfulfilled). The final aim is to achieve a state of total extinction of desire known as nirvana. Nirvana is essentially a state of extinction of the self. Despite Buddhists' belief in reincarnation, the Buddhist doctrine of *anatta* or "No Soul" is essentially a denial of the existence of a permanent self.

Ken Wilber[158] notes that, while Buddhism denies a permanent existence to the individual soul or self, it does grant a "relative existence" to the soul. Indeed, the doctrine of *anatta* seems directed primarily against the idea that personality patterns and traits have a permanent existence. Thus, seekers of enlightenment should not cling to their present mental states. Rather, each such seeker should see himself or herself as pure consciousness and awareness, something separate from the personality traits, memories, feelings and sensations that may form the source or objects of desire or clinging, preventing one from reaching a state of enlightenment.

The most compelling evidence of reincarnation consists of the spontaneous recall of past life memories. This evidence does not in general suggest the existence of any moral karmic principle governing the assignment of incarnations. Such a karmic principle would also seem to require the existence of theistic "traffic cops" of some sort, although many in the Eastern traditions would equate karma with the unresolved cravings of the mind.

Memoryless Reincarnation. Reincarnation need not involve memory. As the ancient Greeks thought, we may drink of the river of Lethe and remember no more. Like the elementary particles that compose our physical body, our souls or selves (construed as centers of pure consciousness) may be constantly recycled through a succession of living organisms and non-biological structures (some such structures perhaps being beyond our ken at the present time). Memories, like a telephone number scrolled on a note pad, may reside in the structure of the brain, not in the soul, and may be lost in each transition.

Conclusions Regarding the Survival of the Personality. Stevenson's reincarnation research provides the best evidence that personality traits, memories, emotions and other aspects of the Person may survive death.

The vast majority of human beings have no recollections of former lives. However, if memories are stored as patterns of synaptic connections in the brain, as most modern neuroscientists believe, then this lack of memories of former lives would be expected, even if the centers of pure consciousness that comprise our core selves do transmigrate from brain to brain (and even from brain to non-brain and then back again).

Our core selves, if conceived as centers of pure consciousness, appear intuitively to be unitary and not divisible into components. If we are something like the proto-consciousnesses that govern the collapse of remote quantum state vectors, as proposed by Walker,[159] then we likely share the same ontological privileges accorded to fundamental particles, including conservation over time. Perhaps we are even identical with particles or fields already known to physics (much like a proton responding to a complex quantum-mechanical field connecting it to the rest of the universe may be said to be in some sense aware of that universe). On the other hand we may well be fundamental entities yet to be identified by modern science. In either event, our association with any given brain or other physical system is likely to be more temporary than we think. The illusion that you have continuously inhabited your current brain for decades likely arises from the memories stored in the connectome (patterns of neuron connections) of your brain combined with your cognitive construction of the social entity known here as the Person.

The illusion of being the Person, in the sense of the conjunction of our physical bodies and personality traits such as memories and desires, likely arises in part from a false identification with the physical body and its needs, which may serve our biological imperatives but perhaps not our spiritual needs.

This universe is one of conservation, of mass-energy, baryon number and angular momentum. It is a universe of rearrangement, not destruction. If, as centers of pure consciousness, we are granted at least some form of parity with such seemingly (to us) mindless and insignificant entities such as quarks and electrons, then it is likely that we, like they, are recycled from system to system, continually falling into the murky depths of one system of primitive awareness after another, but perhaps from time to time becoming united in a "supersystem," compared to which our present human consciousness will appear like that of an amoeba.

If the materialists are correct in their view that we are nothing but matter and energy and if our intuition is correct that we are unitary, much more like a quark or an electron than like a temporary conglomeration of atoms, then the pro-survivalist may rejoice. The universe conserves mass-energy, recycling it from one part of the cosmic show to another. Uncountable beauties and terrors may await us as we are torn free of our human form and the illusion created by our stories of the self and our identification with the Person.

Souls, Microsouls, Macrosouls, Megasouls, and Gods.

We now consider revised views of souls and gods that may be more compatible with modern neuroscience and modern physics than are the traditional religious conceptions of the soul. We will begin with a consideration of the possibility of spheres of consciousness at different levels, from elementary particles to deities.

Souls. In view of the dependence of our thoughts, memories, emotions and sensations on the activity and structure of the physical "wetware" that is our brains, we are left with pure consciousness as the best candidate for the portion of our selves that could survive the death of the brain. Remember that neuroscience, at least in its current state of development, is fundamentally unable to account for the existence of conscious experiences (in the sense of "raw feels," or "qualia," as contemporary philosophers are wont to call them).

For instance, while neuroscientists may be able to identify the neural activity that is associated with the experience of, say, a red rectangle in the left side of one's visual field, it cannot explain how the electrical discharges in this tangled web of biomatter can produce the conscious experience of a red rectangle. They may be able to predict that this stimulus will generate neural signals leading to mouth and throat movements that will cause the subject to exclaim "I see a red rectangle!" However, for all the outside observers know, the subject could be lying (e.g., could be a philosophical "zombie" with no consciousness whatsoever). Modern cognitive neuroscience has gained remarkable insights into the nature of the brain activities that are associated with various forms of cognitive experience. What it has not thus far achieved is any explanation of how a lump of protoplasm, which is basically nothing more than an ongoing (albeit complex) electrochemical reaction, can give rise to conscious experience in the first place.

As we have seen, due to the replacement of atoms, if each of us does have a continuing self, then that self cannot be identical with any specified collection of material particles. The Person you were ten years ago has long been dead. Death may not be as terrible as that Person expected it to be.

If one is to be identified with a particular physical body, the probability that the set of genes that formed the blueprint for that body would ever have come into combination is virtually zero (and still smaller is the probability that the particular configuration of material particles that comprises one's present physical body would ever have formed, much less exist at the present moment). It is also surprising that the present moment in time just happens to within your lifetime, which is but a flicker of a candle in comparison to the eons that have already passed and those that are still to come. Yet here you find yourself (a field of consciousness that is unique and special to you at any rate) existing at the present time. This is most surprising (indeed virtually impossible) based on the view that you are identical with, or dependent on, the existence of a particular collection and arrangement of material particles at a particular moment in time.

Just as the collection of atoms and elementary particles making up your physical body undergoes continual change and replacement, so do your thoughts, emotions, memories and personality traits. Your essential self persists, despite these continual changes in the contents of your consciousness (and, we might add, subconscious and unconscious minds as well). Thus, you cannot be your personality or its "contents," such as your thoughts, emotions, and memories.

As already noted, over the past four decades, neuroscientists have amply demonstrated that one's sensations, feelings, thoughts, emotions, memories, ideas, and even personality can be radically altered through electromagnetic, surgical, chemical, and accidental interventions in the brain. If relatively minor modifications of brain states can substantially alter the nature of one's experience and personality, how could your personality and experiences manage to continue on in a more or less uninterrupted fashion after the far more drastic event of the destruction of your entire brain? Also, many of the concerns that drive the structure of your personality have to do with the preservation of your own physical body and those of people who are closely related to you. What would be the point of the continuance of these concerns once your physical body has been returned to dust and your ability to intervene in the physical world perhaps radically curtailed?

The self that seems to persist over long time periods (from birth to death in the popular, common view) is not the conglomeration of one's thoughts, feelings, memories, and sensations themselves, but rather the field of pure consciousness in which these qualia act out their drama. In other words, we are vessels of consciousness rather than the contents of that vessel.

Creators. If one's true self is Atman, or pure consciousness, is there any Brahman or larger consciousness for it to merge into, or be identical with? In recent times, scientists have turned their backs on the concepts of deities and a Creator. Arguments for a Designer have largely been abandoned as regressive. After all, if there was a Designer, who designed Him (or Her or Them or It)? If there was a "preuniverse," then what preceded that?

The answer for some is consciousness. Recall that the noted mathematician and physicist Sir James Jeans asserted that pondering the subtleties of the mathematics of laws of physics and the seeming dependence of material events upon observation by conscious minds, observed that the "universe begins to look more like a great thought than a great machine"[160] More recently, Henry Stapp[161] avers that, under quantum mechanics, the world has an essentially "idea-like" structure." As noted above, Richard Conn Henry, a physicist at Johns Hopkins University, asserts that that the universe is "entirely mental" in nature and "consists of nothing but ideas."[162] Indeed, the base reality of the world appears to be one of quantum probability waves inhabiting an abstract, multidimensional mathematical space rather than solid, marble-like electrons and protons zipping around in a four-dimensional spacetime continuum that we imagine to be the firm underpinnings of our material existence.

The philosopher Galen Strawson asserts that "there is no good reason to believe that anything nonexperiential exists" and that "we have good reason to believe that nothing nonexperiential exists.[163]

But if the universe is a Dream, whose Dream is it anyway?

Are our individual consciousnesses just aspects of the Creator's (or Creators') consciousness, lost in an unimaginable form of contemplation of the myriad creatures It has managed to generate from Its mathematical inventions, much as we may become lost in the adventures of a goldfish in the bowl in our living room?

The Participatory Universe. We ourselves may be more like antiprotons than to angels, small islands of consciousness born to force the amorphous clouds of quantum possibilities into the crystallized raindrops of actualized events. In the view of many interpreters of quantum mechanics, observation by consciousness is what causes such quantum collapse (i.e., collapse of the state vector containing an array of possibilities into one definite outcome). As already noted, the physicist Harris Walker proposed the existence of "mini-consciousnesses" or "proto-consciousnesses" that govern the collapse of quantum vectors that are remote from human observers.[164] Decades of psychological research indicate humans can hold only about seven items in working memory at one time. We ourselves may thus be mini-consciousnesses or microsouls.

Through the collapse of quantum state vectors, conscious minds may well produce the experience of "time flow" (the sensation that we ride the "now," as events in the future are carried to us and then recede into the inaccessible past). It would seem that in the last few decades philosophers and scientists have generally given up any attempts to explain the phenomenon of time flow, surely one of the most basic facets of our existence, along with the centers of consciousness that comprise our selves. Science and mainstream philosophy have not made much (if any) progress in explaining either of these core elements of the world.

As just noted, conscious observers may be more akin to Walker's "proto-consciousnesses" than to human brains with full-fledged information-processing capabilities (including both subconscious and unconscious activity). If physics suggests anything, it is that the fundamental constituents of the universe are more likely to be very small in comparison to the human observers that formed the center of the cosmos in the medieval ontology that we are just now abandoning. Our essential selves may be more likely to resemble an electron or electromagnetic field than a human body.

Indeed, the fact that souls, if they exist, seem to get "stuck," however temporarily, in physical brains suggests that they reside, at least partially, in spacetime. Thus, they may be quasi-material entities.

Microsouls and Macrosouls. We each seem to be single conscious selves (fields of consciousness) which in some mysterious manner became attached to our brains shortly after our conceptions and will persist in those brains until we die. But our brains are powerful and unimaginably large in comparison to our single-celled ancestors, who, we might suppose, bore the glimmerings of consciousness. Our brains and bodies are in essence colonies of trillions of one-celled animals. Many of us may ride in a single brain. For instance, as noted above, when a human brain is split into its two hemispheres by severing the corpus callosum (the primary bundle of neural fibers connecting the two hemispheres), two fields of consciousness seem to exist, sometimes with such differences in motivation that the right hand (controlled by the left hemisphere) may forced to grab the left hand (controlled by the right) in order to prevent the latter from carrying out an assault on one's spouse. Metzinger[165] denies selfhood to the right hemisphere in such cases of "alien hand" syndrome on the grounds that it has no self model. Perhaps not, but it may have a doozy of a wife model. Schechter[166] reports a case in which a split-brain patient slapped his oversleeping right-hemisphere awake with his left hand. Schechter asserts that such patients have two global workspaces rather than one.

The findings of split-brain research are precisely the evidence "neuro-philosopher" Patricia Churchland[167] uses to refute the existence of a nonphysical self or soul in human beings . Churchland is likely correct so far as the "single soul" theory goes, but the evidence suggests that multiple centers of consciousness or "souls" may exist within a single brain, with perhaps many of them falling under the delusion that they are the single center that is "in charge of" the body.

Philosopher Andy Clark asserts that the human brain is modular, with no central processor. These brain modules can integrate into "surprisingly integrated (although temporary) wholes"[168] Free will denier Sam Harris similarly notes that there are too many separable components for there to be a single entity standing as a "rider to the horse" (brain).[169]

Michael Gazzaniga,[170] a prominent neuropsychologist, proposes that the left hemisphere of the brain hosts an "interpreter," which in split-brain patients fabricates explanations for emotion and behaviors that are caused by the now isolated right hemisphere, and thus creates the illusion of a unified self. Perhaps each such "self" identifies itself with the entire body in much the same way each member of a football audience may identify herself with the whole team. Gazzaniga views humans as the "last word" on evolution[171] There are probably lurking viruses laughing at him right now.

Blindsight. Consider also the phenomenon of blindsight. "Blindsight" is a term coined by Lawrence Weiskrantz[172] to describe a syndrome in which cortically-blind subjects respond appropriately to visually presented stimuli even though they report no conscious awareness of such stimuli. Cortical blindness refers to blindness that is a result of damage to the visual cortex in the occipital lobes of the brain. Even though the eyes of such patients may be normal, they may be blind in part of their visual field because of such damage to their visual cortex. If you present a small dot of light to such patients in the blind areas of their visual fields, they will say that they saw nothing. However, if you ask them to just take a guess by pointing to where the dot of light might have been, they frequently point at the exact location that the dot occupied. If you present erotic pictures to such a patient in the blind area of the visual field, the patient may blush or giggle or say things such as "That's quite a machine you've got there, Doc!"

Marshall and Halligan[173] cite a case in which a blindsight patient's rating of the desirability of a house was influenced by flames that she could not see consciously.

Many researchers have speculated that blindsight is mediated by a secondary visual center in a subcortical area of the brain known as the superior colliculus. Thus, the phenomenon of blindsight also suggests there may be multiple centers of consciousness within a single human brain.

A Hierarchy of Selves. The notion that the human mind may be composed of an assembly of interacting centers of consciousness is an old one. It may be traced as far back as Aristotle, who postulated the existence of a "vegetative soul," a "sensitive soul" and a "rational soul" in each person. F. W. H. Myers[174] hypothesized the existence of several independent selves within the unconscious or "subliminal" mind. William McDougall[175] proposed that the normal human mind is composed of a hierarchy of "coconscious personalities," each carrying out its own separate function. McDougall used Morton Prince's term "coconscious" rather than the usual terms "subconscious" or "unconscious" to describe such secondary personalities in order to emphasize their self-awareness.[176]

In support of McDougall's hierarchical model of the mind, many lines of psychological research, including studies of subliminal perception, posthypnotic suggestion, preattentive filters, and automatic motor performance, suggest that the human mind is capable of conducting a great deal of sophisticated mental activity outside of the field of awareness of the primary center of consciousness.

In 1923, the biologist William Mackenzie proposed a hierarchical model of the mind in which new entities arise through the aggregation of lower entities. These entities could be either biological or psychical. Insect colonies and living cells would examples of such integration.[177]

Freud's one-time rival for the leadership of the psychoanalytic movement, C. G. Jung postulated the existence of complexes, or centers of psychic activity that, like Prince and McDougall, he described as "coconscious."[178] William James[179] also suggested that such "secondary selves" are personal centers of consciousness.

Based on his investigations into hypnotic phenomena, Ernst Hilgard proposed what he called the "neodissociation" theory of hypnosis.[180] Hilgard asserted that the hypnotized person was associated with a subconscious "hidden observer" that was aware of events for which the primary, conscious personality had no knowledge. Hilgard based this theory on phenomena such as hypnotically-induced amnesia, anesthesia, or negative hallucinations (e.g., when a hypnotized subject is instructed not to see a particular person or object). Hilgard was even able to hold conversations with such "hidden observers," who frequently reported awareness of events (posthypnotic suggestions, pain, etc.) for which the primary personality claimed no knowledge, such as pain in the case of hypnotic anesthesia. However, many scientists have asserted that Hilgard's "hidden observers" were created by Hilgard's hypnotic suggestions rather than being autonomous entities that were "discovered" by Hilgard. For instance, Spanos and Hewitt[181] were

411

able to evoke a hidden observer that felt less, rather than more, pain than the primary subject under hypnotic anesthesia. They hypothesize that this "hidden observer" was an artifact manufactured through their own hypnotic suggestions.

Ramachandran and Blakeslee[182] cite dreams in which another dream character tells an unexpected joke to the dreaming self as further evidence of the existence of multiple centers of consciousness within a single brain.

In the decades since the "cognitive revolution" (i.e., overthrow of behaviorism) in psychology, research into the "cognitive unconscious" has led to the creation of many hierarchical models of the mind, such as the "Massachusetts modularism" proposed by Jerry Fodor,[183] in which the mind is seen as being split into modular "computational" components.

Michael Gazzaniga[184] likewise rejects the notion of a unitary consciousness in favor of the view that the mind is composed of a collection of independently-functioning modules that he, following William McDougall, describes as "coconscious." As evidence for this modular view of the mind, Gazzaniga cites post-hypnotic suggestions, apparent unconscious (or coconscious) problem-solving activity (in which the solution to a complex problem suddenly emerges full-blown into consciousness), blindsight, the existence of separate procedural and episodic memory systems, and split-brain research. Gazzaniga tends to identify the "conscious self" with the module that is in control of the language centers of the brain, and he refers to this module as the "executive module." This is likely consistent with one's own introspective experience. For instance, I seem to be the one choosing which words to type; however, when I think about it, I am always amazed that my fingers and my body obey my commands. How this is accomplished is outside of my introspective knowledge. That's somebody else's job.

Gazzaniga cites many instances in which the executive module uses confabulation to explain behavior that was in fact generated by other modules. For instance, a person who acts under a posthypnotic suggestion to close a window may claim that he was cold. Gazzaniga also cites several instances of confabulation by the left hemisphere to explain actions performed in response to directions given to the right hemisphere in split-brain patients. It might not be far-fetched to suppose that all or most modules might likewise subscribe to the illusion that they are the sole center of consciousness or in sole control of the body. For instance, modules listening to the mouth as it issues verbal utterances may be under the illusion that they were primarily responsible for producing those utterances. They might naturally identify with the body as a whole rather than with the particular brain region in which they are located.

Gazzaniga and Roser[185] contend that the "left-hemisphere interpreter" may be responsible for the feeling that one's consciousness is unified. They suggest that either consciousness has a "graded relationship" to brain activity or that consciousness results whenever brain activity exceeds a particular threshold. They note that brain activations associated with consciously perceived stimuli differ from those associated with unseen stimuli in terms of their intensity and spatial extent.

Daniel Wegner, in his book *The Illusion of Conscious Will,* [186] notes that the well-known brain researcher Jose Delgado[187] found that movements produced by direct electrical stimulation of the motor areas of the brain were experienced as voluntarily produced, thus supporting the hypothesis that "free will" may in many cases be an illusion. Wegner does however affirm the existence of the self, which he defines in terms of a continuous memory structure. He asserts that in cases of fugue, multiple personality or apparent "possession" (if any genuine cases in fact exist), a new self exists if the person has amnesia for the prior self.

Multiple Personality and Dissociation. Ostensible cases of multiple personality and dissociation (if genuine) might represent instances in which one or more subordinate personalities or centers of consciousness within a brain have rebelled against the primary, executive personality.

Megasouls. The prominent sociobiologists Bert Hölldobler and E. O. Wilson[188] propose that communities of insects comprise "superorganisms" and that evolutionary selection acts on the colony as a unit, rather than on the individual insects. Can the whole of humanity be considered as a single super-brain, perhaps associated with global spheres of consciousness? As noted above, Stephen Goldberg, a neuroscientist and physician, has even suggested that in the future the Internet may develop into an "advanced intrinsic consciousness."[189] Would this be a center of pure consciousness at a higher level in the hierarchy than our individual selves, a "megasoul" if you will?

Koestler's Holons. The noted writer Arthur Koestler[190] called such entities as a world mind, a society, a Person, an organ, or a cell "holons," a term he coined to denote an entity that is simultaneously a whole and a part of some larger system. He contended that there is a hierarchy of holons, with each holon being a part of a some holon on the next highest level.

Holt[191] notes that it is a mystery how micro-minds can coalesce into a macro-mind or a mega-mind. Holt calls this the Combination Problem, and he notes that William James, who was otherwise friendly to panpsychism, found this to be the greatest stumbling block for a panpsychist account of the world. Holt notes that, based on current theories of quantum mechanics, even two elementary particles may not be separate things but may be quantum-mechanically entangled. Thus, in this case, the fundamental entity may be the system of particles rather than the individual particles. Finally, the fields of consciousness that we take ourselves to be seem to have arisen from the multispecies free-for-alls that we call our bodies. These are the selves that we know most directly, and we know that there are cognitive systems far below us and far above us in the physical hierarchy. Are these conscious systems as well? Or does the *meso-level* we directly experience form the only ground of awareness?

Gods. Now we will turn to the ultimate (or perhaps penultimate,) megasoul: God. When two people argue about the existence of God (or gods), their disagreements are often semantic rather than substantive. The word "god" may (and usually does) denote very different things to different people.

The omnipotent and benevolent God of the Abrahamic religious tradition would seem to be a more powerful god than those of the mythological and shamanistic traditions. In what is called the *theistic* view of God, the deity still intervenes in the world, causing some events to happen and preventing others from happening. However, the existence of an all-powerful and omnibenevolent

God is difficult to square with the existence of catastrophes such as tsunamis, wars and other forms of suffering and injustice.

Deism Redux. Deism is the belief in a being who designed and created the universe, but no longer participates in it. This was the view of Einstein, the late mathematician Martin Gardner and many of the founding fathers of the United States, its first ten Presidents, and Abraham Lincoln,[192] as well as philosophers such as Spinoza. The anthropic principle discussed above might be taken as support for the deistic view that the universe was created by an intelligent being or beings. However, as we have seen above, concerns were expressed that physicists at the Large Hadron Collider might create black holes that could give birth to new universes. Thus, the intelligent creators of the universe might well have had no clue as to what they were creating (and may not even know of its accidental existence).

Pantheism, Pandeism, and Panentheism. In some religious views, God does not stand outside the universe, but participates in it. In the *pantheistic* view, God is the universe and is thus present in all things. Thus, everything in the world is identical to, or part of, God. If one equates God with consciousness, this is very similar to the panpsychist view. "Theism" is the view that God sometimes intervenes in the universe. If one subscribes to a deistic view of the universe in which God does not intervene in the universe once it has been created, the corresponding term is pandeism.

In the related theological doctrine of *panentheism*, God interpenetrates the universe and is present in all things, but God also extends beyond the present universe rather than being identical to the universe. The corresponding term for deists is *panendeism* Under both of these views, one's self is part of God.

Philosopher and theologian John W. Cooper[193] has provided a recent encyclopedic review of panentheism. He cites the 18th century theologian Jonathan Edwards' view that minds as continuing entities exist only in that God forms and communicates a coherent series of ideas. Edwards asserted that God literally thinks minds into existence and the whole of creation is in God's mind. Thus, in Edwards' view, God could therefore be conceptualized as a "World-Soul."

Cooper notes that within Islam, the 20th century theologian Sir Muhammed Iqbal asserted that there is nothing but Allah. He characterizes Iqbal's view as a form of panpsychism, citing Iqbal's remark that "every atom of Divine energy is an ego."[194] Iqbal contended that the "world and everything in it, from atoms to humans, are "ego-unities." Cooper also cites Iqbal's view that the emergence of egos endowed with the power of spontaneous and hence unforeseeable action represents, in a sense, a limitation of the freedom of the all-inclusive Ego (i.e., God).

Cooper discusses the work of Sarvepalli Radhakrishnan, a Hindu philosopher and the President of India from 1962 to 1967. Radhakrishnan proposed a form of panentheism that sought common ground with Western and non-Hindu religions.

Cooper describes Radhakrishnan as a panentheist about current reality and a pantheistic monist about ultimate reality. Cooper notes that the Hindu tradition embraces both views. The great Hindu philosopher Sankara (who lived from 788 to 820) held that God is absolutely one and that all differences and distinctions were merely temporary illusions. The 12th century philosopher Ramanuja held that the world is the body of Brahman or God and, that individual souls are real and do not disappear into God. Radhakrishnan proposed an amalgamation of these views. In temporal existence (i.e., within spacetime) God is personal and souls are real, as asserted by Ramanuja. However, ultimately all things become indistinguishable, as held by Sankara.

Cooper classifies the popular Anglican priest turned Zen Buddhist Alan Watts, who died in 1973, as a panentheist. Indeed as noted above, Watts often described the universe as God playing hide-and-seek with himself.

However, this conclusion seems at best premature in light of the fact that neuroscience can offer no explanation of how brain activity gives rise to a unified center of consciousness and conscious experience. These are deep mysteries that are unlikely to be solved in the foreseeable future, if ever.

But who knows? Tonight we sleep, perchance to dream, perchance to be released from our bondage, only to be eventually imprisoned in yet another host.

Prognostications. It is possible that one day we will be able scientifically describe and detect microsouls and macrosouls (especially if they have a physical aspect tying them to brains and other types of physical systems) and maybe even megasouls. The search for such entities will likely be confined to the present universe (but who knows?) and will likely be more fruitful than a quest for the First Cause, or a pre-universe, that might entail our exploration of a nested labyrinth of pre-universes, each giving birth to the next.

Conclusions

There is no unified view of the soul at the present time. When people use the words "soul," "self," "god," "heaven," and "the afterlife," they may mean many different things by these terms. This may sometimes lead to confusion and seemingly intractable differences in religious viewpoints when the only disagreement is semantic. Under the irrefutable doctrine of solipsism, you might be the only center of consciousness that exists in the universe. The rest may be an elaborate dream. If so, the physical universe is a very complex dream, obeying complex laws that seem well beyond the capacity of our unconscious minds to conjure up. But who knows what megasouls with their vast resources and information channel capacities might be capable of. Within the major religious traditions there is a wide range of beliefs as to the nature of the thanatope. For instance, within the Abrahamic tradition, a fundamentalist Christian may believe that his personality and physical body will be resurrected on Judgment Day, based on a literal reading of the Bible, whereas a humanistic reformed Jew may not believe in an afterlife (or God for that matter).

Segal[195] notes that the Bible of the Abrahamic traditions actually has little to say about the nature of the afterlife. He speculates that the Biblical silence on this issue may reflect an aversion to foreign cults and gods. Discussion of possible afterlives may have been perceived as opening the door to idolatry or the veneration of ghosts.

Similarly, some atheists believe in an afterlife, despite their disavowal of God. For instance, Buddhism is often described as an atheistic religion and yet embraces the doctrine of reincarnation, although they deny the existence of souls, which might be thought to be a precondition for reincarnation. (Of course at a more popular level, there are pantheons of Buddhist and Hindu deities, along with dreamlike heavens and hells.) Even resurrection need not imply a deity. For instance, an atheist might believe that she could survive death by having her personality uploaded into the cybernetic brain of an android replica of her body, which might be considered a form of survival of the Person.

Based on the nature of the thanatope, there are a variety of possible afterlives, including the resurrection world, an astral or dream world, a collective mind containing the remnants of one's personality, reincarnation with and without memory, a world of pure consciousness or nirvana, or nothing (which is also a form of nirvana, according to some versions of Buddhism).

As noted above, some distinguished philosophers and scientists, including Henri Bergson, F. W. H. Myers, and William James.[196] believed that the brain acts as a filter of consciousness, keeping one's focus on the everyday need for survival, rather than a source or transmitter of consciousness. Under this view, a damaged (and even better yet dead) brain may in fact open you to a wider realm of consciousness. The question then becomes one of whether the expanded consciousness would be so dissimilar to one's premortem personality (with its primary attention no longer focused on biological survival) that it would not be recognizable. There is a body of parapsychological research aimed at detecting the survival of at least parts of the personality. The strongest evidence in this regard is provided by children who spontaneously report memories of previous lives and who often manifest personality traits and birthmarks related to the previous life. In many such cases, these memories of previous lives have been verified as accurate, by interviewing the relatives of the ostensible previous personality. However, this evidence is controversial, and skeptics both within and outside the parapsychological community assert that such reported previous lives may be based on cryptomnesia (forgotten memories of having heard the details of the claimed past life) and other normal processes.

Thus, there is really is no Person in the sense of a continuing aggregation of matter or a and/or personality traits. Like the mayfly, who lives for only a day, we may be the universe temporarily lost in itself.

The Person is likely to be, just as Blackmore[197] and Dennett[198] insist, simply a story we tell ourselves. However, it is a very useful story, just like the story of one's car or my house. It helps credit card companies to obtain payments for purchases we made the preceding month and guides our interactions with former classmates at a high school reunion. But in an absolute sense, the Person is only a cognitive construct, much like the ever-changing body of water that is now called the Mississippi River.

The reason that we think that we ride our present brains from birth to death is likely that we have fallen under the powerful illusion that we are the Person. Much like an oxygen atom temporarily trapped in one's body, we may have jumped on board well after birth and may depart well before death. One should perhaps give up the illusion of the Person! It is a big cognitive adjustment, but you may find it to be an exhilarating and profoundly soothing one, as I have.

We are not the Person, we are not even Atman (in the sense of a sphere of pure consciousness inhabiting the same body from birth until death), and are likely no longer Brahman, although it is possible that we were once conjoined in an aggregate of consciousnesses that may have somehow "designed" the world.

References

Baars, B. C. (1988). *A cognitive theory of consciousness.* New York: Cambridge University Press.

Baars, B. C. (1997). *In the theater of consciousness: The workspace of the mind.* New York: Oxford University Press.

Baker, M. C., and Goetz, S. (Eds.) (2011). *The soul hypothesis: Investigations into the existence of the soul.* New York: The Continuum International Publishing Group.

Barker, D. (2016). *God: The most unpleasant character in all fiction.* New York: Sterling.

Barrow, J. D., and Tipler, F. S. (1986). *The anthropic cosmological principle.* New York: Oxford University Press.

Bergson, H. (1911), *Matter and memory.* London: Swain Sonnenschein.

Bergson, H. (1914). Presidential address to the Society for Psychical Research (1913). *Proceedings of the Society for Psychical Research, 27,* 157–175.

Blackmore, S. J. (2002). There is no stream of consciousness. *Journal of Consciousness Studies,* 9(5/6), 17-28.

Blackmore, S.J. (2017). *Consciousness" A Very Short Introduction.* New York: Oxford Univesity Press.

Bostrum, N. (2003). Are you living in a computer simulation? *Philosophical Quarterly, 53,* 243-255.

Bray, D. (2009). *Wetware: A computer in every living cell.* New Haven, CT: Yale University Press.

Bryan, R. (2009). Consciousness and quantum-mechanical wave functions. *Australian Journal of Parapsychology, 9,* 33-55.

Butler, J. (1736/1852). *The analogy of religion, natural and revealed.* London: Harry G. Bohn.

Carington, W. (1949). *Mind, matter and meaning.* New Having, CT: Yale University Press.

Churchland, P. M. (1989). *A neurocomputational perspective.* Cambridge, MA: MIT Press.

Churchland, P. M. (1995). *The engine of reason, the seat of the soul: A philosophical journey into the brain.* Cambridge, MA: MIT Press.

Churchland, P. S. (1986). *Neurophilosophy.* Cambridge, MA: MIT Press.

Churchland, P. S. (2002). *Brain-wise: Studies in neurophilosophy.* Cambridge, MA: MIT Press.

Clark, A. (2008). *Supersizing the mind: Embodiment, action and cognitive extension.* New York: Oxford University Press.

Clayton, P. (2010) Unsolved dilemmas: The concept of matter in the history of philosophy and in contemporary physics. In Davies, P. C. W., and Gregorsen, N. H. (Eds). *Information and the nature of reality: From physics to metaphysics* (pp. 38-62). Cambridge, UK: Cambridge University Press.

Cohen, D. (1999). *The Manhattan Project.* Minneapolis, MN: 21st Century.

Coons, P. M. (1988). Psychophysiological aspects of multiple personality disorder. *Dissociation, 1,* 47-53.

Cooper, J. W (2006). *Panentheism: The other god of the philosophers.* Grand Rapids, MI: BakerAcademic.

Crick, F. C. (1994). *The astonishing hypothesis: The scientific search for the soul.* New York: Charles Scribner's Sons.

Crick, F. C. and Koch, C. (1990). Toward a neurobiological theory of consciousness. *Seminars in Neuroscience, 2,* 263-275.

Crick, F. C. and Koch, C. (2003). A framework for science. *Nature Neuroscience, 6, 119-126.*

Davies, P. C. W. (2008). A quantum origin of life? In Abbot, D., Davies, P. C. W., and Pati, A. K. (Eds.), *Quantum aspects of life* (pp. 3-14). London: Imperial College Press.

De Chardin, P. T. (2008). *The phenomenon of man.* New York: Harper Perennial Modern Classics.

Delgado, J. M. R. (1969). *Physical control of the mind: Toward a psychocivilized society.* New York: Harper & Row.

Dennett, D. C. (1988). Quining qualia. In Marcel, A. J., and Bisiach, E. (Eds.), *Consciousness in contemporary science* (pp. 42–77). Oxford, England: Oxford University Press.

Dennett, D. C. (1991). *Consciousness explained.* Boston: Little, Brown.

Earle, W. (1955). *Objectivity: An essay on phenomenological ontology.* New York: Noonday Press.

Eddington, A. S. (1920/1959). *Space, time and gravitation: An outline of the general relativity theory.* New York: Harper & Row.

Eddington A. S (1935). *The nature of the physical world.* New York: MacMillan.

Edwards, J. C. W. (2005). Is consciousness only a property of individual cells? *Journal of Consciousness Studies, 12(4/5),* 60-76.

Edwards, J. C, W. (2006). *How many people are there in my head, and in hers? An exploration of single-cell consciousness.* Exeter, UK: Imprint Academic.

Edwards, P. (1997). Introduction. In Edwards, P. (Ed.), *Immortality* (pp. 1-70). Amherst, NY: Prometheus Books.

Everett, H. (1957) Doctoral dissertation.

Fjermedal, G. (1987). *The tomorrow makers.* New York: MacMillan.

Fodor, J. (1983). *The modularity of mind.* Cambridge: MIT Press/Bradford Books.

Gasperini, L. (2012). [Review of *Metapsichica Moderna* by William MacKenzie] *Journal of Scientific Exploration, 26,* 911-912.

Gazzaniga, M. S. (1985). *The social brain: Discovering the networks of the mind.* New York: Basic Books.

Gazzaniga, M. S. (1989). Organization of the human brain. *Science, 245,* 947–952.

Gazzaniga, M. S. (2011) *Who's in charge? Free will and the science of the brain.* New York, HarperCollins.

Gazzaniga, M. S., and Roser, M. (2004). Automatic brains - interpretive minds. *Current Directions in Psychological Science, 13,* 56-59.

Göcke, B. P. (Ed.). (2012). *After physicalism*. Notre Dame, IN: University of Notre Dame Press.

Goldberg, S. (2009), *Anatomy of the soul: Mind, god and the afterlife*. Miami, FL: Medmaster, Inc.

Griffin, D. R. (1988a). Introduction: The reenchantment of science. In Griffin, D. R. (Ed.), *The reenchantment of science* (pp. 1–46). Albany: State University of New York Press.

Griffin, D. R. (1988b). Of minds and molecules: Postmodern medicine in a psychosomatic universe. In Griffin, D. R. (Ed.), *The reenchantment of science* (pp. 141–163). Albany, NY: State University of New York Press.

Griffin, D. R. (1994). Dualism, materialism, idealism and psi. *Journal of the American Society for Research, 88*, 23–29.

Griffin, D. R. (1997). Panexperientialist physicalism and the mind-body problem. *Journal of Consciousness Studies, 4*(3), 248-268.

Goetz, S. (2001). Modal dualism: A critique. In Corcoran, K. (Ed.), *Soul, body and survival* (pp. 89-104). Ithaca: NY: Cornell University Press.

Goetz. S., and Taliaferro, C. (2011). *A brief history of the soul*. West Sussex, UK: Wiley-Blackwell.

Goswami, A. (1993). *The self-aware universe: How consciousness creates the material world*.

Haisch. B. (2006). *The God theory: Universes, zero-point fields and what's behind it all*. San Francisco: Weiser Books.

Harris, S. (2010). *The moral landscape*. New York: Free Press.

Hasker, W. (2001). Persons as emergent substances. In Corcoran, K. (Ed.), *Soul, Body and Survival*, (pp. 107-119). Ithaca: NY: Cornell University Press.

Hasker, W. (2010). Persons and the unity of consciousness. In Coons, R. C and Bealer, G. (Eds.), *The waning of materialism* (pp. 175-190). New York: Oxford University Press.

Hasker, W. (2011). Souls beastly and human. In Baker, M. C. and Goetz, S. (Eds.), *The soul hypothesis: Investigations into the existence of the soul* (pp. 202-217). New York: Continuum International Publishing, Inc.

425

Henry, R. C. (2005). The mental universe. *Nature, 436*, 29.

Henry, R. C. (2007). [Review of *Quantum enigma: Psychics encounters consciousness.*] *Journal of Scientific Exploration, 21*, 185-191

Hilgard, E. (1977). *Divided consciousness.* New York: Wiley.

Hill, T. (2005). [Letter to the Editor.] *Skeptical Inquirer, 29(1)*, 61.

Höldobler, B., and Wilson, E. O. (2008). *The superorganism: The beauty, elegance and strangeness of insect societies.* New York: Norton.

Holt, J. (2012). *Why does the world exist? An existential detective story.* New York: Liveright Publishing Corporation.

Hood, B. (2012). *The self illusion: How the social brain creates identity.* New York, NY: Oxford University Press.

Hume, D. (1739/1978). *A treatise of human nature.* Oxford, UK: Clarendon Press.

Humphrey, N. (2011). *Soul dust: The magic of consciousness.* Princeton, NJ: Princeton University Press.

Husserl, E. (1954). *The crisis of European sciences and transcendental philosophy.* New York: Oxford University Press.

Huxley, A. (1945/2009). *The perennial philosophy.* New York: Harper Perennial Modern Classics.

Huxley, T. H. (1874). On the hypothesis that animals are automata, and its history. *The Fortnightly Review 16* (New Series): 555–580. Reprinted in *Method and results: essays by Thomas T. Huxley,* New York: D. Appleton and Company, 1898.

Huxley, T. H. (1892). *Essays upon some controverted questions.* New York: D. Appleton and Company.

James, W. (1890). *The principles of psychology. Volume I.* New York: Dover.

James, W. (1898). *Human immortality: Two supposed objections to the doctrine.* Boston: Houghton Mifflin.

James, W. (1902). *The varieties of religious experience: A study in human nature.* New York: Longmans, Green & Co.

James, W. (1911). *Some problems in philosophy.* New York: Library of America..

Jeans, J. (1937). *The mysterious universe*. Cambridge, England: Cambridge University Press.

Jung, C. G. (1973). *Synchronicity: An acasual connecting principle*. Princeton, NJ: Princeton University Press.

Jung. C. G. (1978). *On the nature of the psyche. The structure and dynamics of the psyche. (Collected works of C. G. Jung Volume 8)*. Princeton, NJ: Princeton University Press.

Jung. C. G. (1981). *The archetypes and the collective unconscious. (Collected works of C. G. Jung Volume 9, Part 1)*. Princeton, NJ: Princeton University Press.

Kelly, E. F. (2007). Toward a psychology for the 21st century. In Kelly, E. F., Kelly, E. W., Crabtree, A., Gauld, A., Grosso, M., and Greyson, B., *Irreducible mind: Toward a psychology for the 21st century* (pp. 577-643). Lanham, MD: Rowan & Littlefield Publishers.

Klein, S. B. (2012). The self and science: Is it time for a new approach to the study of human experience? *Current Directions in Psychological Science, 4*, 253-257.

Koch, C. (1996). Toward the neuronal substrate of visual consciousness. In Hameroff, S. R., Kaszniak, A. W., and Scott, A. C. (Eds), *Toward a science of consciousness. The first Tuscon discussions and debates* (pp. 247-257). Cambridge, MA: MIT Press.

Koch, C. (2012). *Consciousness: Confessions of a romantic reductionist*. Cambridge, MA: MIT Press.

Koch, C., and Crick, F. (1991). Understanding awareness at the neuronal level. *Behavioral and Brain Sciences, 4,* 683–685.

Koestler, A. (1967). *The ghost in the machine*. New York: Macmillan.

Koestler, A. (1972). *The roots of coincidence*. New York: Random House.

Koestler, A. (1978). *Janus*. New York: Random House.

Koons, R. C., and Bealer, G. (Eds.). (2010). *The Waning of Materialism*. New York, NY: Oxford University Press.

Krauss, L. M. (2012). *A universe from nothing*. New York. NY: Free Press.

Kuhn, R. L. (2007). Why this universe? A taxonomy of explanations. *Skeptic, 13(2)*, 28- 35.

Kurzweil, R. (2006). *The singularity is near: When humans transcend biology*. New York: Penguin Books.

LeShan, L. (1969). *Toward a general theory of the paranormal.* New York: Parapsychology Foundation.

Locke, J. (1975). *An essay concerning human understanding.* Oxford, UK: Clarendon Press.

Lueptow, L. B. (2009). Will physicists destroy the world? *Skeptic, 15* (2). 24-59.

Lund, D. H. (1985). *Death and consciousness.* Jefferson, NC: McFarland.

Lund, D. H. (2009) *Persons, souls and death: A philosophical investigation of an afterlife.* McFarland & Co., 2009.

Marshall, J., and Halligan, P. (1988). Blindsight and insight in visuo-spatial neglect. *Nature, 336,* 766-777.

Martin, M. and Augustine, K. (Eds.) (2015). *The myth of the afterlife: The case against life after death.* New York: Rowman & Littlefield.

Martin, R., and Barresi, J. (2006). *The rise and fall of the soul and self: An intellectual history of personal identity.* New York: Columbia University Press.

McDougall, W. (1920). Presidential address. *Proceedings of the Society for Psychical Research, 31,* 150-123.

McDougall, W. (1926). *An outline of abnormal psychology.* London: Methuen.

McGinn, C. (1999). *The Mysterious flame: Conscious minds in a material world.* New York: Basic Books.

Metzinger, T. (2003). *Being no one: The self-model theory of subjectivity.* Cambridge, MA: MIT Press, 2003.

Metzinger, T. (2009). *The ego tunnel: The science of the mind and the myth of the self.* New York: Basic Books, 2009.

Miller, G. A. (1956). The magical number seven, plus or minus two: Some limits on our capacity for processing information. *Psychological Review 63(2),* 81–97.

Miranker, W. (2005). The Hebbian synapse: Progenitor of consciousness. *Mind and Matter, 3(2),* 87-102.

Mlodinow, L. (2012). *How your unconscious mind rules your behavior.* New York: Pantheon Books.

Moravec, H. (1988). *Mind children: The future of robot and human intelligence.* Cambridge, MA: Harvard University Press.

Myers, F. H. W. (1903). *Human personality and its survival of death.* London: Longmans.

Nagel T. (1974). What is it like to be a bat? *Philosophical Review, LXXXIII(4)*, 435-450.

Nagel, T. (2012). *Mind and cosmos: Why the materialist neo-Darwinian conception of nature is almost certainly false.* New York: Oxford University Press.

Oppenheimer, P. (1986). [Letter to the Editor.] *The Sciences*, 26(2), 12.

Parfit, D. (1986). *Reasons and Persons.* New York: Oxford University Press.

Parfit, D. (1987). Divided minds and the nature of persons. In Blakemore, C. and Greenfield, S. (Eds.), *Mindwaves: Thoughts on intelligence, identity and consciousness* (pp. 19–26). New York: Basil Blackwell.

Pashler, H. (1998). *The psychology of attention.* Cambridge, MA: MIT Press.

Peake, A. (2006). *Is there life after death: The extraordinary science of what happens when we die.* London: UK: Arcturus Publishing Limited.

Plantinga, A. (2012). Against materialism. In Göcke, A. (Ed.), *After Physicalism* (pp. 104-145). Notre Dame, IN: University of Notre Dame Press.

Plato (1961). *The collected dialogues of Plato.* Princeton, NJ; Princeton University Press.

Priest, S. (2012). The unconditioned soul. In Göcke, A. (Ed.), *After Physicalism* (pp. 295-334). Notre Dame, IN: University of Notre Dame Press.

Prince, M. (1906). The dissociation of a personality. New York: Longmans, Green, & Co.

Ramachandran, V. S., and Blakeslee, S. (1998). *Phantoms in the brain.* New York: HarperCollins.

Reid, T. (1872). *The works of Thomas Reid.* Edinburgh, UK: Maclachlan & Stewart.

Ryle, G. (1949). *The concept of mind.* New York: Rutledge.

Schechter, E. (2018). *Self-consciousness and "split" brains.* New York: Oxford University Press.

Seager, W. (1995). Consciousness, information and panpsychism. *Journal of Consciousness Studies, 2*, 272–288.

Segal, A. (2004). *Life after death: A history of the afterlife in the religions of the West.* New York: Doubleday.

Skinner, B. F. (1953). *Science and human behavior.* Toronto: Collier-Macmillan.

Skrbina, D. (2003). Panpsychism as an underlying theme in Western philosophy: A survey paper. *Journal of Consciousness Studies, 10*(3), 4-46.

Skrbina, D. (2005). *Panpsychism in the West.* Cambridge, MA: MIT Press.

Spanos, N. P., and Hewitt, E. C. (1980). The hidden observer in hypnotic analgesia: discovery or experimental creation? *Journal of Personality and Social Psychology, 46,* 688-696.

Stapp, H. P. (2005). Commentary on Hodgson. *Journal of Consciousness Studies, 12(1),* 70-75.

Stapp, H. P. (2011). *Mindful universe: Quantum mechanics and the participating observer.* Heidelberg, Germany: Springer-Verlag.

Stokes, D. M. (2014) *Reimagining the soul.* Jefferson, NC: McFarland.

Stokes, D. M. (2015). The case against psi. In E. Cardeña, J. Palmer and D. Marcusson-Clayavertz (Eds.) *Parapsychology: A handbook for the 21st century* (pp. 40-48 Jefferson, NC: McFarland.

Strawson, G. (2009). *Selves: An essay in revisionary metaphysics.* New York: Oxford University Press.

Strawson, G. (2017) Mind and being: The primacy of panpsychism. In G. Brüntrip, and L. Jaskolla , (Eds.) *Panpsychism: Contemporary Perspectives.* New York, NY: Oxford University Press (pp. 75-112)

Strawson, G. (2018). *Things that bother me.* New York: New York Review of Books.

Tegmark, M. (1997). The interpretation of quantum mechanics: Many words or many words? In Ruben, M. H., and Shih, Y. H. (Eds.), *Fundamental Problems in Quantum Theory.* New York: Wiley.

Tegmark, M. (2003) Parallel universes. *Scientific American.* (May 2003), 41-51.

Tegmark, , M. (2014). *Our mathematical universe.* New York: Knopf.

Tegmark, M. (2017). *Life 3.0.* New York Vintage Books

Tertullian (1997). The refutation of the Pythagorean doctrine of transmigration. In Edwards, P. (Ed.), *Immortality* (pp. 88–90). New York: Macmillan.

Tipler, F. J. (1994). *The physics of immortality.* New York: Doubleday.

Tononi, G. (2012). *PHI: A voyage from the brain to the soul*. New York: Pantheon Books

Tryon, E. P. (1973). Is the universe a vacuum fluctuation? *Nature, 246*, 396–397.

Tyrrell, G. N. M. (1953). *Apparitions*. New York: Macmillan.

Walker, E. H. (2000). *The physics of consciousness*. Cambridge, MA: Perseus Books.

Ward, K. (2010). God as the ultimate informational principle. In Davies, P. C. W., and Gregorsen, N. H. (Eds). *Information and the nature of reality: From physics to metaphysics* (pp. 281-300). Cambridge, UK: Cambridge University Press.

Watson, J. (1924/1970). *Behaviorism*. New York: W. W. Norton.

Watts, A. (1989). *The book: On the taboo against knowing who you are*. New York: Vintage Books.

Wegner, D. (2002). *The illusion of conscious will*. Cambridge, MA: MIT Press.

Weiskrantz, L. (1986) *Blindsight: A case and implications*. Oxford: Oxford University Press.

Wheeler, J. A. (1983). Law without law. In J. A. Wheeler and W. H. Zurek (Eds.), *Quantum theory and measurement* (pp. 182-213). Princeton, NJ: Princeton University Press.

Whitehead, A. N. (1929/1978). *Process and reality: An essay in cosmology*. New York: Free Press.

Wilber, K. (1990). Death, rebirth and meditation. In Doore, G. (Ed.), *What survives? Contemporary explorations of life after death* (pp. 176–191). Los Angeles: Tarcher.

Wigner, E. (1960). The unreasonable effectiveness of mathematics in the natural sciences. *Communications on Pure and Applied Mathematics, XIII*, 1-14.

Wilson, E. O. (2010). *Anthill*, New York: Norton & Co.

Yantis, S. (2008). The neural basis of selective attention: Cortical sources and targets of attentional modulation. *Current Directions in Psychological Science, 17*, 86-90.

1 Koons and Bealer (2010).
2 Göcke (2012).
3 Kelly, Crabtree, and Marshall (2015).
4 Baker and Goetz (2011).
5 Goetz and Taliaferro (2011).
6 Humphrey (2011).
7 Martin and Augustine (2015).
8 Stokes (2014).
9 Martin and Augustine (2015).
10 Ryle (1949).
11 See Stokes (2014, 2015) for a more detailed discussion of this issue.
12 See Watson (1924/1970) and Skinner (1953).
13 Dennett (1988).
14 Dennett (1991).
15 Blackmore (2002, 2013).
16 Metzinger (2003, 2009).
17 Churchland (1989, 1995).
18 Churchland (1986, 2002).
19 Hood (2012).
20 Strawson (2018), p. 130.
21 Baars (1988, 1997).
22 See Crick and Koch (1990) and Koch (2012).
23 See Crick and Koch, 1990, for instance).
24 Plantinga 2012).
25 See Edwards (2005, 2006).
26 Koestler (1967, 1978),
27 For instance, Hölldobbler and Wilson (2008).
28 LeShan (1969).
29 Huxley (1945/2009).
30 Barker (2016).
31 Everett (1957).
32 Skrbina (2003, 2005).
33 Edwards (2005,2006).
34 Crick and Koch (2003), Koch (1996, 2012), Koch and Crick (1991).
35 DeChardin (2008).
36 Skrbina (2003, 2005).
37 Dennett (1988,1991).
38 Blackmore (2002).
39 Metzinger (2003, 2009).
40 Edwards (2005, 2006).
41 Jung (1973, 1981).
42 de Chardin (2008).
43 Hölldobler and Wilson (2008).
44 Kurzweil (2006).
45 Segal (2004).
46 Plato 1961).
47 Lund (2009).
48 Martin and Berresi (2006).
49 Butler. (1736/1852).
50 Goetz and Taliaferro (2011).
51 Goetz (2001).
52 Martin and Berresi (2006).
53 Martin and Berresi (2006).
54 Husserl (1954).
55 Ward (2010, p .295).
56 Goetz and Taliferno (2011).
57 Locke (1975).

[58] Goetz and Taliferro (2011).
[59] Reid (1872).
[60] Edwards (2005, 2006).
[61] Krauss (2012).
[62] Holt (2012).
[63] James (1902).
[64] Huxley (1945/2009).
[65] Strawson (2009).
[66] Hume (1739/1698).
[67] Holt 2012).
[68] Parfit (1986).
[69] Whitehead (1929/1978).
[70] Stapp (2011).
[71] James (1890, p. 401).
[72] Stapp (2011).
[73] Carington,(1949).
[74] Klein (2012, p. 255).
[75] Earl (1955, p. 89, as cited by Klein, 2012, p. 256).
[76] Lueptow (2009).
[77] Cohen (1999).
[78] Jeans (1937, p. 134).
[79] Jeans (1937, p. 134).
[80] Bostrum (2003).
[81] Holt (2012, p. 5).
[82] Tegmark (1997, 2003, 2014).
[83] See Kuhn (2007).
[84] Eddington (1920/1959).
[85] Stapp (2005).
[86] Henry (2005, p. 25).
[87] Wheeler (1983).
[88] Walker (2000).
[89] McGinn (1999).
[90] Holt (2012, p.131).
[91] Barrow and Tipler (1986).
[92] Tryon (1973).
[93] Everett (1957).
[94] See Watts (1989), for instance.
[95] Skinner (1953).
[96] Watson (1924/1975).
[97] Nagel (2012), p. 15.
[98] Huxley (1874).
[99] Hasker (2001).
[100] Hasker (2010, 2011).
[101] Haisch (2006).
[102] Goswami (1993).
[103] Eddington (1935).
[104] Priest (2012).
[105] Pashler (1998).
[106] Miller (1956).
[107] Mlodinow (2012).
[108] Tegmark (2017).
[109] Stapp (2011).
[110] James (1890, 1911).
[111] Whitehead (1929/1978).
[112] See Stapp (2011, pp. 134-135).
[113] McGinn (1999).
[114] McGinn (1999).
[115] Griffin (1988a, 1988b, 1994, 1997).
[116] Höldobler and Wilson (2008).
[117] Wilson (2010).
[118] Goldberg (2009), p. 54
119 Edwards (2005, 2006).
[120] Miranker (2005).
[121] Edwards (2006, p. 69).
[122] Zeki (2002).
[123] Bray (2009).
[124] Clayton (2010).
[125] Goetz (2001).
[126] Yantis (2008).
[127] Skrbina (2003, 2005).
[128] Bryan (2009).
[129] Kuhn (2007).
[130] Seager (1995).

131 Nagel (2012).
132 Nagel (1974).
133 Humphrey (2011).
134 Humphrey (2011, p. 196).
135 Koch (2012).
136 Prince (1906).
137 Koch (2012, p. 133).
138 Tononi (2012).
139 Peake (2006).
140 Tegmark (2017).
141 Kurzweil (2006).
142 Moravec (1988).
143 Fjermedal (1987).
144 Tipler (1994).
145 Kurzweil (2006).
146 Oppenheimer (1986).
147 Parfit (1987).
148 Martin and Augustine (2015).
149 Myers (1903).
150 Tyrrell (1953), p.119.
151 Tertullian (1997).
152 Edwards (1997).
153 Walker (2000).
154 Hill (2005).
155 Martin and Augustine (2015).
156 Wilber (1990).
157 Stokes (2014).
158 Wilber (1990).
159 Walker (2000).
160 Jeans (1937, p.122).
161 Stapp (2011).
162 Henry (2005, p. 29).
163 Strawson (2017, p. 98).
164 Walker (2000).
165 Metzinger (2009).
166 Schechter (2018).
167 Churchland (2002), pp. 46-47.
168 Clark (2008), p. 138.

169 Harris (2010).
170 Gazzagina (2011).
171 Gazzagina (2011, p.3).
172 Weiskrantz (1986).
173 Marshalla and Halligan (1988).
174 Myers (1903).
175 McDougall (1920, 1927).
176 Prince (1906).
177 Gasperini (2012).
178 Jung (1978).
179 James (1890).
180 Hilgard (1977).
181 Spanon and Hewitt (1980).
182 Ramachandran and Blakeslee (1998).
183 Fodor (1983).
184 Gazzaniga (1985, 1989, 2011).
185 Gazzaniga and Roser (2004).
186 Wegner (2002).
187 Delgado (1969).
188 Hölldobler and Wilson (2008).
189 Goldberg (2009).
190 Koestler (1967, 1972, 1978).
191 Holt (2012).
192 Henry (2007).
193 Cooper (2006).
194 Cooper (2006, p. 230).
195 Segal (2004).
196 Kelly et al. (2007), Bergson (1911, 1914).
197 Blackmore (2002).
198 Dennett (2009).

Postscript

There is not a right or wrong way to read this book. Every essay stands on its own feet, and the book as a whole stands on its own—though, if you've found it to your liking, there are predecessor volumes and potential future volumes with many additional perspectives of thought. As you may have noticed, our goal in assembling this has not been to persuade you of the rightness of any one theology, but to inform you of the choices available, a much broader universe of ideas than the average person may imagine.

And now, with increased knowledge.... go forth and love. Go forth and learn. Bring all of those loving and learning experiences back to your second reading, or next reading after that, of this work. We build our understanding of the world together.

Song of Myself, Section 48

By Walt Whitman

Walt Whitman (1819–1892) is considered one of America's most important poets. A journalist, editor, and writer, he is most known for publishing nine editions of *Leaves of Grass.* With these contributions to American poetry, he is often considered the father of free verse. His poetry often explores deistic and pandeistic qualities, rejecting views of God as separate from the world.

I have said that the soul is not more than the body,
And I have said that the body is not more than
        the soul,
And nothing, not God, is greater to one than one's
        self is,
And whoever walks a furlong without sympathy walks
to his own funeral drest in his shroud,
And I or you pocketless of a dime may purchase the
        pick of the earth,
And to glance with an eye or show a bean in its pod
        confounds the learning of all times,
And there is no trade or employment but the young
        man following it may become a hero,
And there is no object so soft but it makes a hub
        for the wheel'd universe,
And I say to any man or woman, Let your soul stand
        cool and composed before a million universes.
And I say to mankind, Be not curious about God,
For I who am curious about each am not curious
        about God,
(No array of terms can say how much I am at peace
        about God and about death.)

I hear and behold God in every object, yet understand
	God not in the least,
Nor do I understand who there can be more
	wonderful
	than myself.
Why should I wish to see God better than this day?
I see something of God each hour of the twenty-four,
	and each moment then,
In the faces of men and women I see God, and in
	my own face in the glass,
I find letters from God dropt in the street, and every
	one
	is sign'd by God's name,
And I leave them where they are, for I know
	that wheresoe'er I go,
Others will punctually come for ever and ever.

THE END

Printed in Great Britain
by Amazon